# 3D Origami Platonic Solids & More

## Second Edition in Full Color

Books by John Montroll
www.johnmontroll.com

General Origami

*DC Super Heroes Origami*
*Origami Worldwide*
*Teach Yourself Origami: Second Revised Edition*
*Christmas Origami*
*Storytime Origami*
*Origami Inside-Out: Third Edition*

Animal Origami

*Dogs in Origami*
*Perfect Pets Origami*
*Dragons and Other Fantastic Creatures in Origami*
*Bugs in Origami*
*Horses in Origami*
*Origami Birds*
*Origami Gone Wild*
*Dinosaur Origami*
*Origami Dinosaurs for Beginners*
*Prehistoric Origami: Dinosaurs and other Creatures: Third Edition*
*Mythological Creatures and the Chinese Zodiac Origami*
*Origami Under the Sea*
*Sea Creatures in Origami*
*Origami Sea Life: Third Edition*
*Bringing Origami to Life*
*Bugs and Birds in Origami*
*Origami Sculptures: Fourth Edition*
*African Animals in Origami: Third Edition*
*North American Animals in Origami: Third Edition*

Geometric Origami

*Origami Stars*
*Galaxy of Origami Stars: Second Edition*
*Origami and Math: Simple to Complex*
*Origami & Geometry*
*3D Origami Diamonds*
*3D Origami Antidiamonds*
*3D Origami Pyramids*
*Classic Polyhedra Origami*
*A Constellation of Origami Polyhedra*
*A Plethora of Polyhedra in Origami: Second Revised Edition*
*Origami Polyhedra Design*

Dollar Bill Origami

*Dollar Origami Treasures*
*Dollar Bill Animals in Origami: Second Revised Edition*
*Dollar Bill Origami*
*Easy Dollar Bill Origami*

Simple Origami

*Fun and Simple Origami: 101 Easy-to-Fold Projects: Second Edition*
*Super Simple Origami*
*Easy Dollar Bill Origami*
*Easy Origami Animals*
*Origami Twelve Days of Christmas: And Santa, Too!*

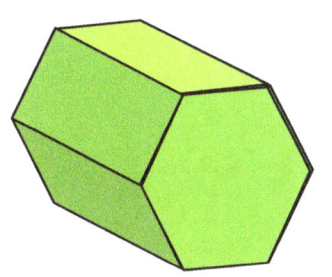
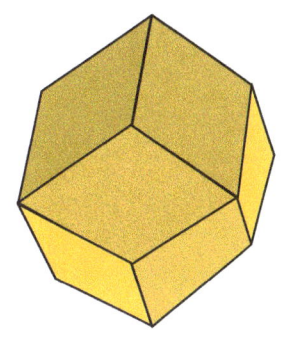

# 3D Origami Platonic Solids & More

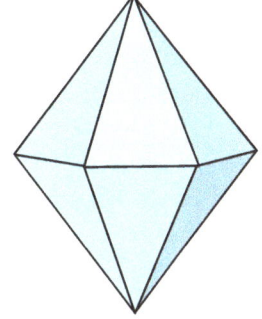
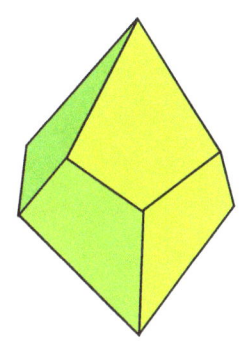

*Second Edition in Full Color*

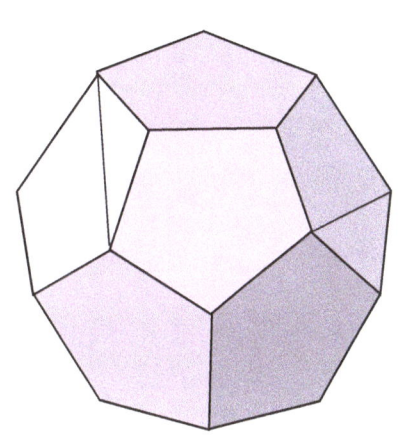

*Each from a single square!*

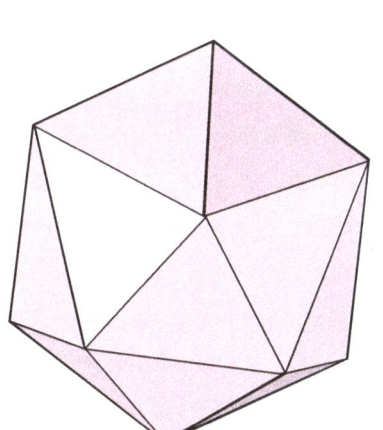
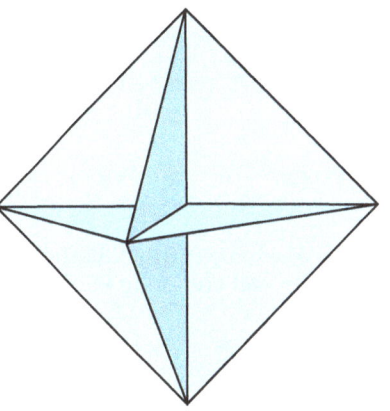

## John Montroll

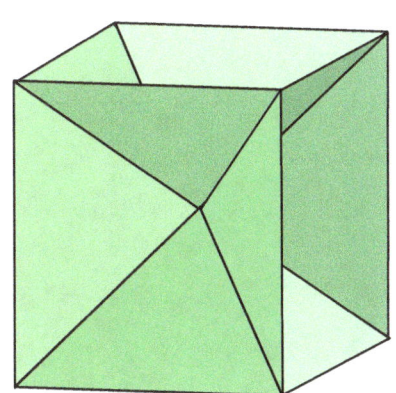
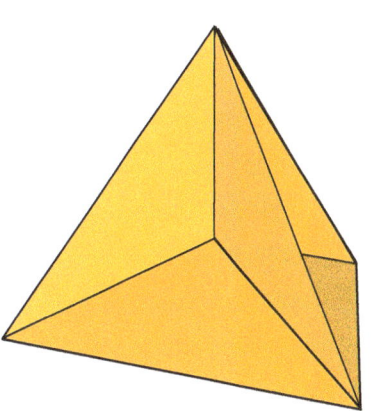

Antroll Publishing Company

**3D Origami Platonic Solids & More**
Second Edition in Full Color

Copyright © 2018 by John Montroll. All rights reserved.
No part of this publication may be copied or reproduced by any means without the express written permission of the author.

ISBN-10: 1-877656-35-6
ISBN-13: 978-1877656-35-4

Antroll Publishing Company

# Introduction

Polyhedra are incredibly beautiful shapes. Here is a collection of around 30 models including the five Platonic Solids, sunken versions of each, models with color patterns, variations on Archimedean Solids, and more.

The folding methods for each of these interesting models are amazingly different. All are original designs, using the latest in folding techniques. Each model is folded from a single square, which makes them more amazing and satisfying. They range from simple to complex.

The folding techniques combine the art of origami with geometry. Many of the models were designed using math so as to fold them as simply as possible. There is information on symmetry, which is used to understand and simplify the folding patterns. Included are sections on Octahedra and Dodecahedra, polyhedra with eight and twelve sides. This adds variety to families of shapes including a prism, antiprism, dipyramid, and trapezohedron.

The illustrations conform to the internationally accepted Randlett-Yoshizawa conventions. You can use any kind of square paper for these models, but the best results can be achieved using standard origami paper, which is colored on one side and white on the other. In these diagrams, the shading represents the colored side. Origami paper can be found in many hobby shops or on several online sites including www.origami-usa.org.

I am a pioneer in designing origami polyhedra from a single sheet. Through origami ideas combined with math, I have been able to create a long list of polyhedra which is not so difficult to fold. Related books on this subject include *Classic Polyhedra Origami*. I hope this collection inspires you to continue with this topic.


John Montroll
www.johnmontroll.com

| | |
|---|---|
| Symbols | 8 |
| Basic Folds | 9 |
| Symmetry | 10 |
| Platonic Solids | 11 |
| Sunken Platonic Solids | 31 |
| Inside-Out Platonic Solids | 49 |
| Dimpled Polyhedra | 68 |
| Octahedra | 85 |
| Dodecahedra | 99 |

# Contents

★ Simple
★★ Intermediate
★★★ Complex
★★★★ Very Complex

―― **Platonic Solids** ――――――――――――――――

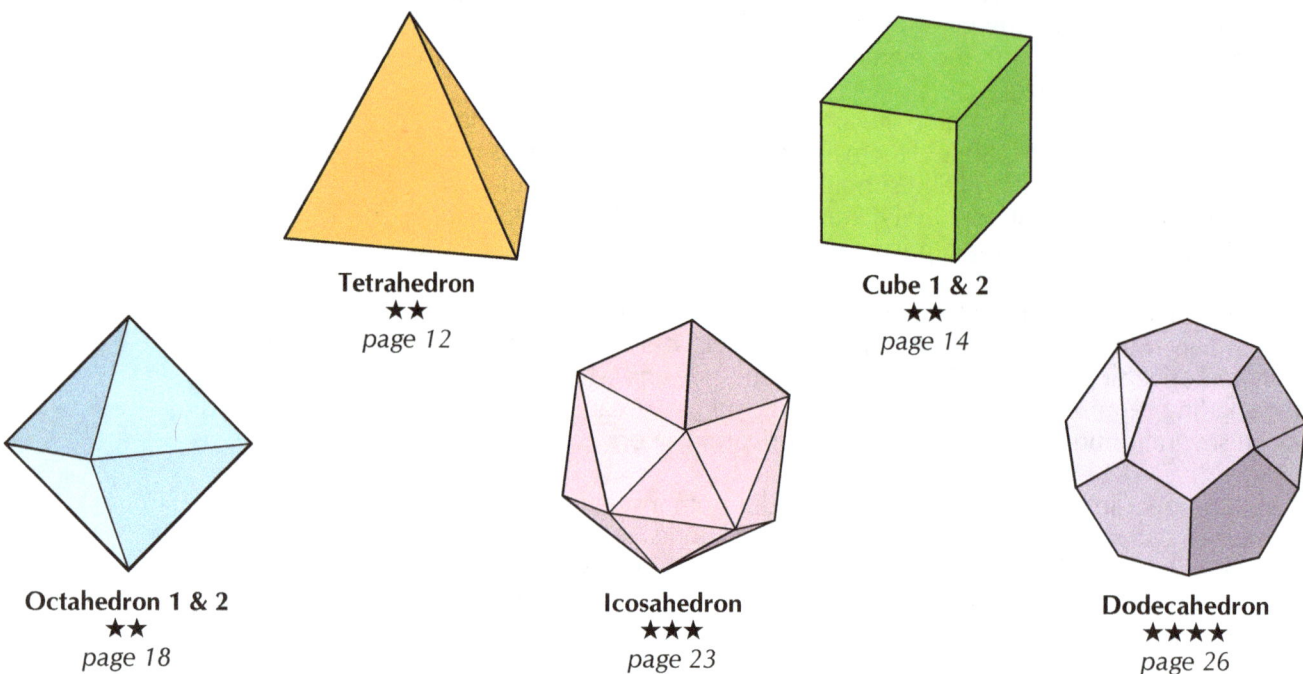

**Tetrahedron**
★★
*page 12*

**Cube 1 & 2**
★★
*page 14*

**Octahedron 1 & 2**
★★
*page 18*

**Icosahedron**
★★★
*page 23*

**Dodecahedron**
★★★★
*page 26*

―― **Sunken Platonic Solids** ――――――――――――

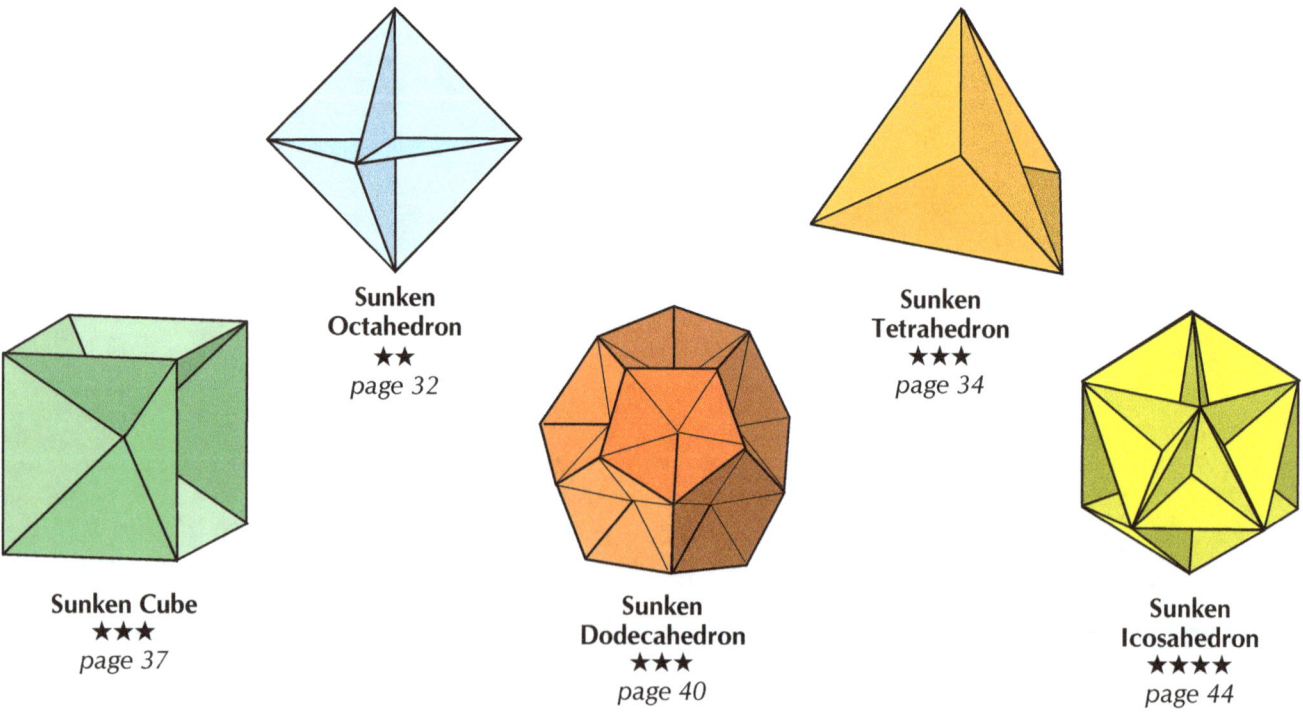

**Sunken Octahedron**
★★
*page 32*

**Sunken Tetrahedron**
★★★
*page 34*

**Sunken Cube**
★★★
*page 37*

**Sunken Dodecahedron**
★★★
*page 40*

**Sunken Icosahedron**
★★★★
*page 44*

6  *3D Origami Platonic Solids & More*

## Inside-Out Platonic Solids

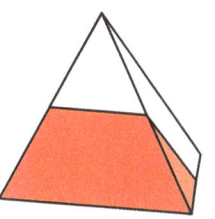
**Duo-Striped Tetrahedron**
★★
page 50

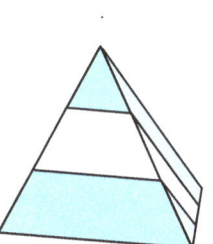
**Layered Tetrahedron**
★★
page 53

**Three-Layered Cube**
★★
page 56

**Fancy Cube**
★★
page 59

**Banded Cube**
★★
page 62

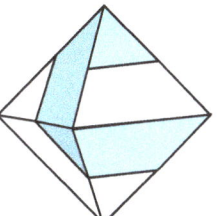
**Banded Octahedron**
★★
page 65

## Dimpled Polyhedra

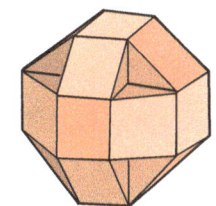
**Dimpled Rhombicuboctahedron**
★★★
page 68

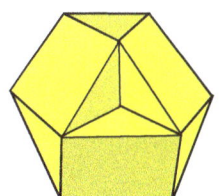
**Cubehemioctahedron**
★★★
page 72

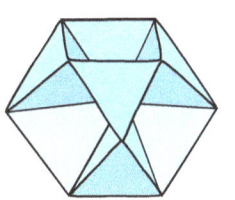
**Octahemioctahedron**
★★★
page 76

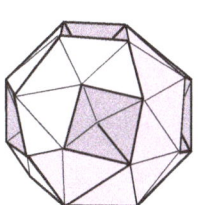
**Dimpled Snub Cube**
★★★
page 80

## Octahedra

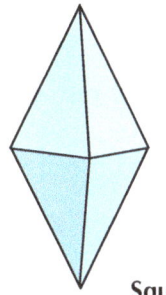
**Square Dipyramid**
★★
page 86

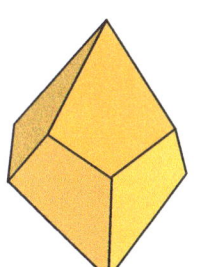
**Square Trapezohedron**
★★★
page 88

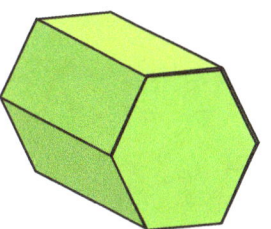
**Hexagonal Prism**
★★★
page 92

**Triangular Antiprism**
★★★
page 96

## Dodecahedra

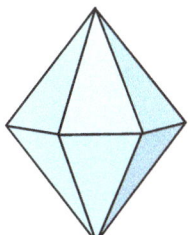
**Hexagonal Dipyramid**
★★★
page 100

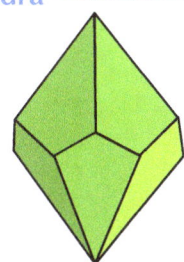
**Hexagonal Trapezohedron**
★★★
page 103

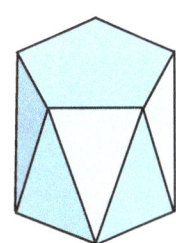
**Golden Pentagonal Antiprism**
★★★
page 107

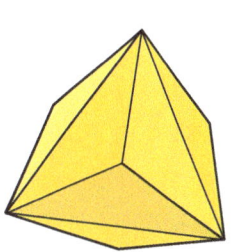
**Triakis Tetrahedron**
★★★
page 111

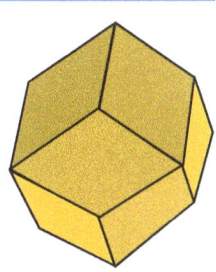
**Rhombic Dodecahedron**
★★★
page 115

Contents 7

# Symbols

## Lines

– – – – – – – – –  Valley fold, fold in front.

–··–··–··–··–··–··–.  Mountain fold, fold behind.

———————————  Crease line.

············································  X-ray or guide line.

## Arrows

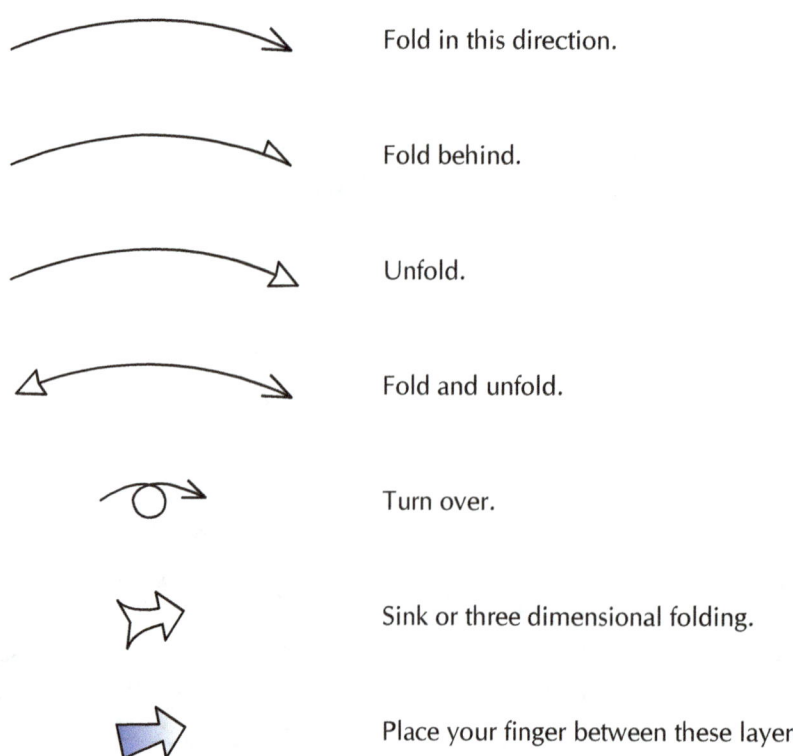

Fold in this direction.

Fold behind.

Unfold.

Fold and unfold.

Turn over.

Sink or three dimensional folding.

Place your finger between these layers.

8   *3D Origami Platonic Solids & More*

# Basic Folds

### Squash Fold.

In a squash fold, some paper is opened and then made flat. The shaded arrow shows where to place your finger.

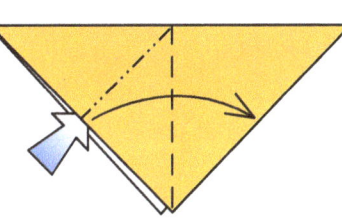
1. Squash-fold.

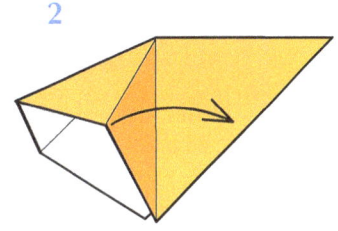
2. A 3D step.

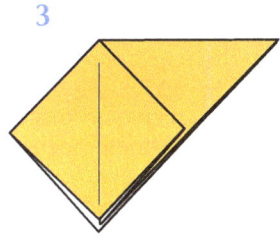
3.

### Inside Reverse Fold.

In an inside reverse fold, some paper is folded between layers. Here are two examples.

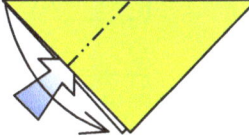
1. Reverse-fold.

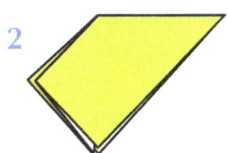
2.

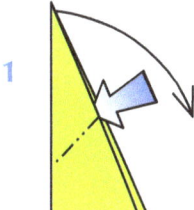
1. Reverse-fold.

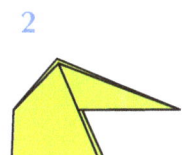
2.

### Preliminary Fold.

The Preliminary Fold is the starting point for many models. The maneuver in step 3 occurs in many other models.

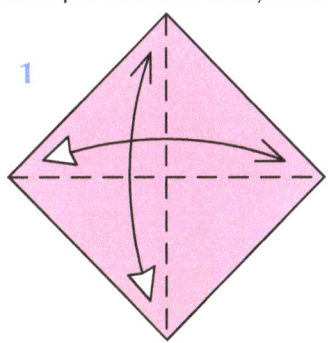
1. Fold and unfold.

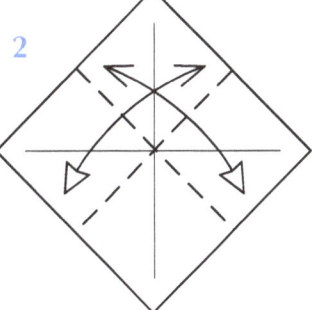
2. Fold and unfold.

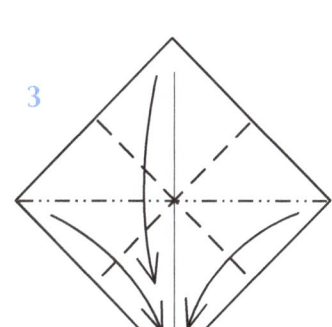
3. Collapse the square by bringing the four corners together.

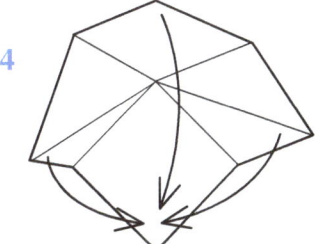
4. This is 3D.

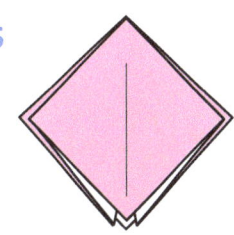
5. Preliminary Fold

Basic Folds 9

# Symmetry

Each model in this collection is folded from a square sheet of paper. To design these complex three-dimensional shapes, I want to satisfy several conditions that include:
1. The model is not too difficult to fold.
2. The paper is used efficiently to produce a shape as large as possible.
3. The model holds together well.
4. Each face has no stray lines, or a minimal number.
5. The folding procedure is as simple as possible, with fewest number of steps.

Symmetry simplifies the folding procedure. Symmetry can be seen by looking at the crease pattern of a model. The crease pattern shows the unfolded square sheet where the shaded regions represent the faces of the model, and the orientation of these regions shows the form of symmetry.

Five forms of symmetry are used in this work, and the five Platonic solids can be folded which use each of them. Here are the forms of symmetry.

**Even Symmetry:** Two sides of the square are mirror images. The tetrahedron uses even symmetry.

Tetrahedron

**Odd Symmetry:** The crease pattern is the same when rotated 180°. The icosahedron uses odd symmetry.

Icosahedron

**Square Symmetry:** The crease pattern is the same when rotated 90°. The octahedron uses square symmetry.

Octahedron

**3/4 Square Symmetry:** The crease pattern is the same when rotated 90°, but one of four quadrants is not used. The cube uses 3/4 square symmetry.

Cube

**No Symmetry:** The crease pattern shows no symmetry. The dodecahedron has no symmetry.

Dodecahedron

10   3D Origami Platonic Solids & More

# Platonic Solids

The five Platonic solids are the tetrahedron, cube, octahedron, icosahedron, and dodecahedron. They are the only polyhedra with the following properties:

1. The faces of each are identical regular polygons.

2. The corners of each are alike.

3. The shapes are convex. For convex polyhedra, line segments connecting any two corners are on or inside the solid.

To Plato, the tetrahedron represented fire, the cube represented earth, the octahedron represented air, the icosahedron represented water, and the dodecahedron represented the universe.

Here are the five Platonic solids with number of faces for each.

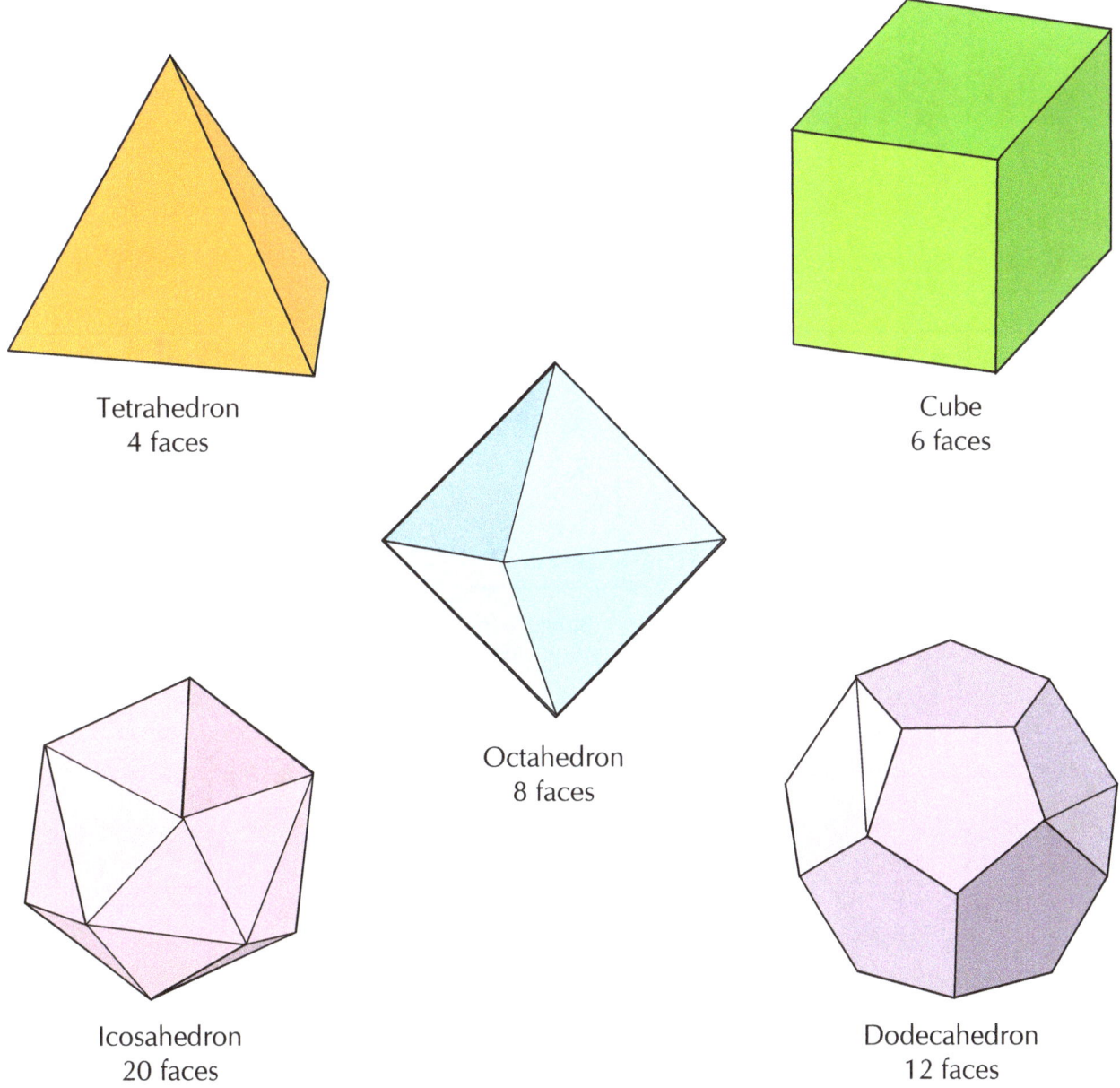

Tetrahedron
4 faces

Cube
6 faces

Octahedron
8 faces

Icosahedron
20 faces

Dodecahedron
12 faces

*Platonic Solids*

# Tetrahedron

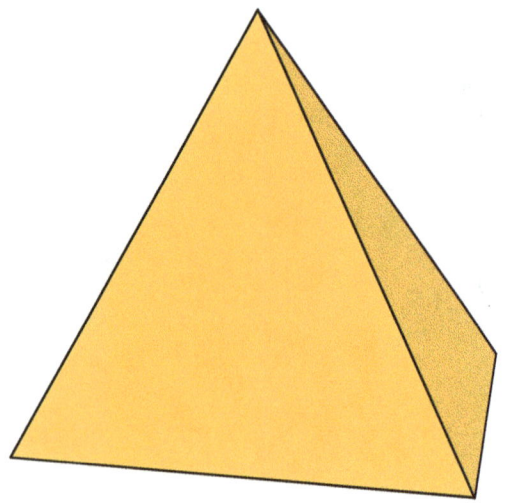

Composed of four equilateral triangles, this is the simplest of the five Platonic solids. Plato believed the tetrahedron represented fire because of its sharpness and simplicity.

The figure above shows the crease pattern. Even symmetry is used.

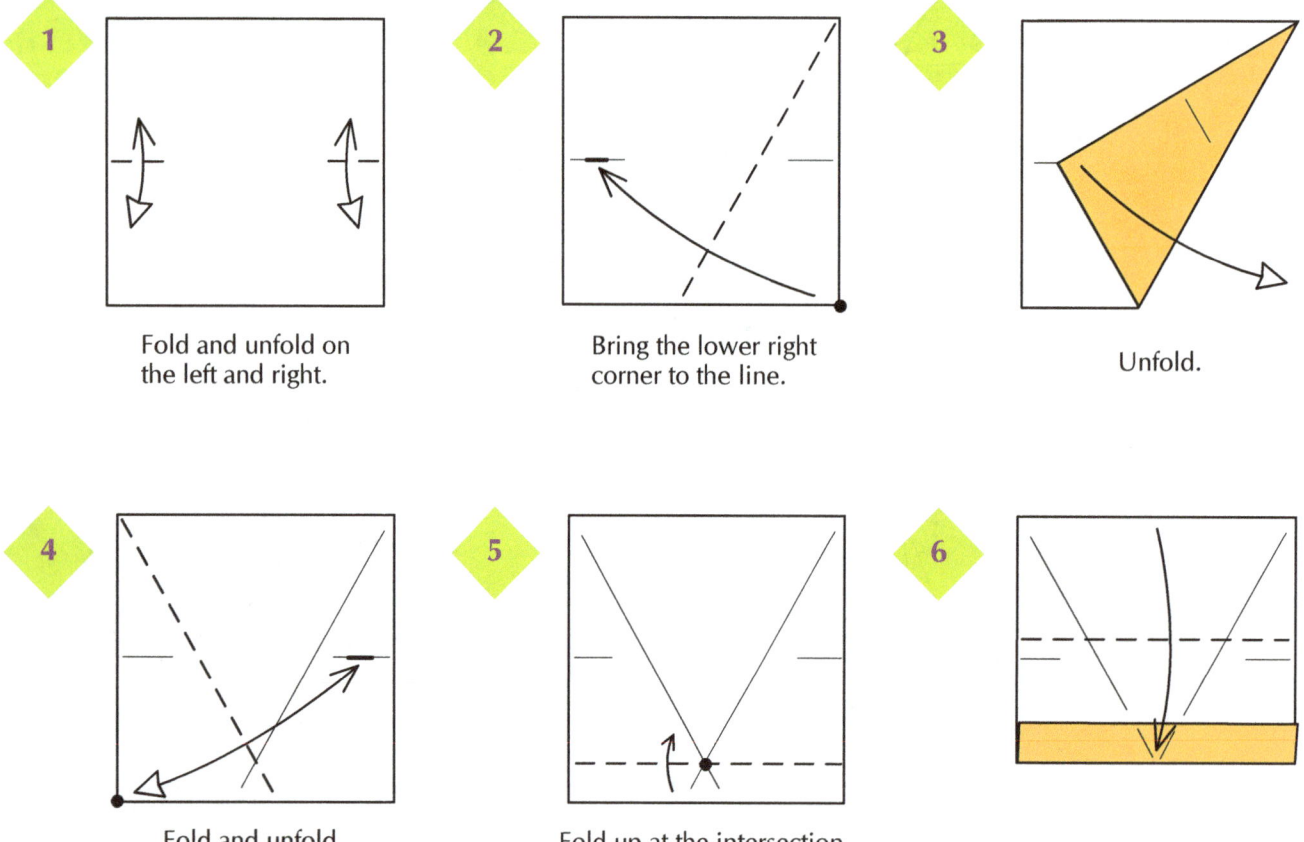

1. Fold and unfold on the left and right.
2. Bring the lower right corner to the line.
3. Unfold.
4. Fold and unfold.
5. Fold up at the intersection.

12  3D Origami Platonic Solids & More

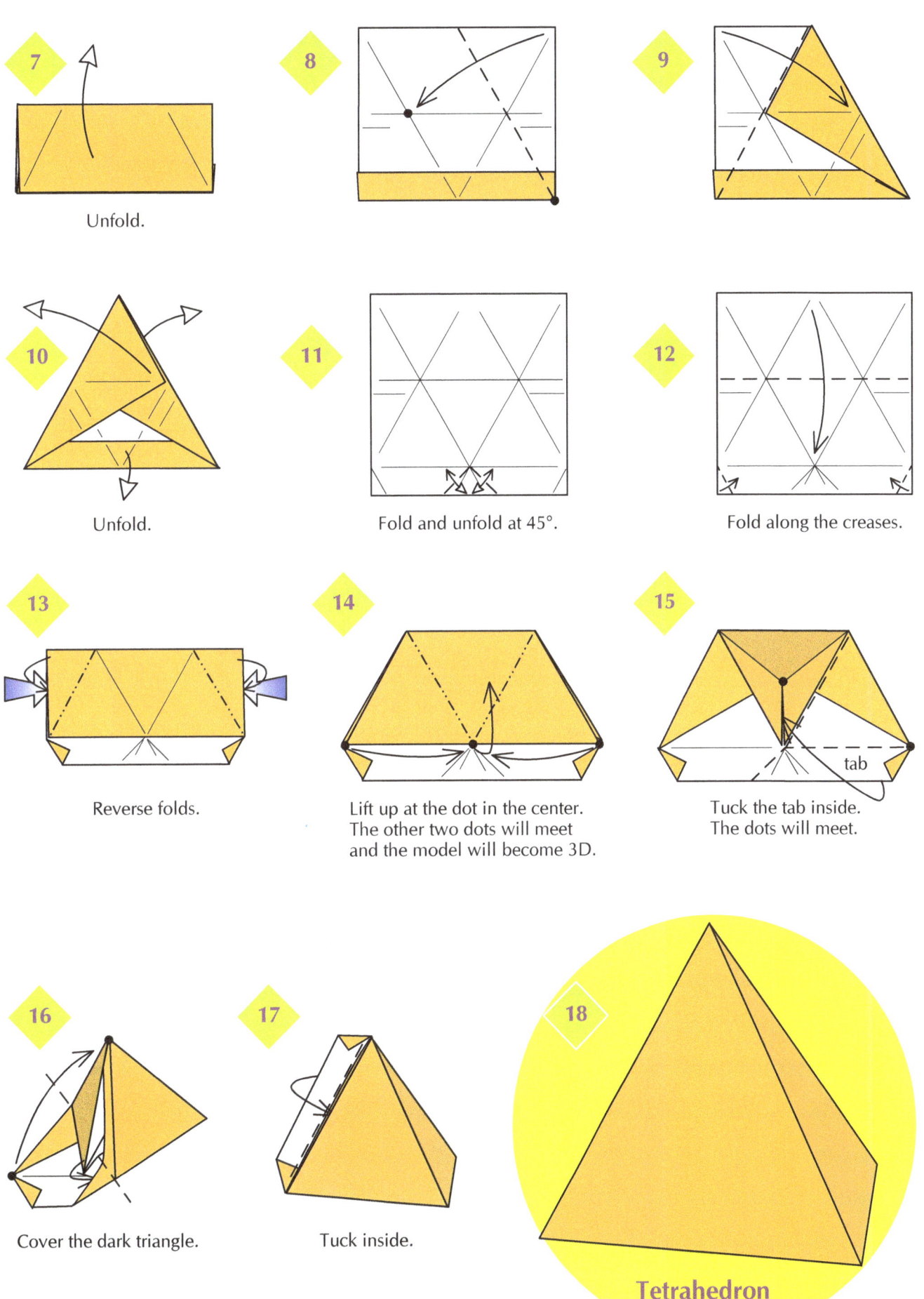

# Cube (1)

Plato believed the cube, with six square faces, symbolized earth because of its stability.

This model uses 3/4 square symmetry and is slighly easier to fold than the next cube.

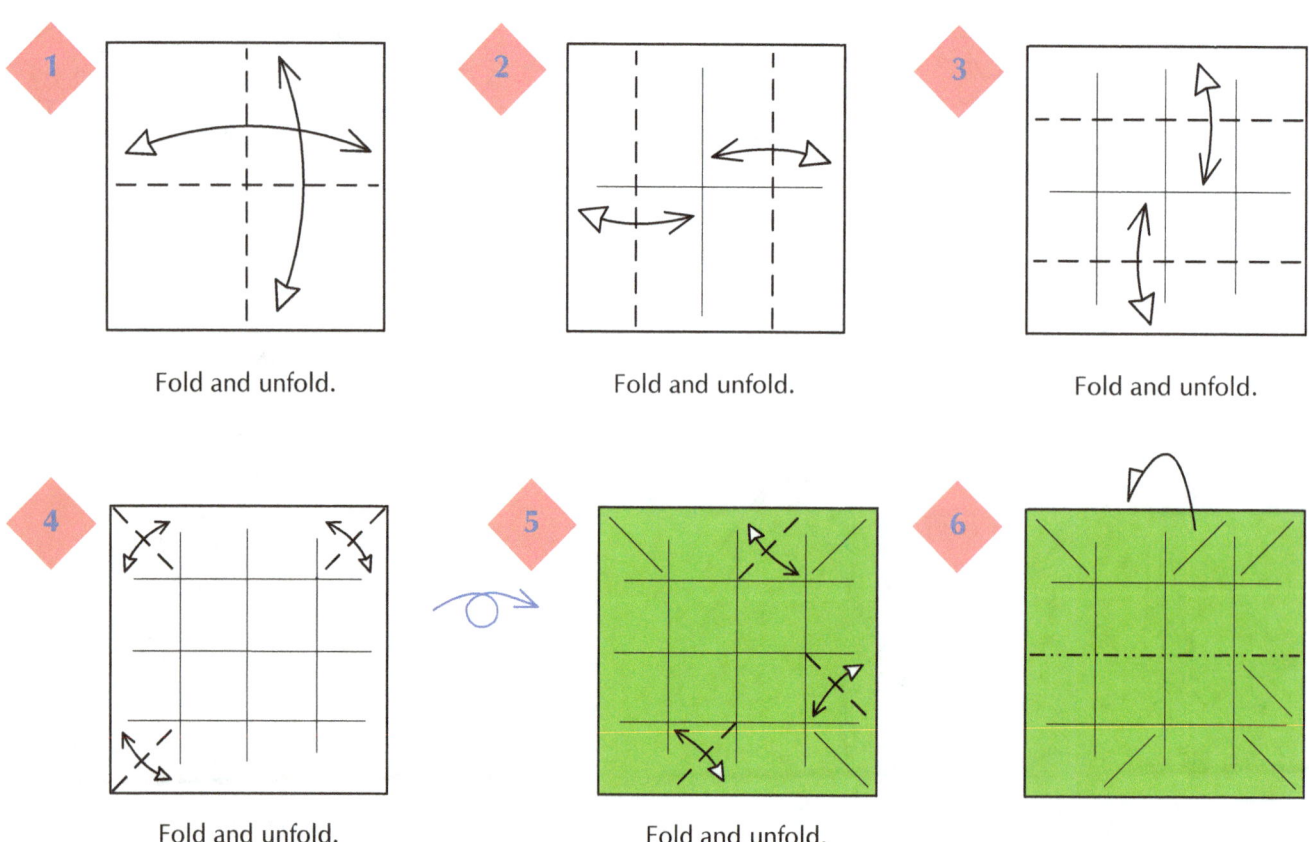

1. Fold and unfold.
2. Fold and unfold.
3. Fold and unfold.
4. Fold and unfold.
5. Fold and unfold.
6. 

14   3D Origami Platonic Solids & More

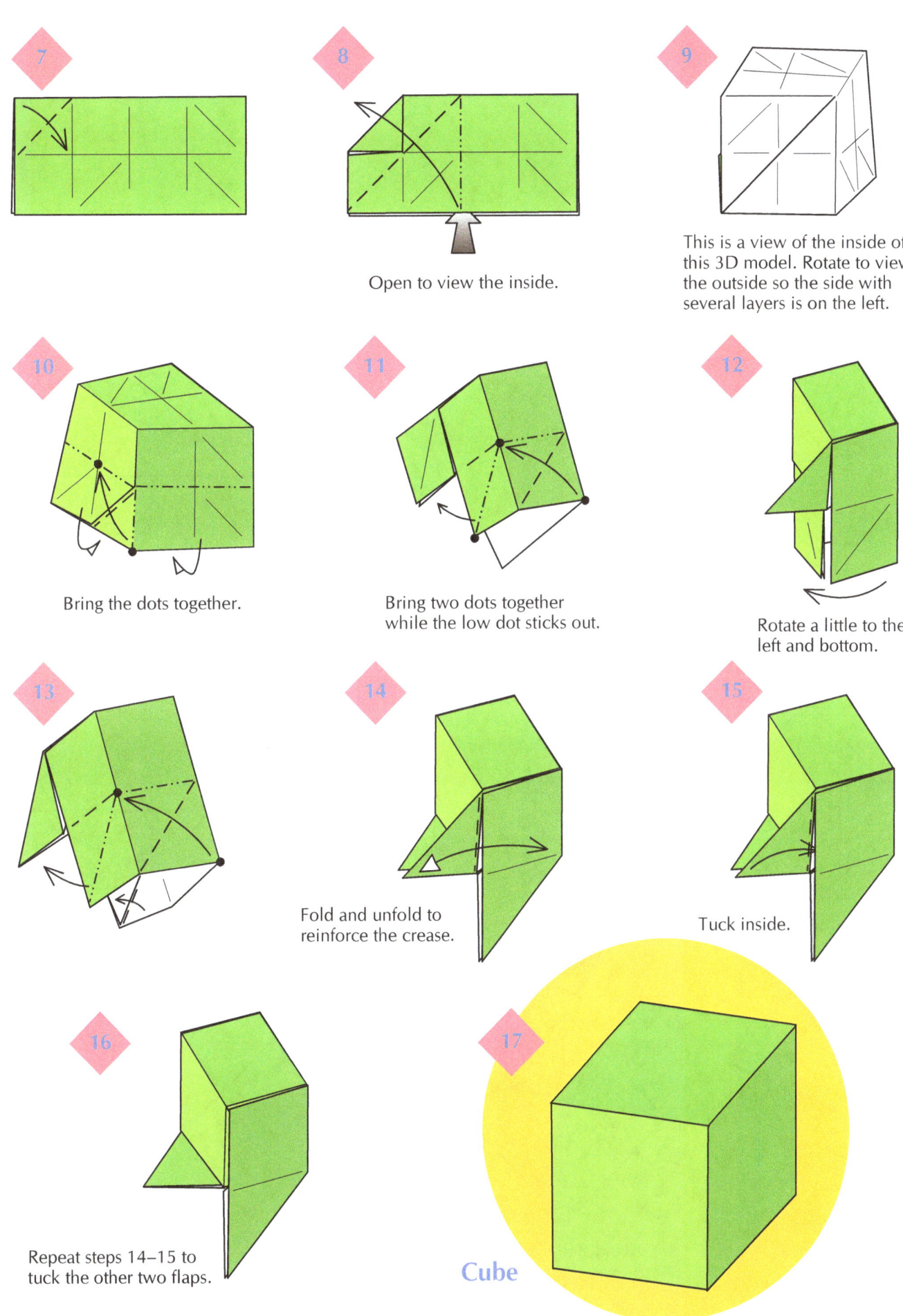

# Cube (2)

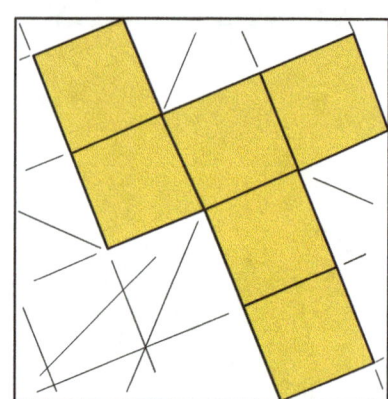

This folding method produces a larger cube than the previous model. However, there is less tab to lock the cube. The crease pattern shows 3/4 square symmetry.

**1.** Fold and unfold on the left.

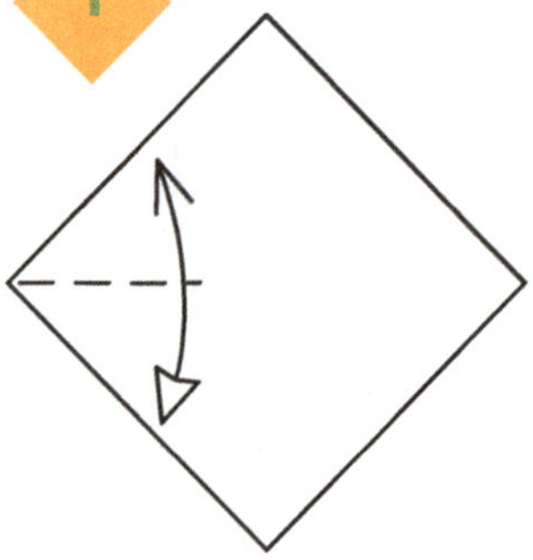

**2.**

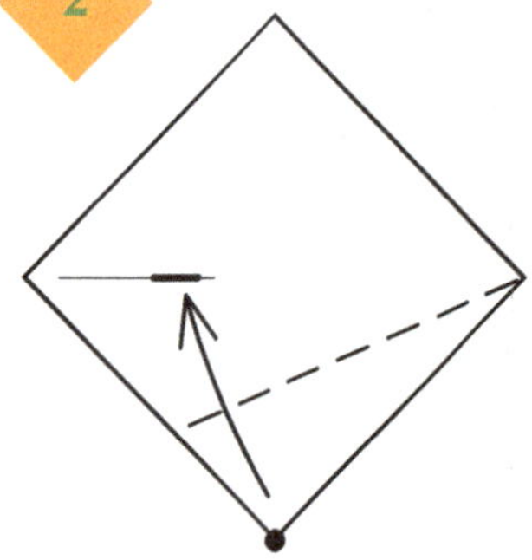

**3.**

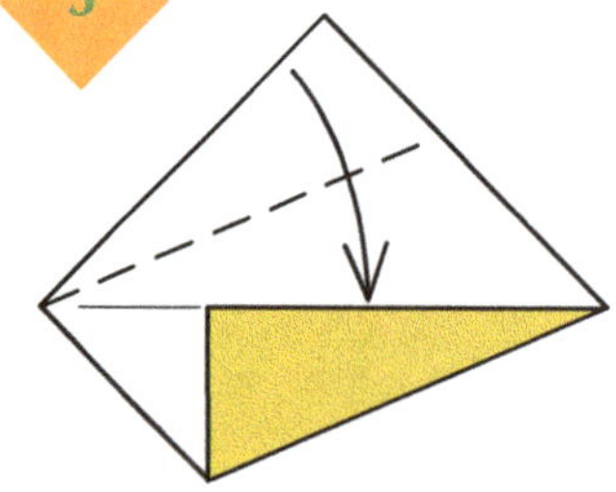

**4.** 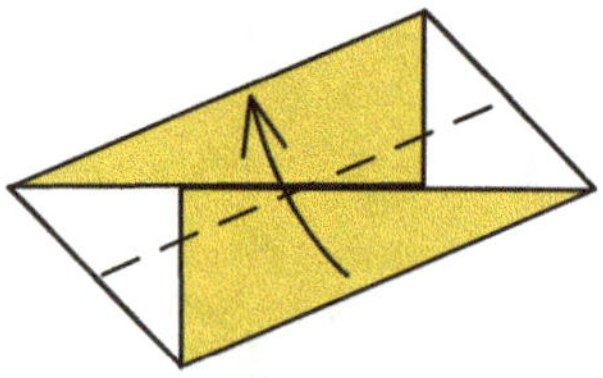 Fold un half.

**5.** Unfold.

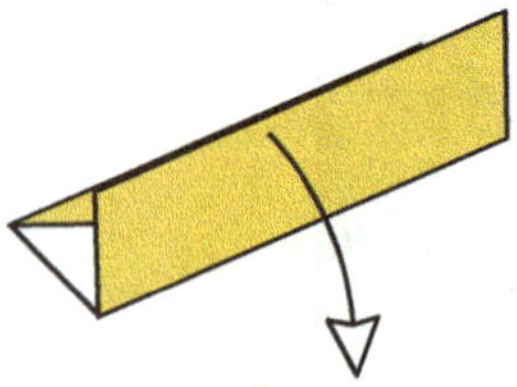

**6.** Fold and unfold.

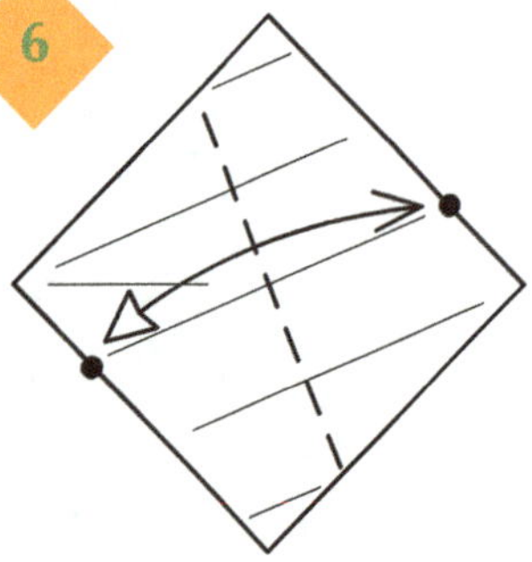

**7.**

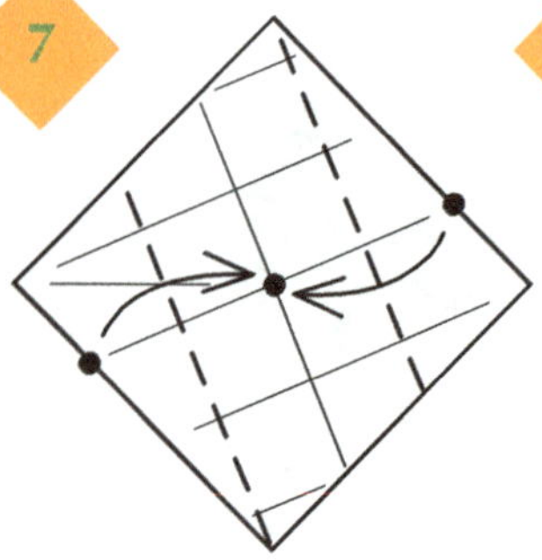

**8.** 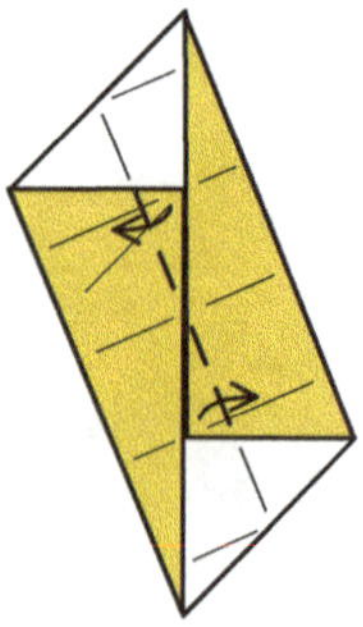 Fold along a partially hidden crease.

16  *3D Origami Platonic Solids & More*

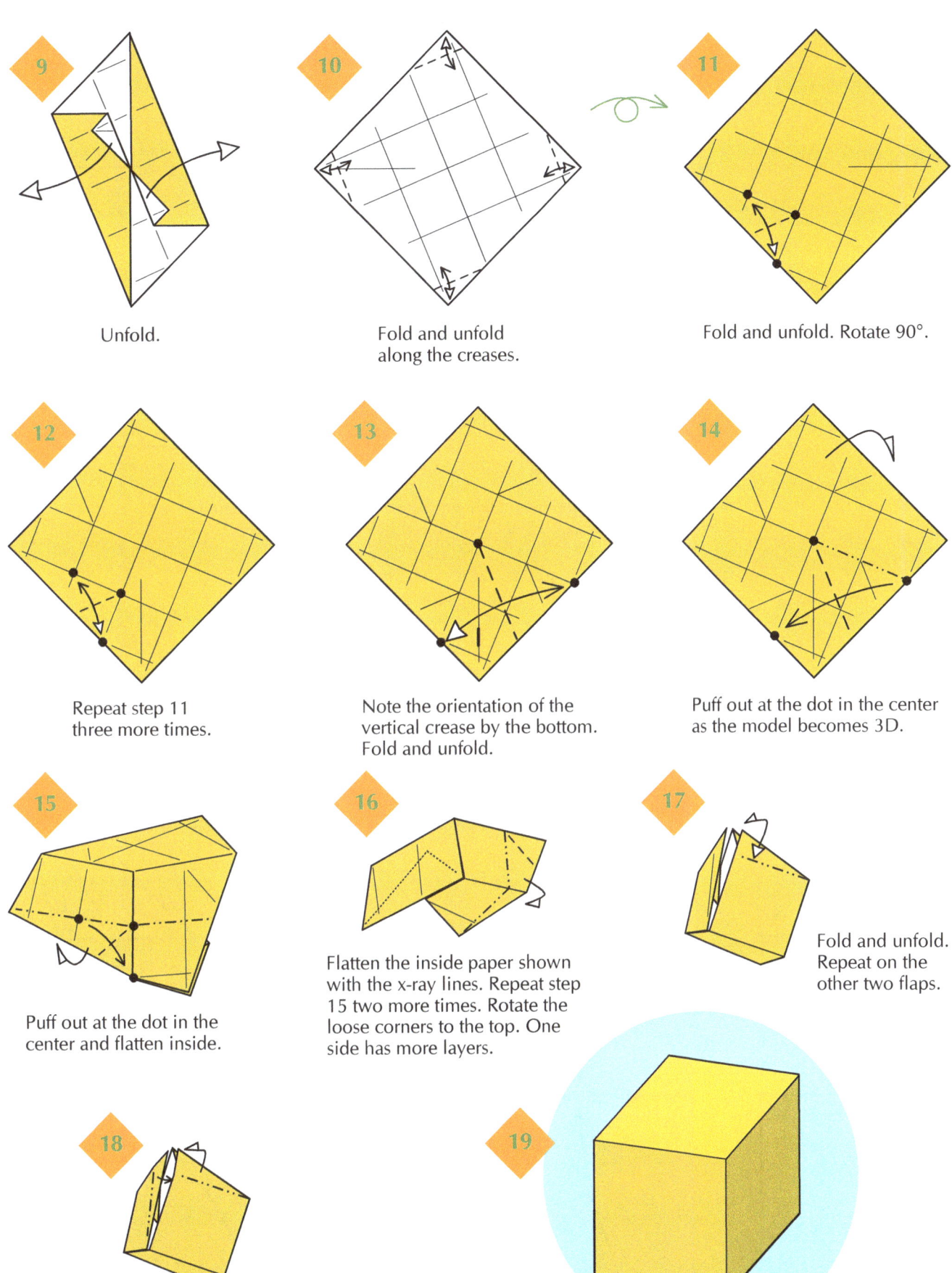

Cube 17

# Octahedron (1)

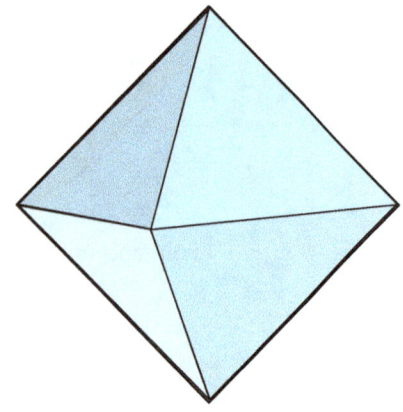
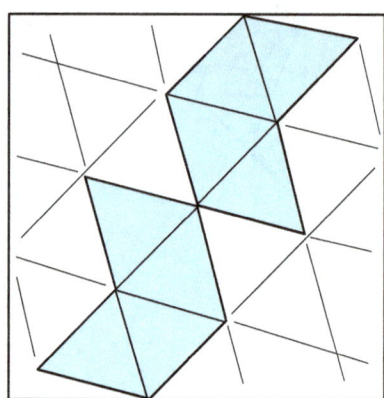

The octahedron, formed from eight equilateral triangles, represented air to Plato because it appears to be suspended.

This version is easier to fold than the next. The folding method is 2D until the last step when it is inflated. Odd symmetry is used.

**1** Fold and unfold.

**2** Fold and unfold at the top and bottom.

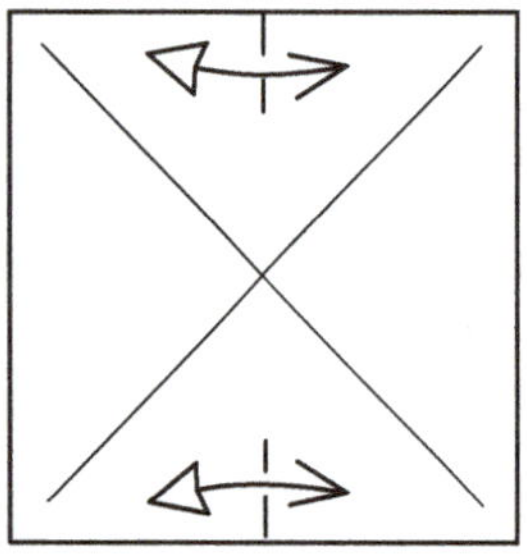

**3** Bring the corners to the lines. Crease at the top and bottom.

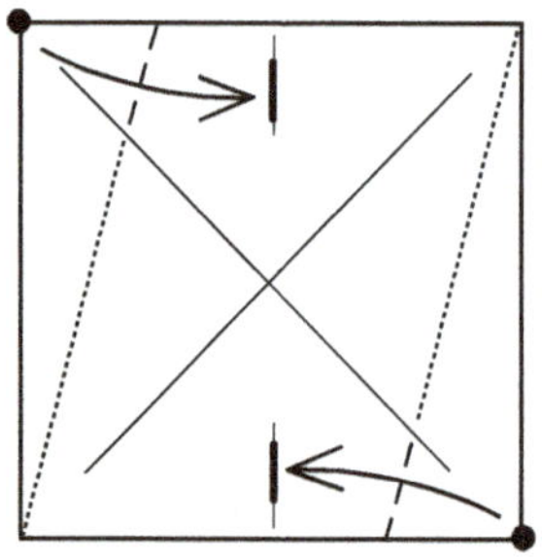

**4** Unfold.

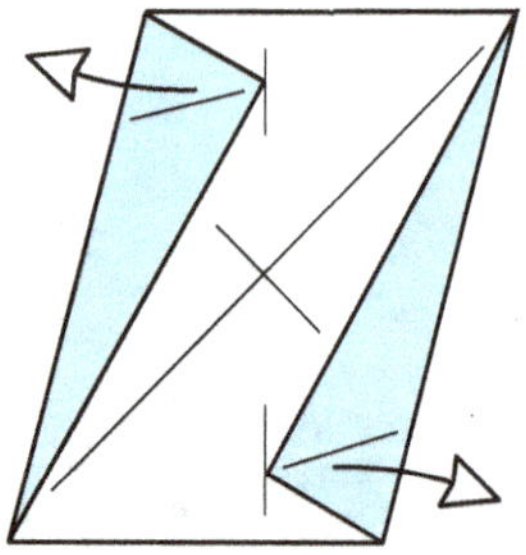

**5** Fold and unfold at the top and bottom.

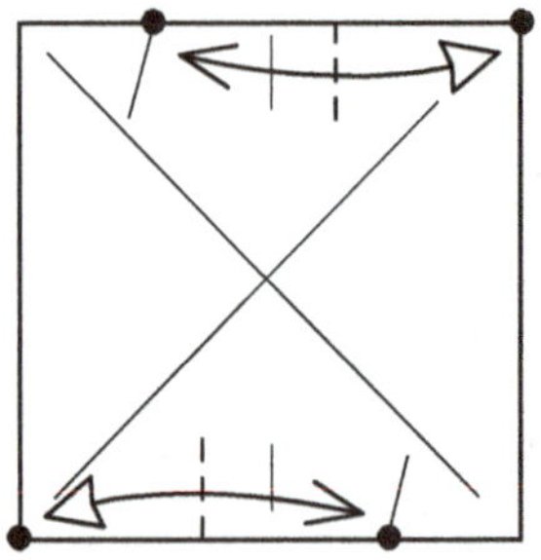

**6** The dots will meet.

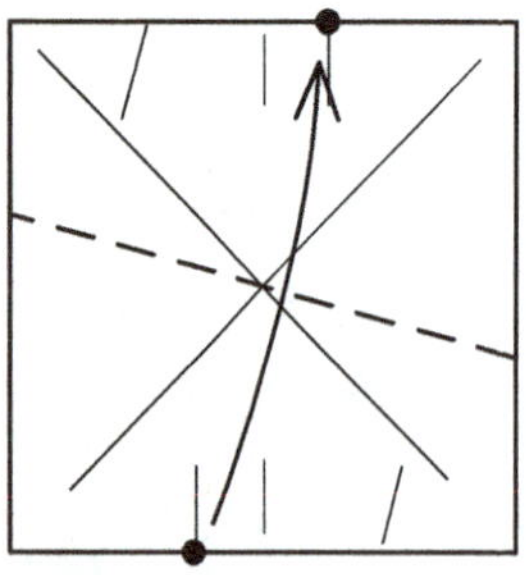

**7**

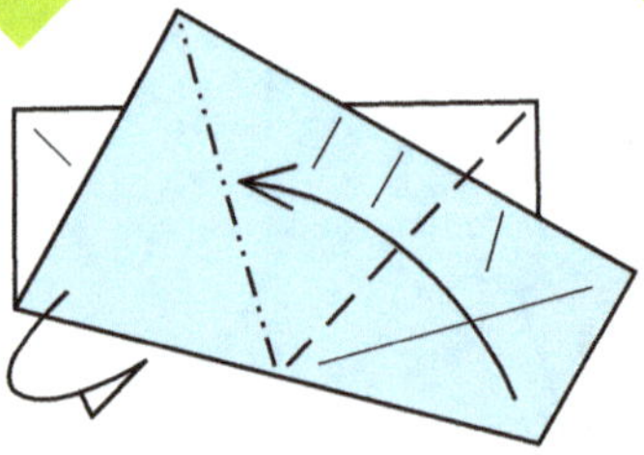

**8**  Turn over and repeat.

18   3D Origami Platonic Solids & More

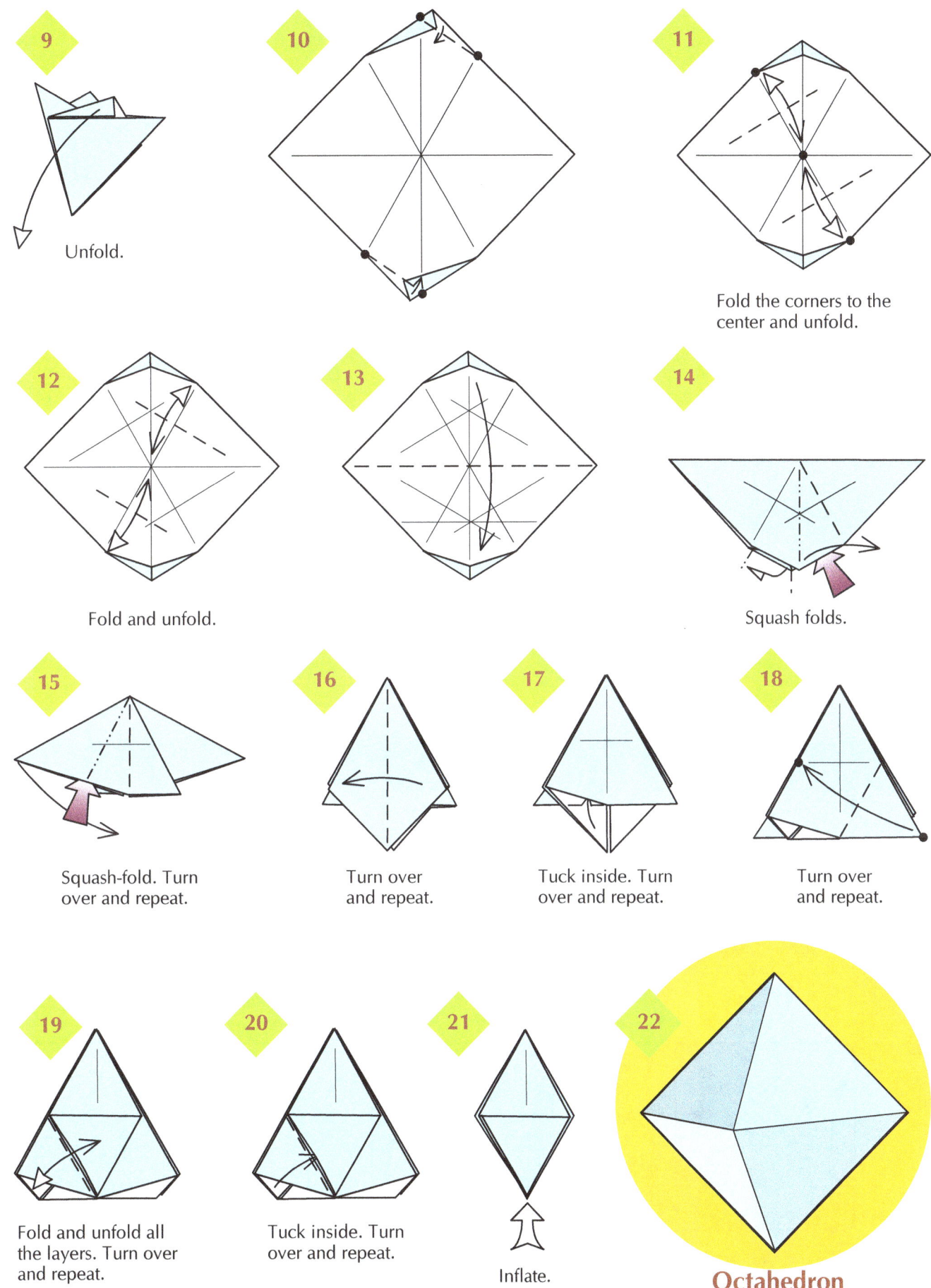

Octahedron 19

# Octahedron (2)

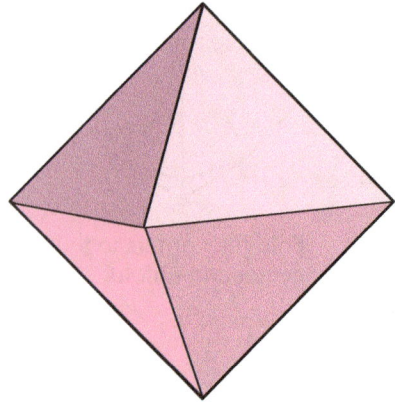
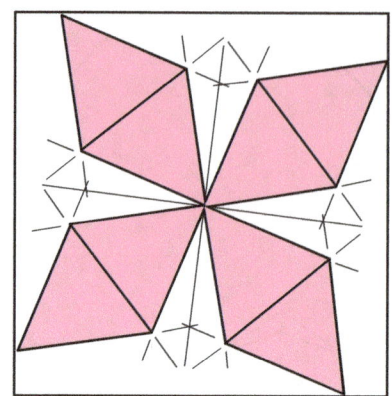

The design for this octahedron has square symmetry. The model closes with four thin tabs interlocking at the top, a concept called the twist lock. The thin tabs allow for efficient use of paper so this version is larger than the previous one.

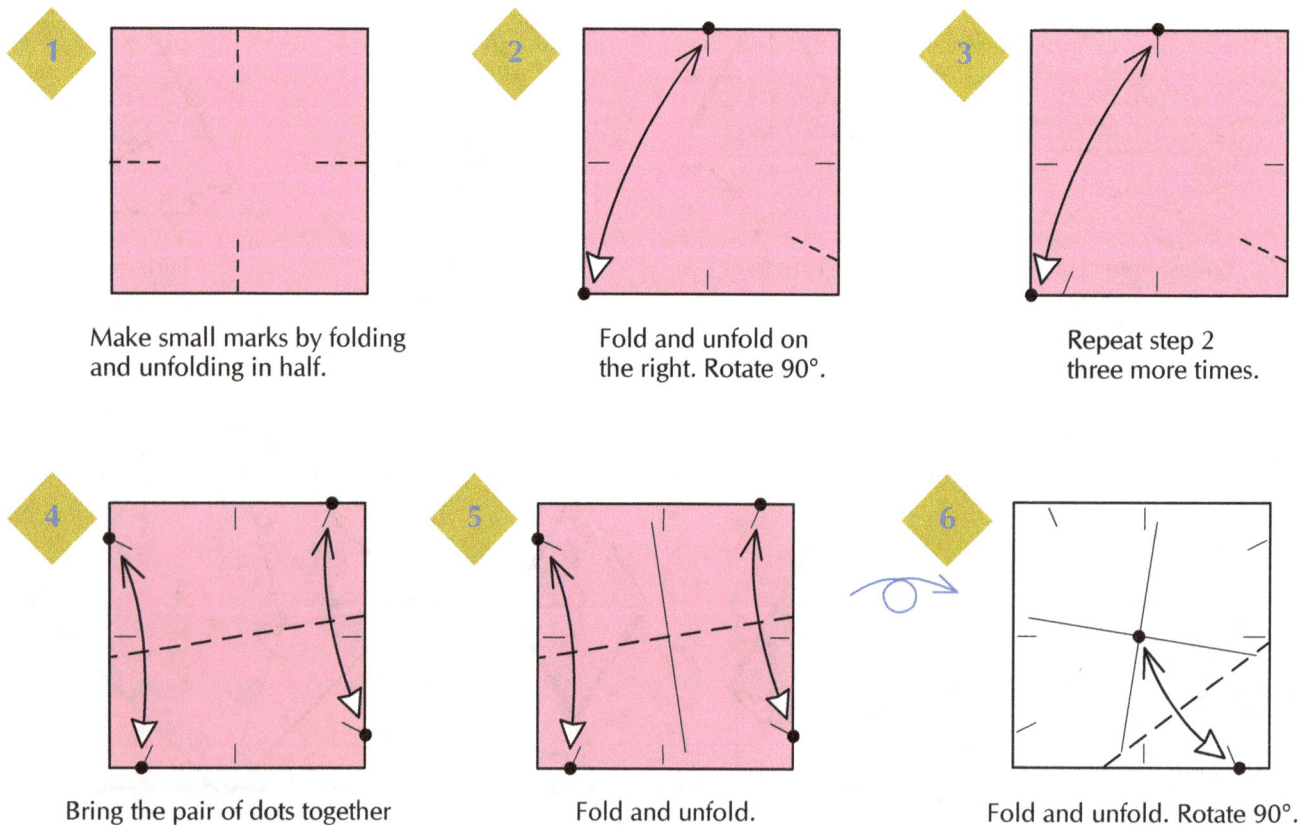

1. Make small marks by folding and unfolding in half.
2. Fold and unfold on the right. Rotate 90°.
3. Repeat step 2 three more times.
4. Bring the pair of dots together and unfold. Rotate 90°.
5. Fold and unfold.
6. Fold and unfold. Rotate 90°.

20  3D Origami Platonic Solids & More

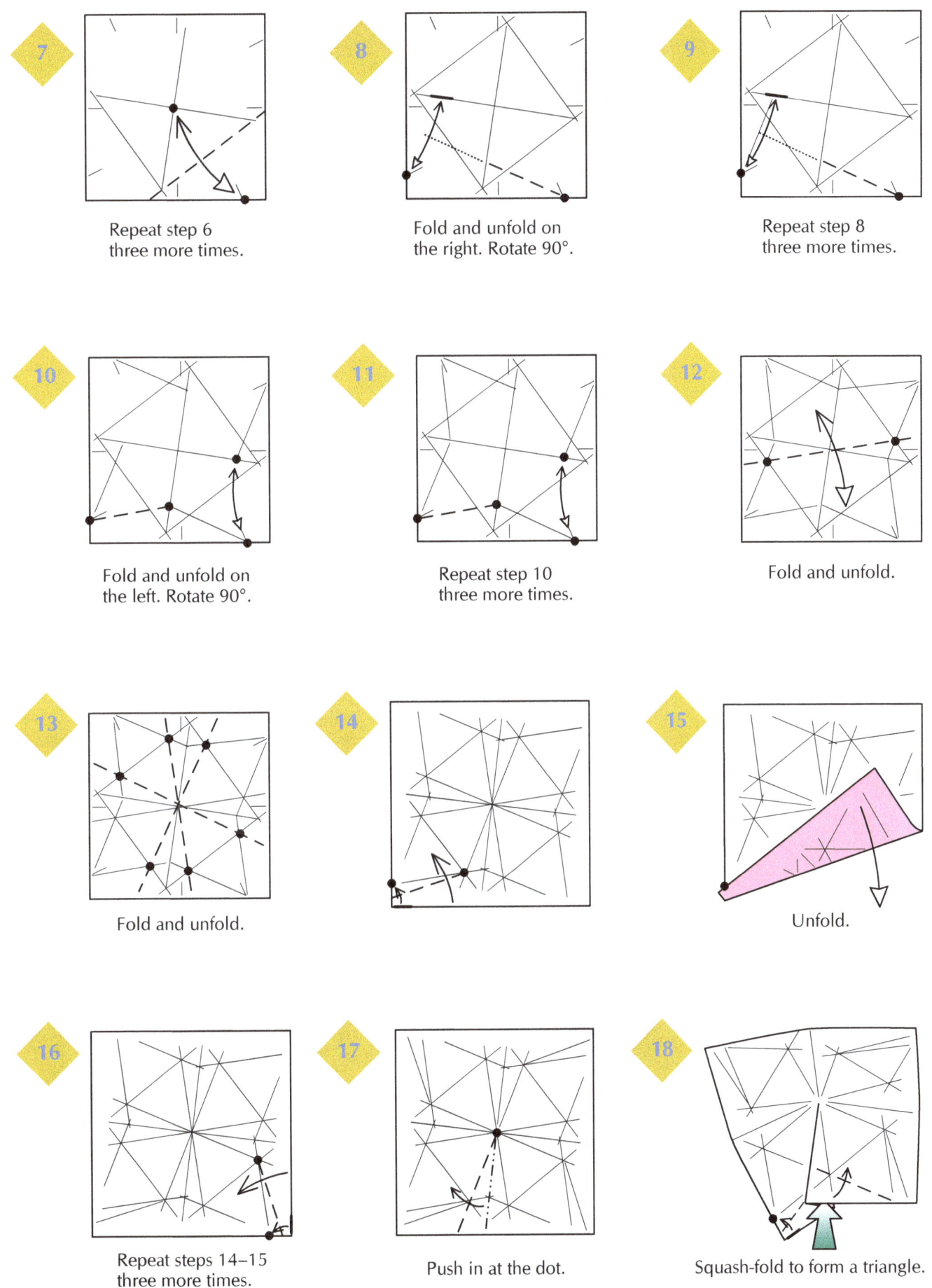

Octahedron 21

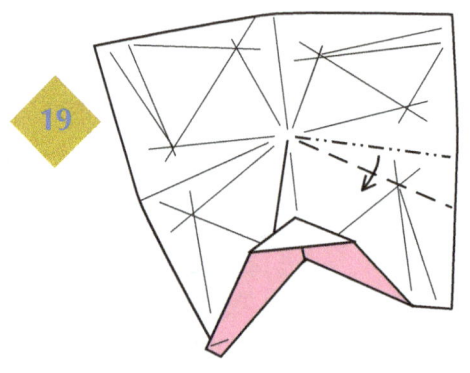

19

The orientation of the white triangle is not important. Repeat steps 17–18 three more times. Rotate to view the outside.

20

Flatten.

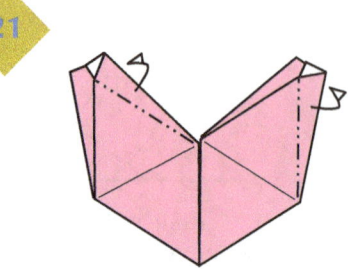

21

Turn over and repeat.

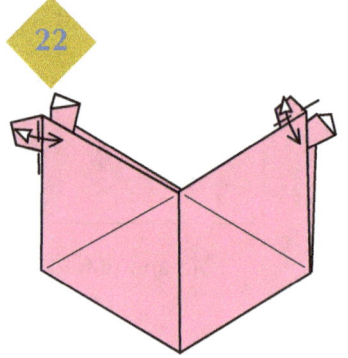

22

Fold and unfold. Repeat behind.

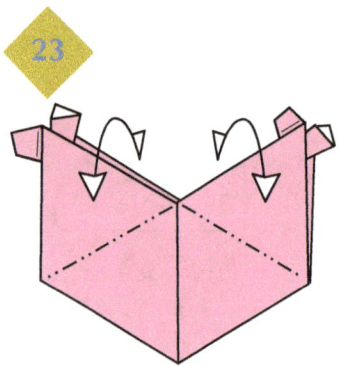

23

Open to fold inside and unfold. Do not flatten. Repeat behind.

24

Open and flatten. Follow the dot in the next step.

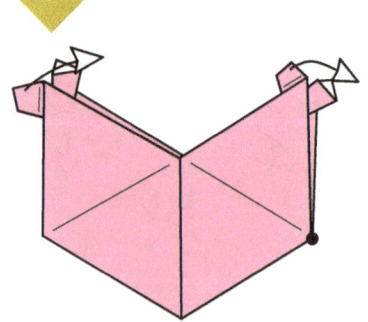

25

Unfold the thin flaps. Repeat behind.

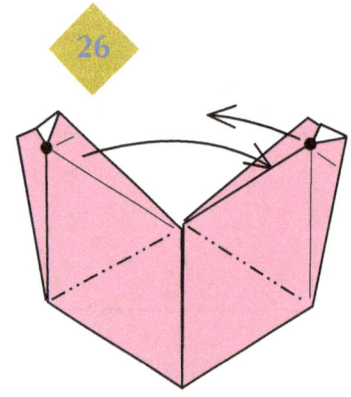

26

Close the model by interlocking the four tabs. The tabs spiral inward. This method is called a twist lock.

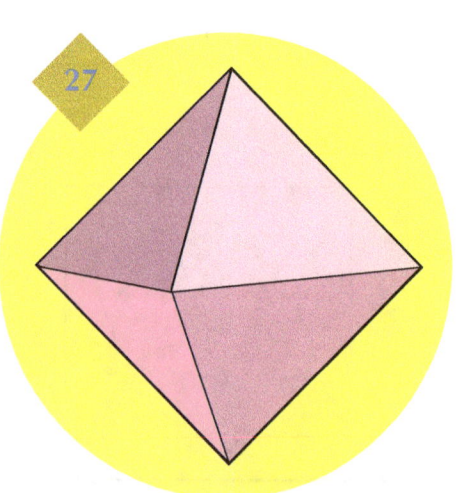

27

**Octahedron**

22    3D Origami Platonic Solids & More

# Icosahedron

The icosahedron is composed of 20 equilateral triangles. Plato attributed this model to water because if its ability to roll.

The layout shows a band of ten triangles down the diagonal with five triangles on each side. Odd symmetry is used.

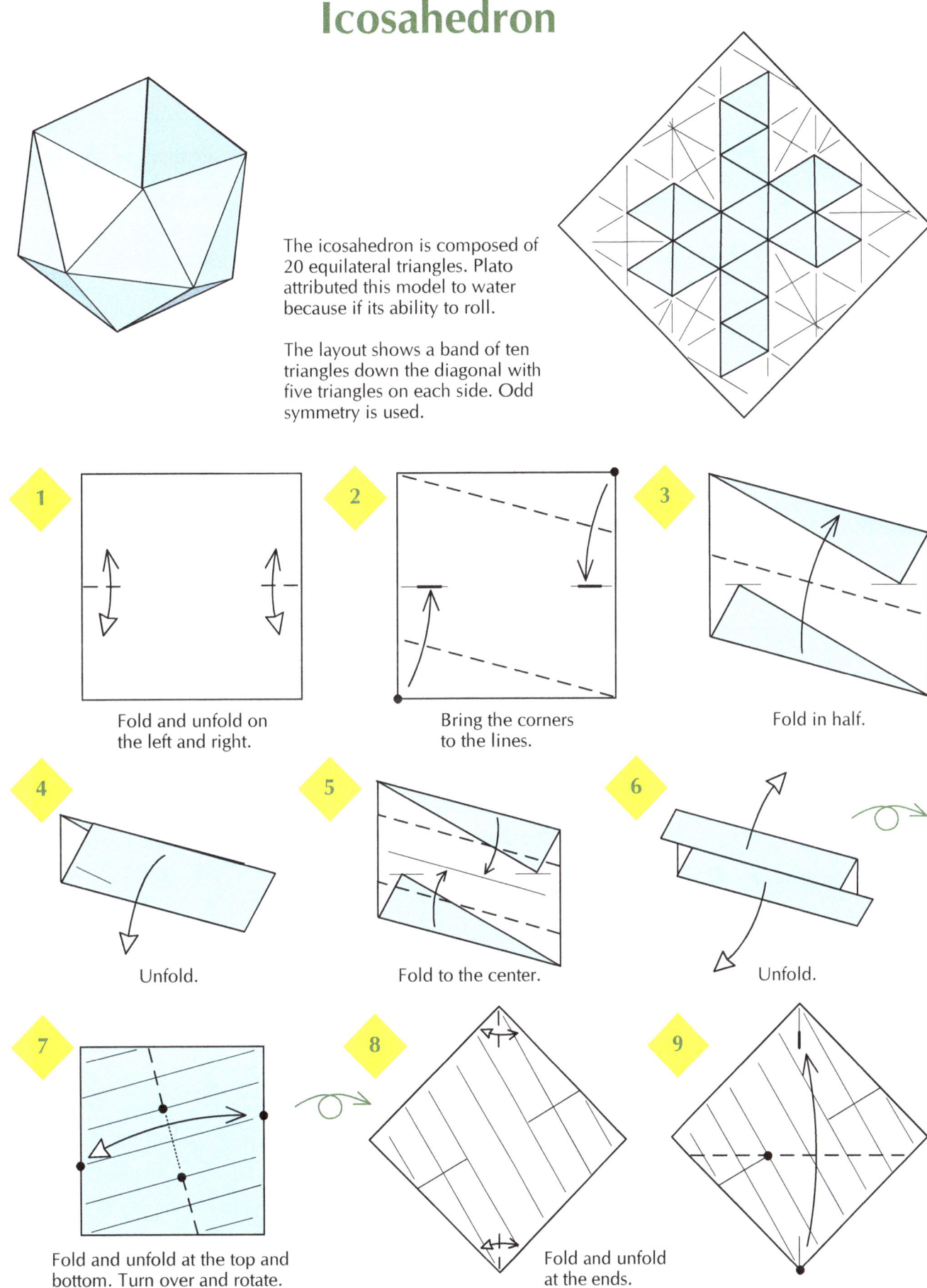

1. Fold and unfold on the left and right.
2. Bring the corners to the lines.
3. Fold in half.
4. Unfold.
5. Fold to the center.
6. Unfold.
7. Fold and unfold at the top and bottom. Turn over and rotate.
8. Fold and unfold at the ends.

Icosahedron 23

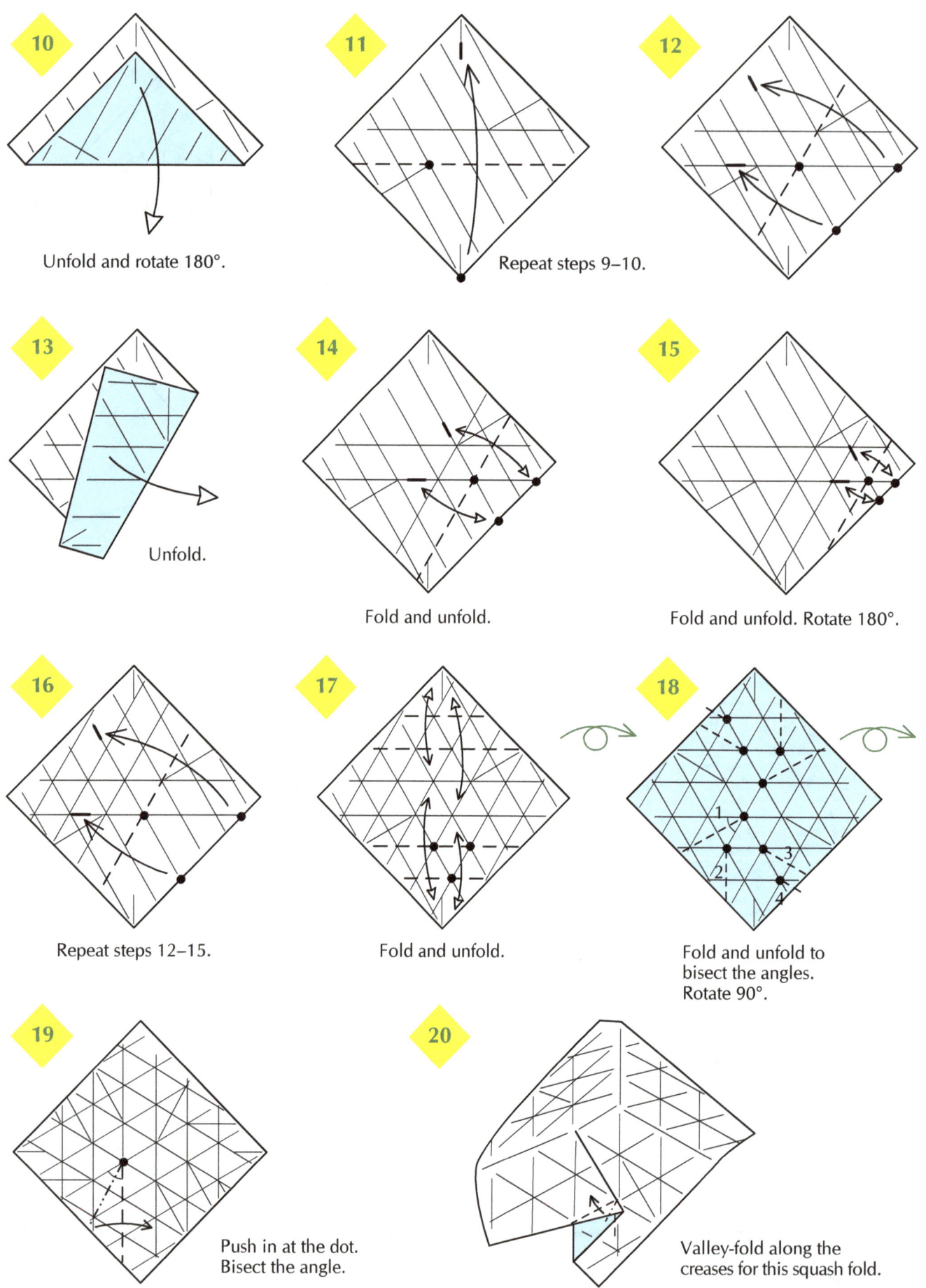

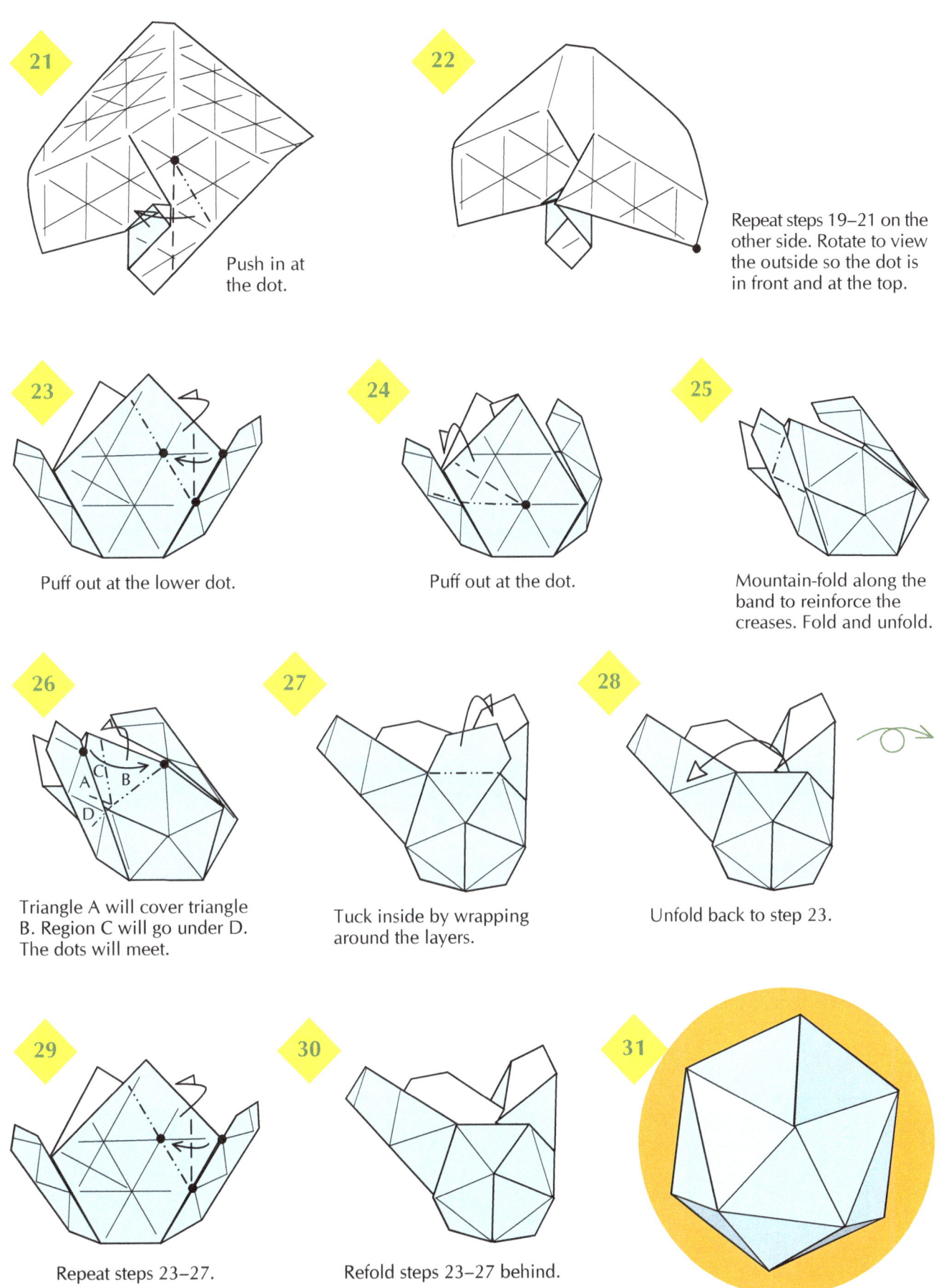

Icosahedron 25

# Dodecahedron

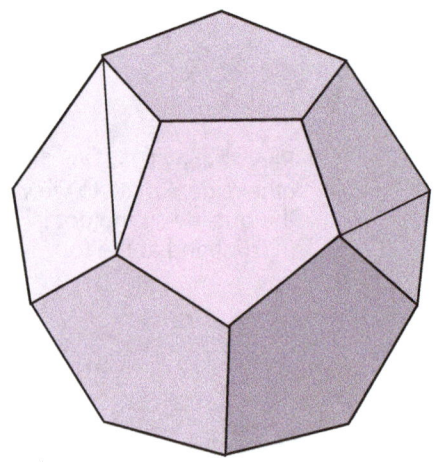
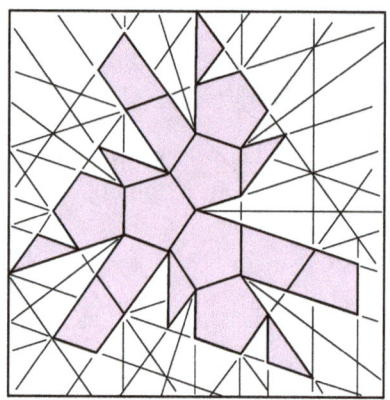

The dodecahedron has twelve pentagonal faces. To Plato, the dodecahedron, the quintessence (the "fifth being"), represented the whole universe.

This was a formidable model to design. I must have made a plethora of different versions before selecting this one to diagram. To simplify the folding, I allowed some faces to have lines through them. This method uses a minimal amount of folding (though plenty of precreasing). A version of the dodecahedron with clean faces can be found in *Classic Polyhedra Origami*.

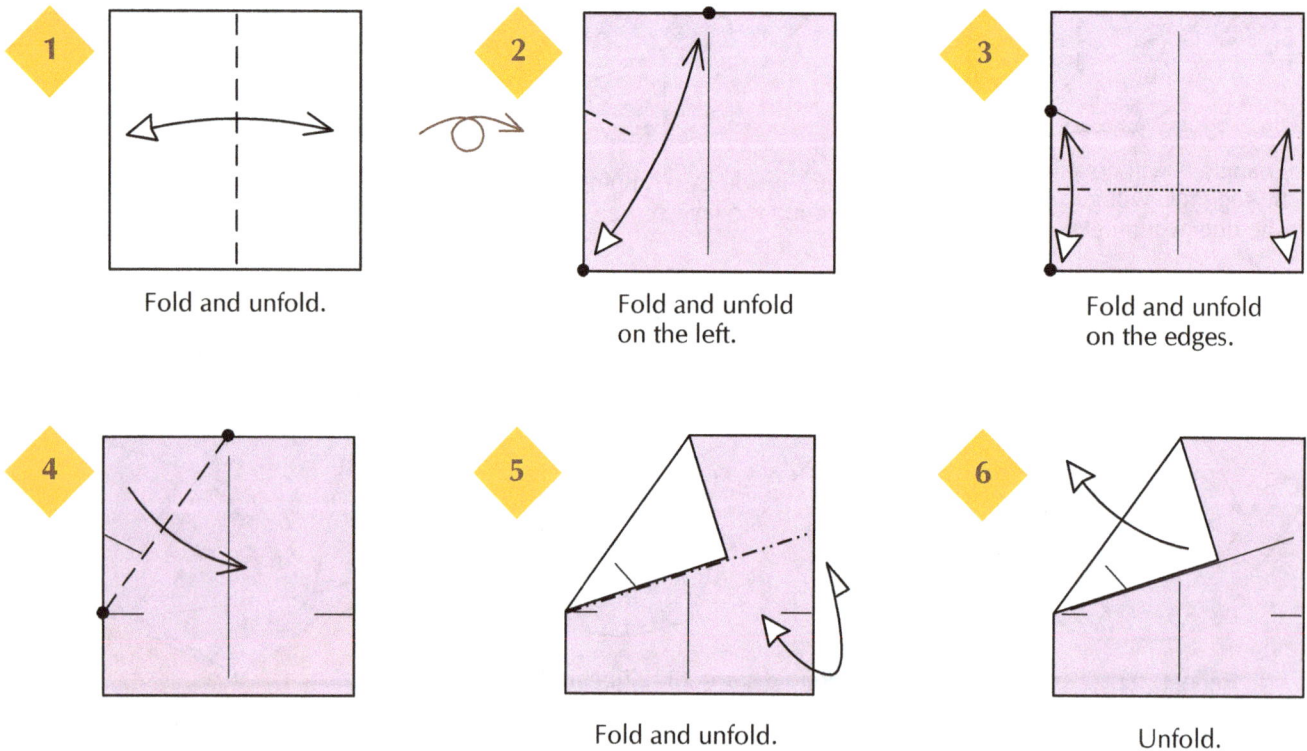

26   3D Origami Platonic Solids & More

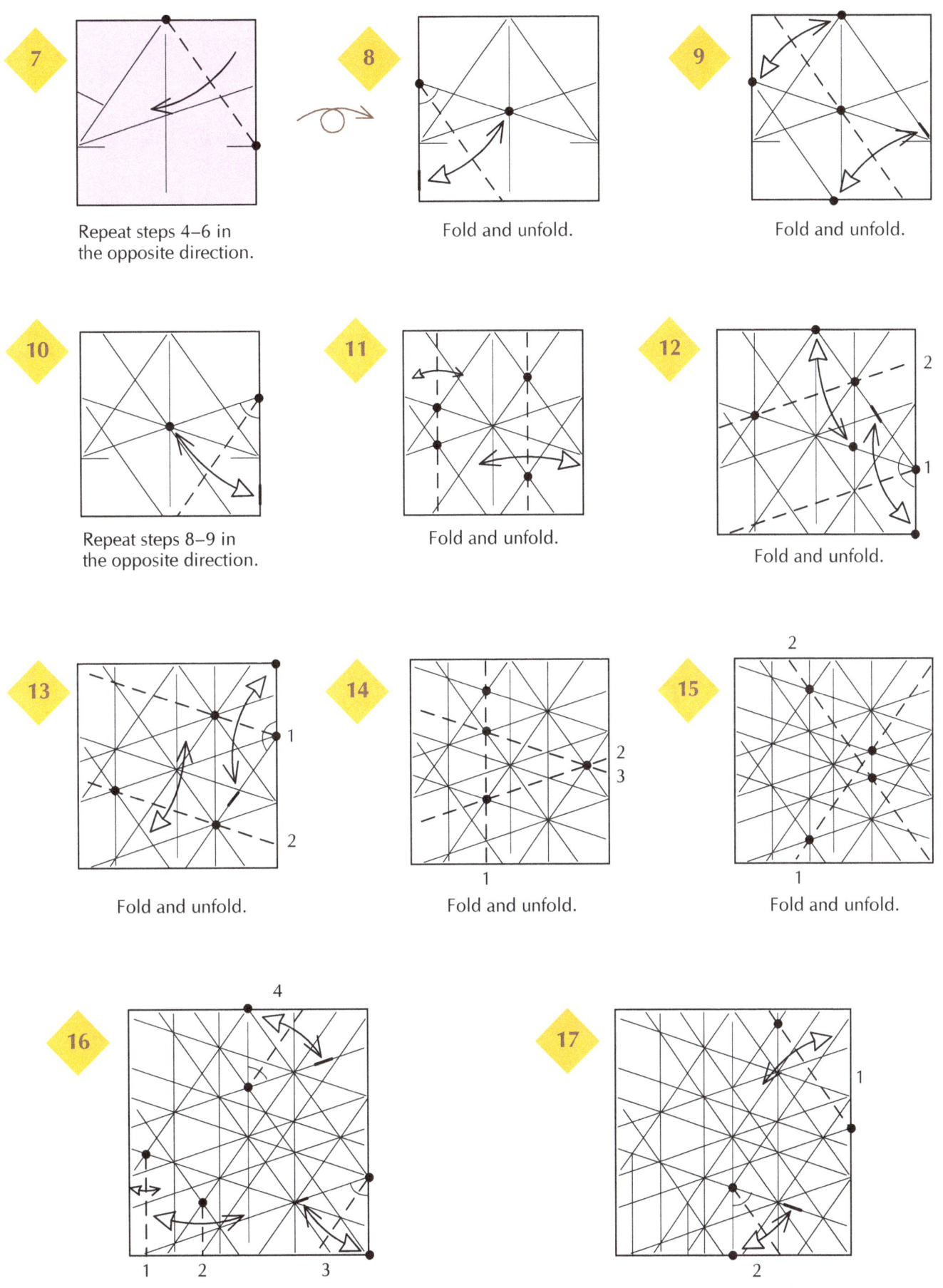

Dodecahedron 27

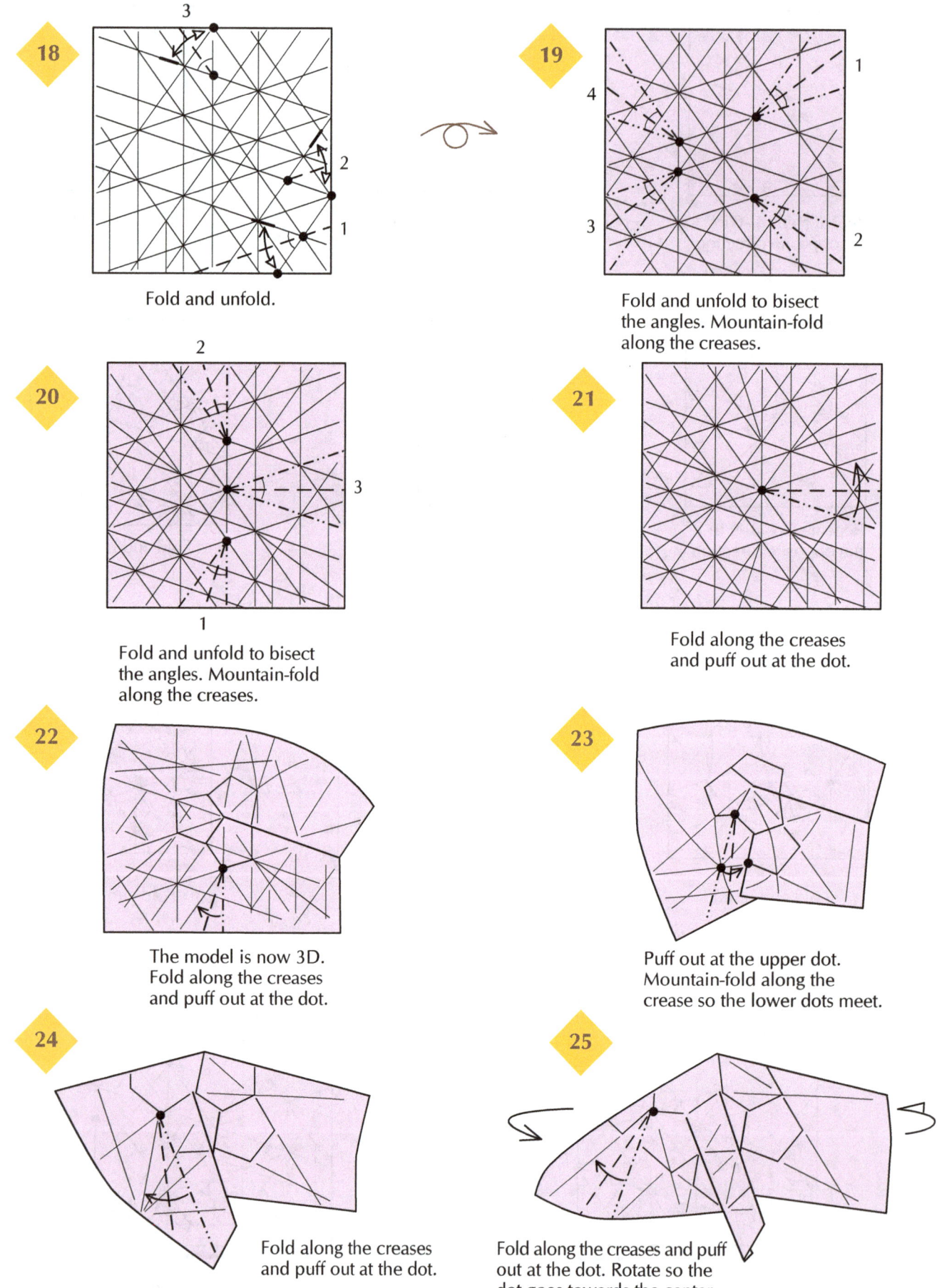

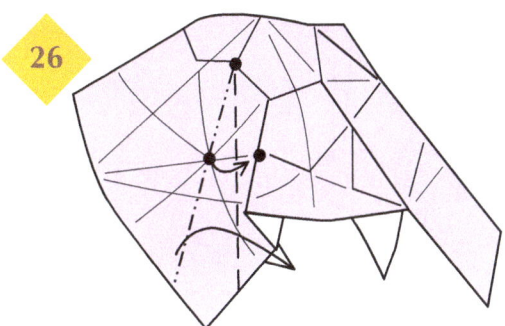

Puff out at the upper dot. Mountain-fold along the crease so the lower dots meet.

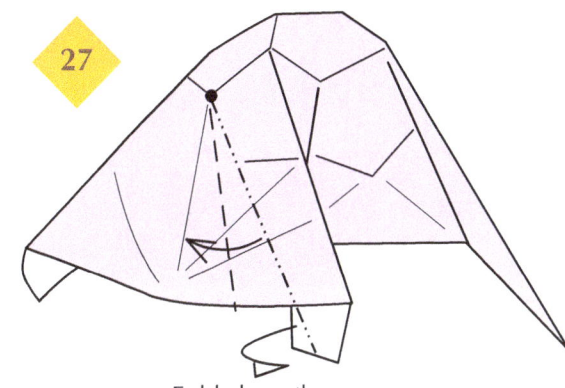

Fold along the creases and puff out at the dot.

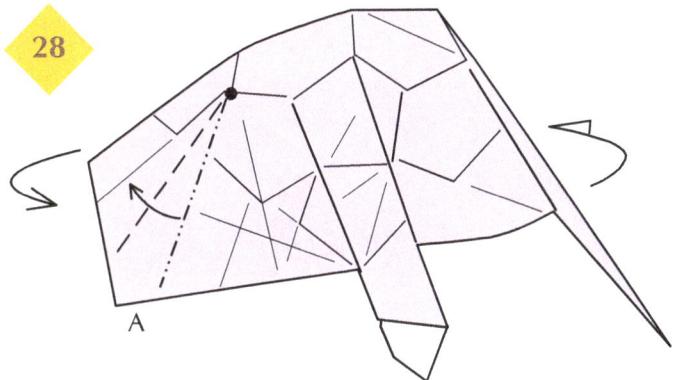

Note corner A. Fold along the creases and puff out at the dot. Rotate so the dot goes towards the center.

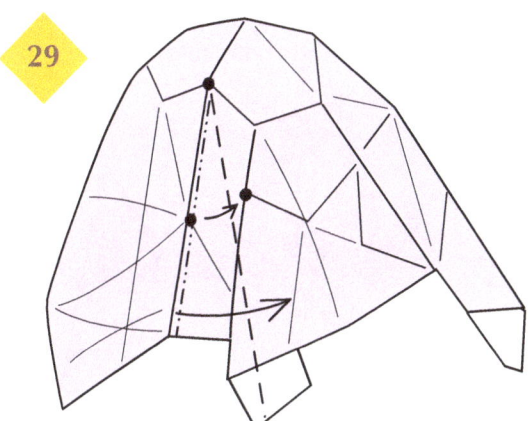

Puff out at the upper dot. Mountain-fold along the crease so the lower dots meet.

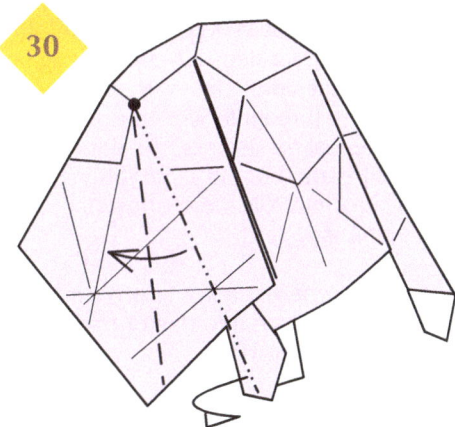

Fold along the creases and puff out at the dot.

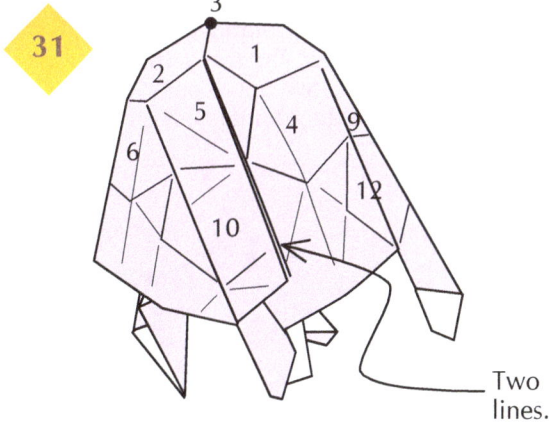

Two lines.

In this picture, the vertex at the dot is at the top. The vertex meets the top three pentagons, labeled 1, 2, and 3. Pentagon 3 is on the back. Below these three are six going around, labeled 4, 5, 6, ... , 9. Pentagons 7 and 8 are behind. (9 is just barely visible on the right.) By the bottom are the last three pentagons—10, 11, 12. 11 is behind. Also, there are two lines at the same location going down on pentagons 5 and 10, and this happens only once. Rotate so the vertex at the dot becomes the bottom, and the 2 lines are showing in front on the left.

*Dodecahedron*

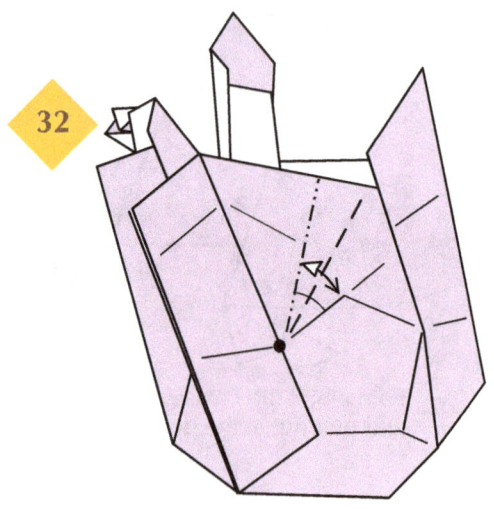

Fold and unfold.

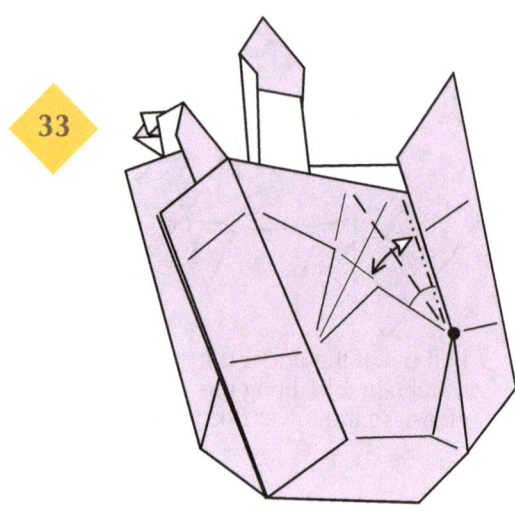

Fold and unfold.

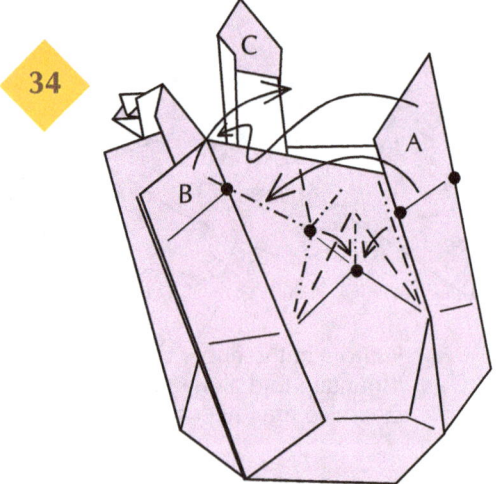

Bring the dots together by folding tabs A and B toward each other. The three lower dots will meet and the two upper ones will meet. Tab A will tuck under B.

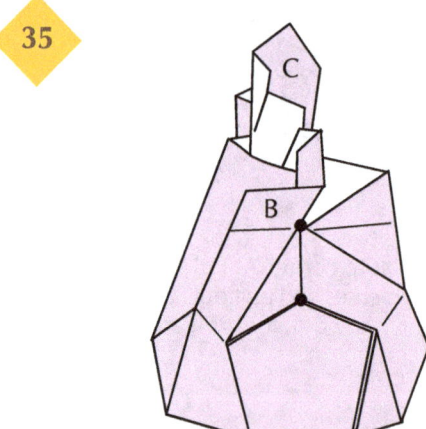

Unfold to step 32, then repeat steps 32–34, unfold back to step 32, and repeat steps 32–34 once again, each time on a different side. Tabs A, B, and C interlock as if they are three interwoven ribbons. As you go around to repeat these steps, the edges and tabs are all a bit different, but the same folding process is used. Since tab A is the shortest one, it is easiest to tuck that one in last.

There are three sides where the last tabs were tucked inside, it is possible to inflate into one of these sides to round out the dodecahedron.

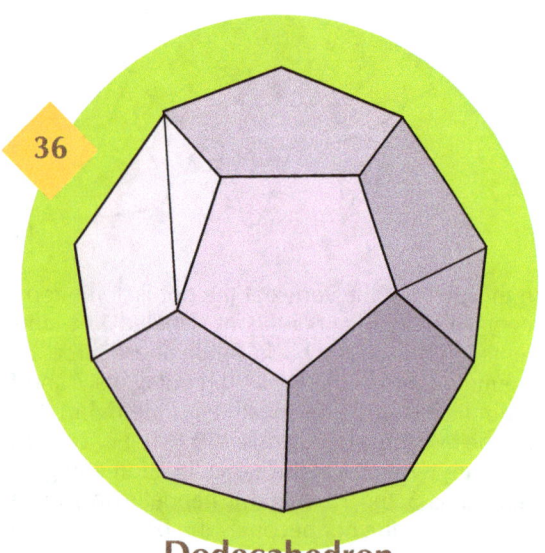

**Dodecahedron**

30   3D Origami Platonic Solids & More

# Sunken Platonic Solids

The shapes of the five sunken Platonic solids are variations of the regular solids. Each face of the regular solid is divided into several isosceles triangles which indent towards the center of the model.

The sunken Platonic solids are nonconvex polyhedra. For each model, the faces are identical isosceles triangles.

This imaginative set makes for a beautiful and powerful display. The folding methods for each of these challenging models are amazingly different.

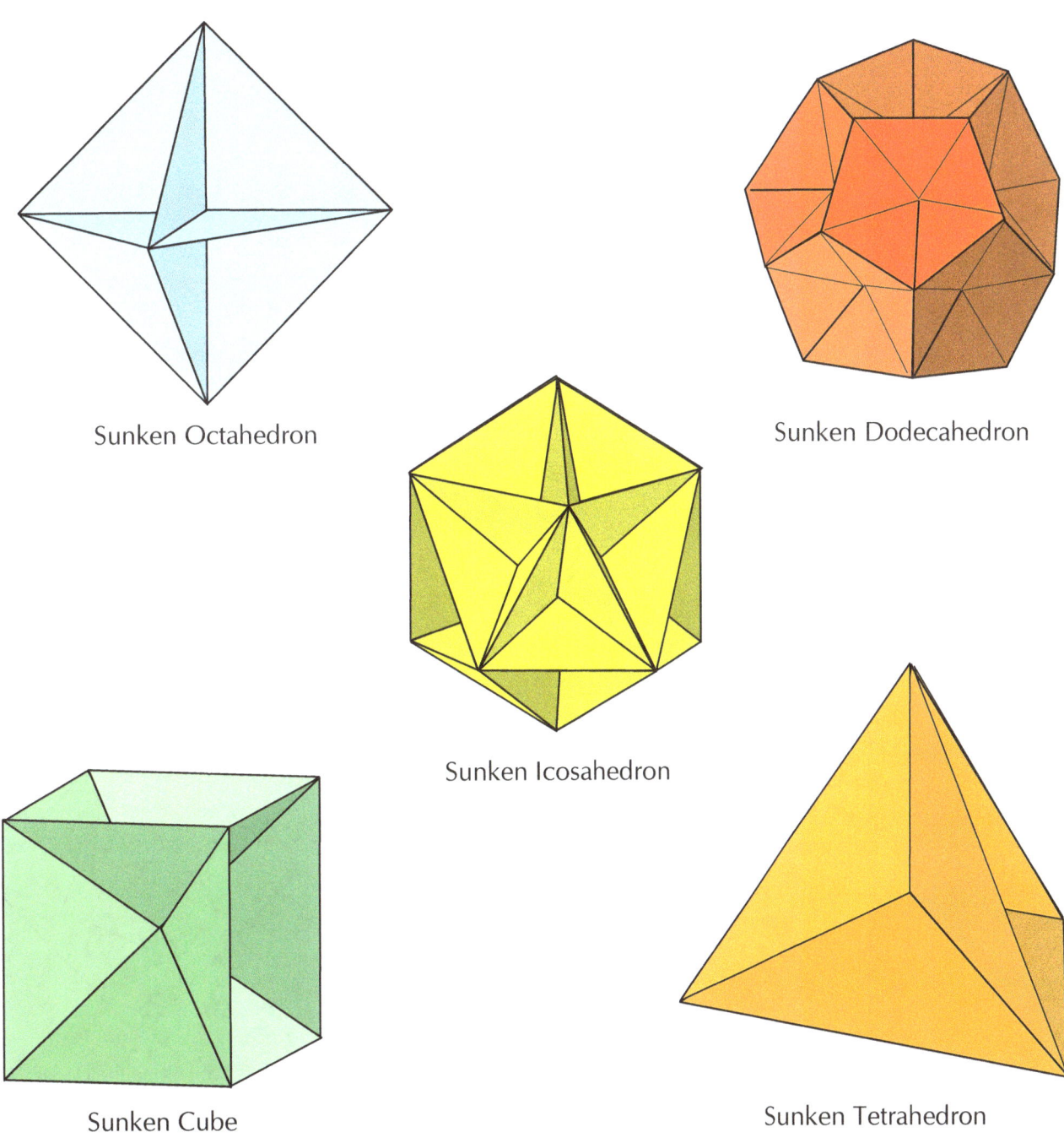

Sunken Octahedron

Sunken Dodecahedron

Sunken Icosahedron

Sunken Cube

Sunken Tetrahedron

*Sunken Platonic Solids*

# Sunken Octahedron

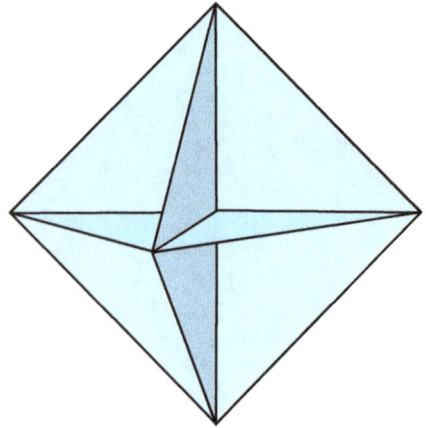
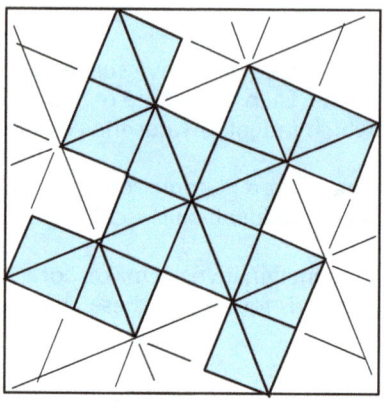

All the faces meet at the center, and this model can be viewed as three intersecting squares in three dimensions. Square symmetry is used.

**1.** Fold and unfold.

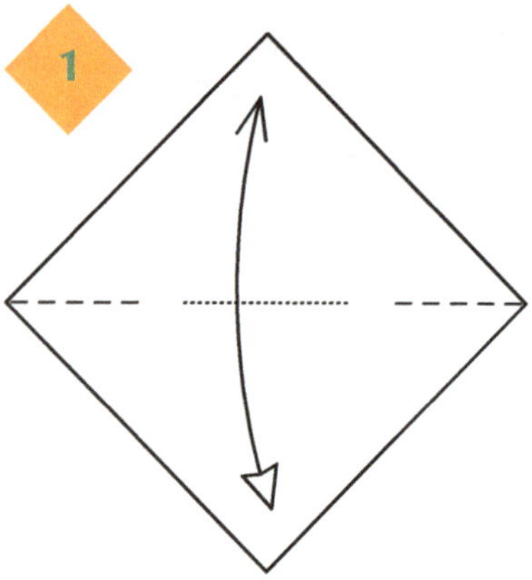

**2.** Fold to the center.

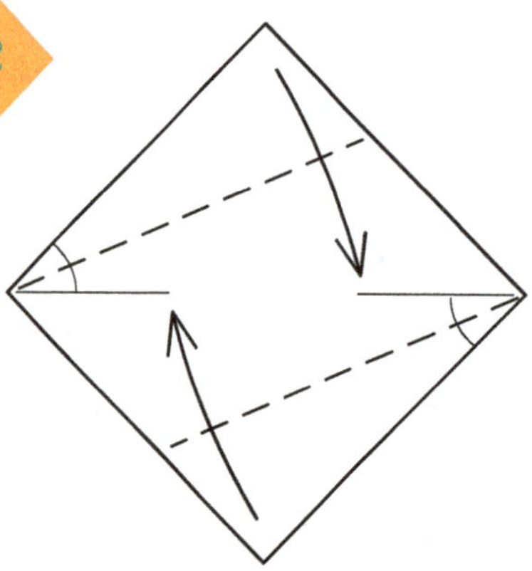

**3.** Fold in half.

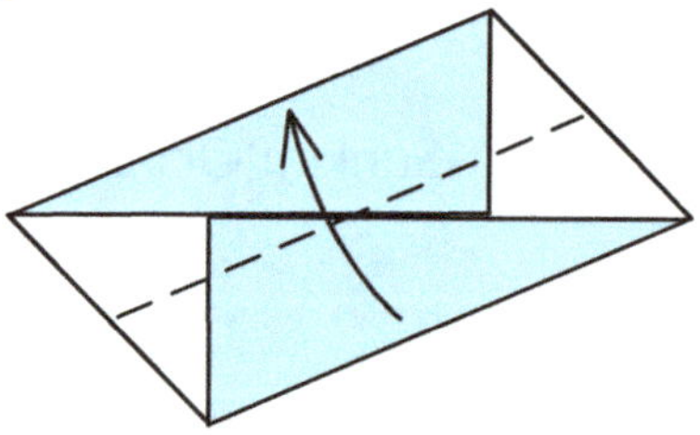

**4.** Unfold and rotate 90°.

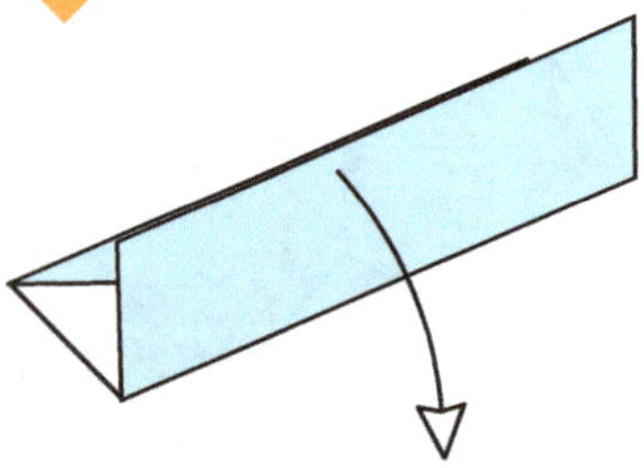

**5.** Repeat steps 1–4.

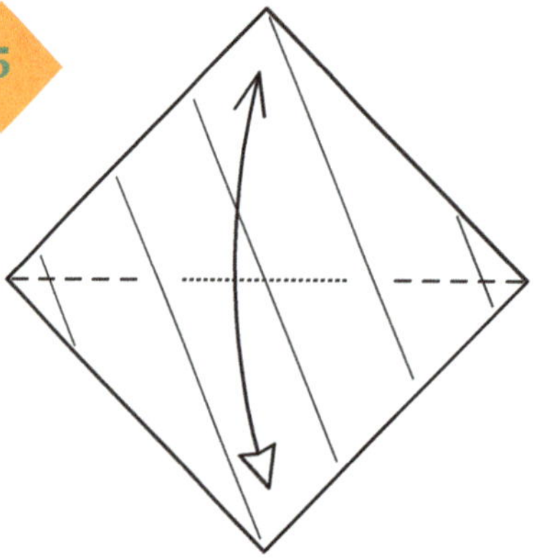

**6.** 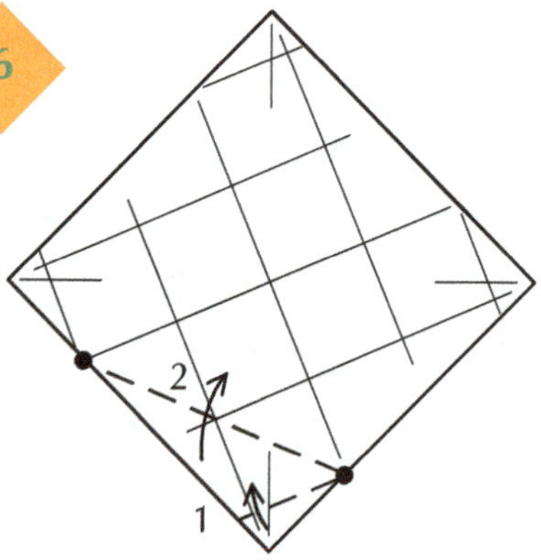 
1. Fold along the crease.
2. Fold by the dots.
Rotate 90°.

32   3D Origami Platonic Solids & More

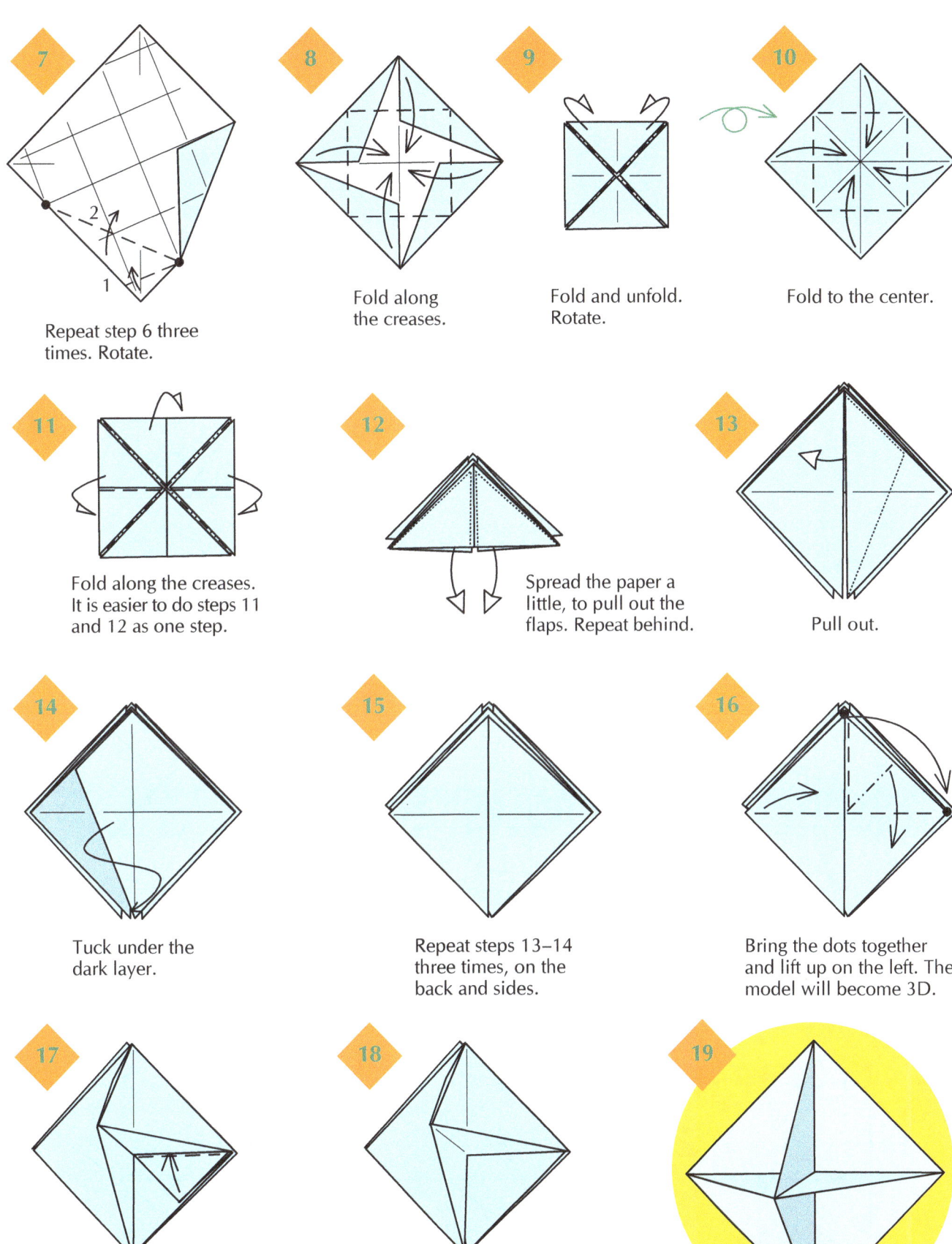

Sunken Octahedron 33

# Sunken Tetrahedron

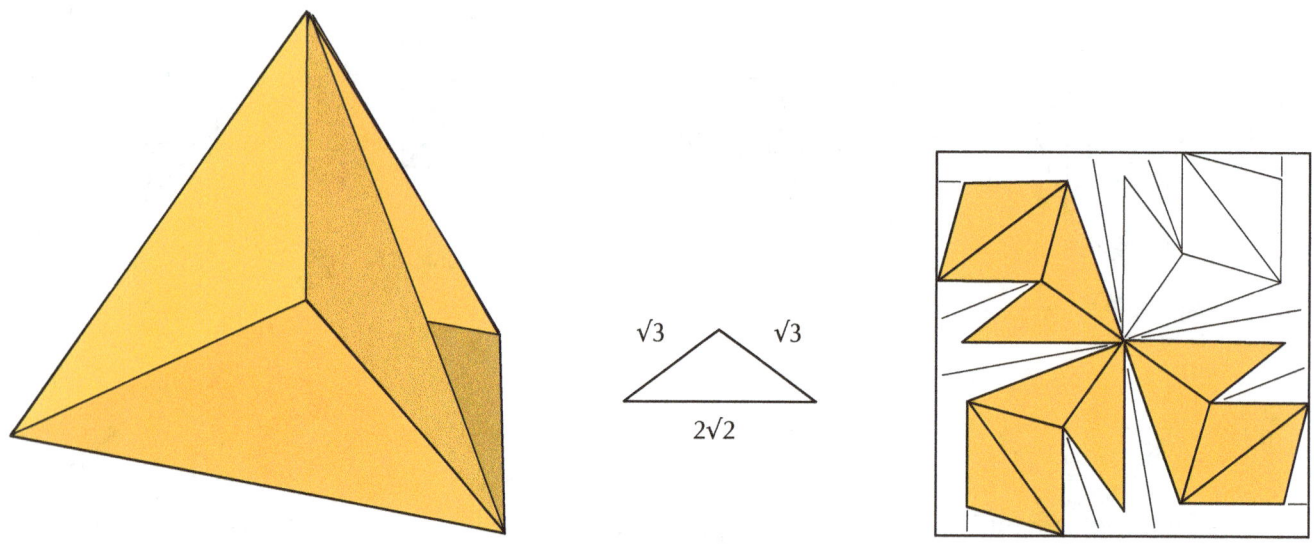

The twelve faces of the sunken tetrahedron are isosceles triangles. The sides of each triangular face are proportional to 2√2, √3, and √3. The crease pattern shows 3/4 square symmetry.

**1.** Fold and unfold.

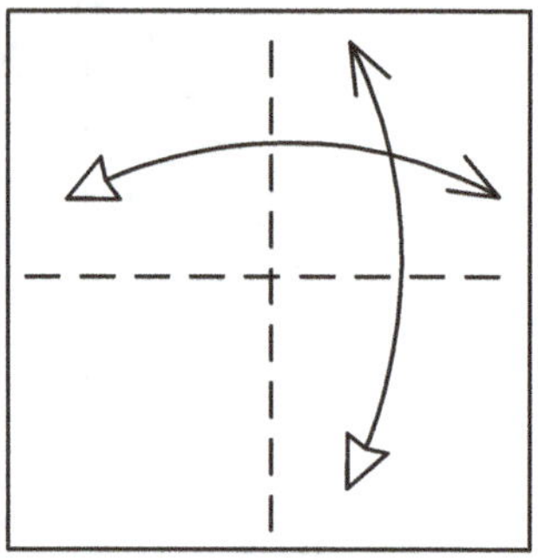

**2.** Bring the edges to the center creasing on the edges.

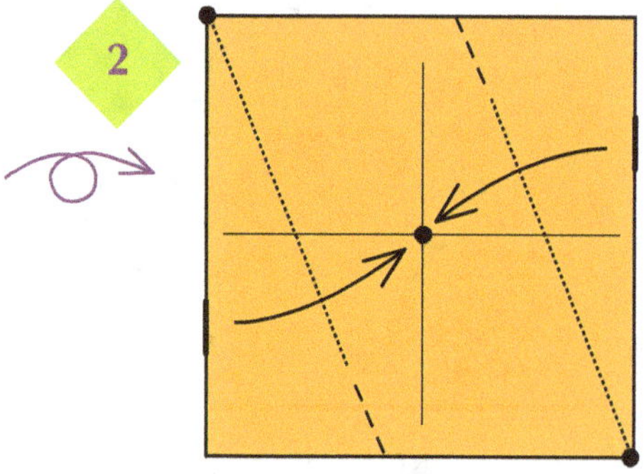

**3.** Unfold.

**4.** Fold and unfold.

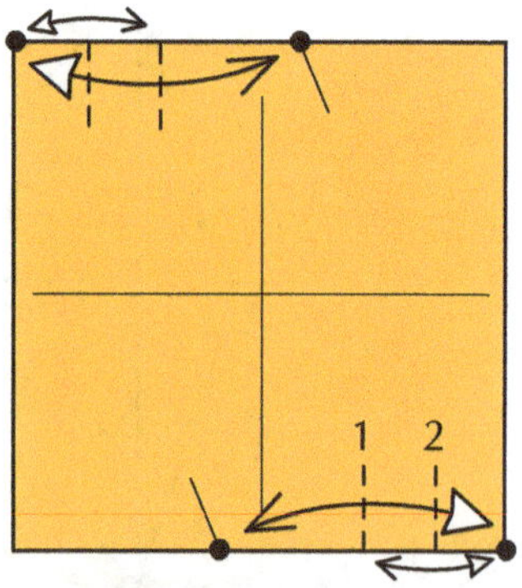

**5.**

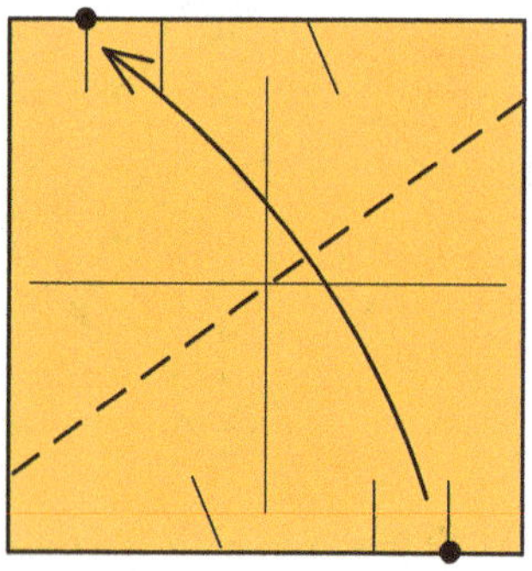

**6.**
1. Fold along the crease. 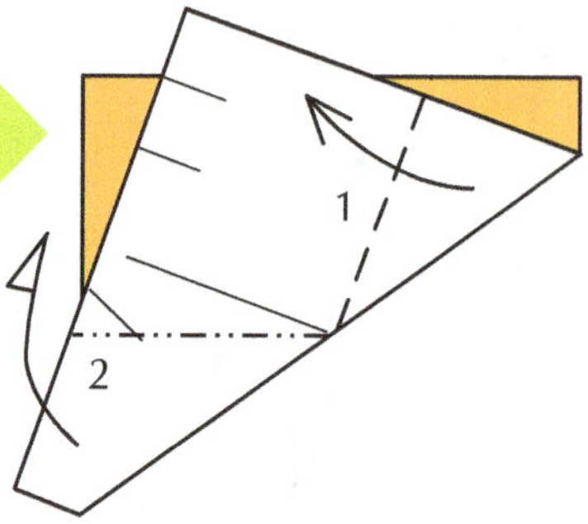
2. Fold along a hidden crease.

34   *3D Origami Platonic Solids & More*

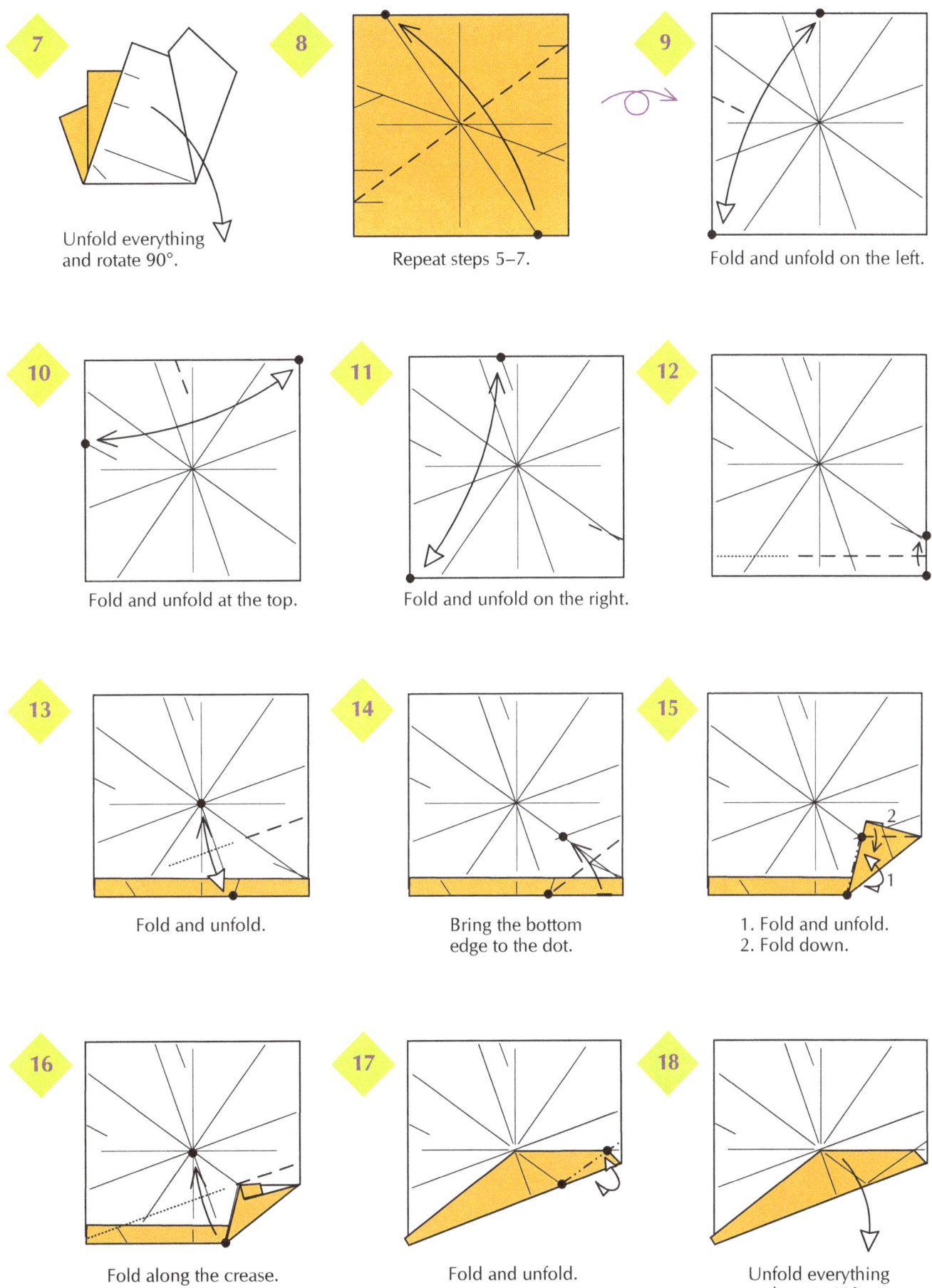

*Suken Tetrahedron* 35

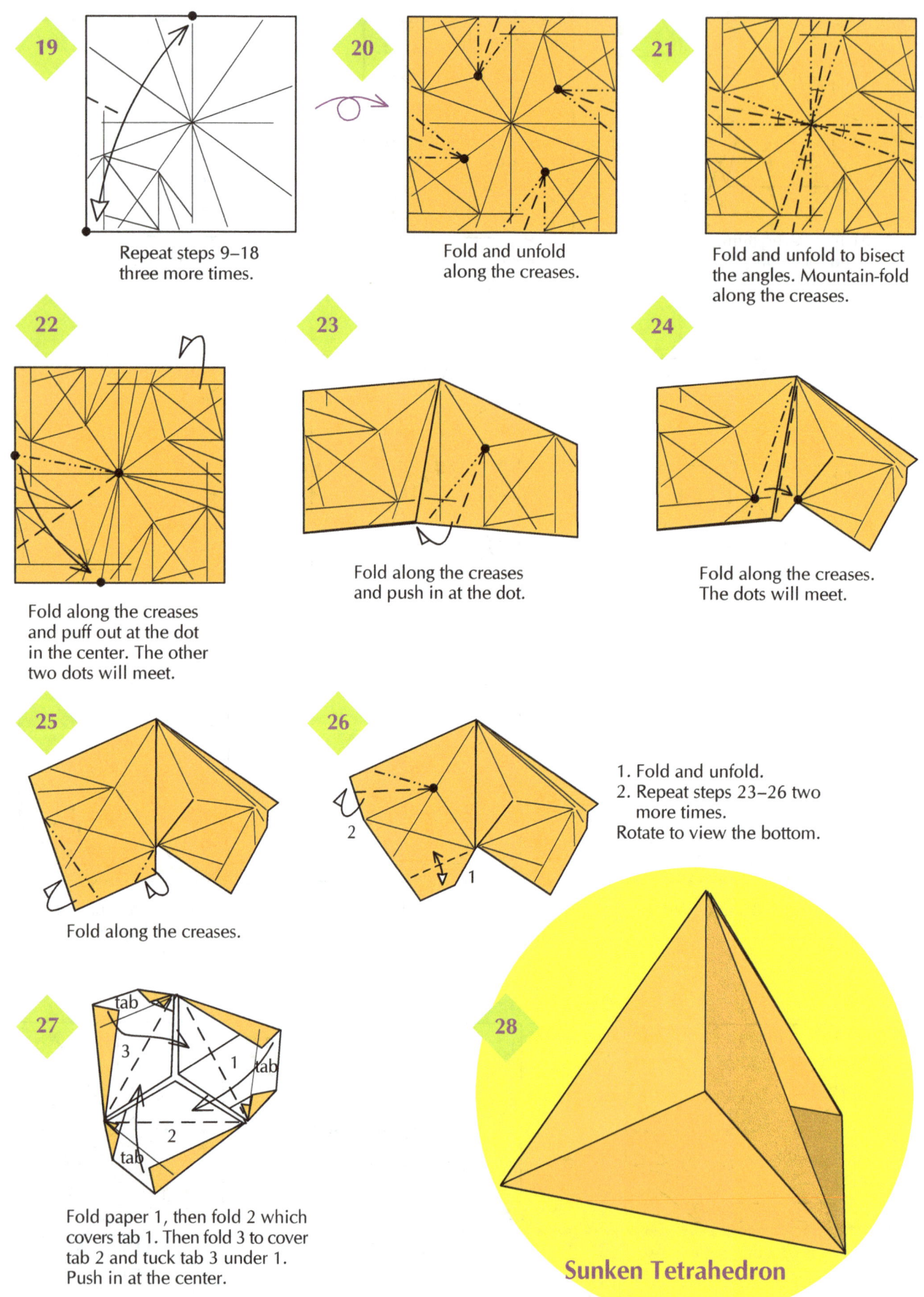

# Sunken Cube

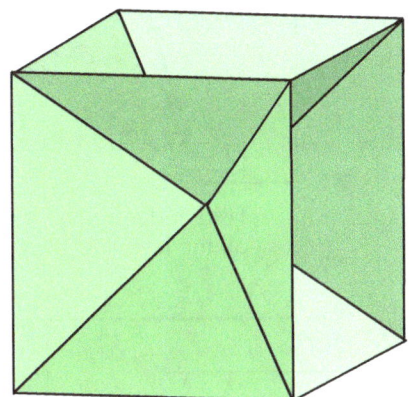
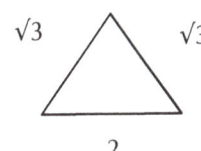
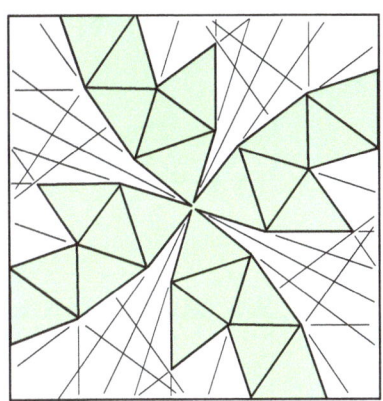

The sunken cube is composed of 24 isosceles triangles all meeting at the center. Each face has sides proportional to 2, $\sqrt{3}$, and $\sqrt{3}$. The crease pattern shows square symmetry.

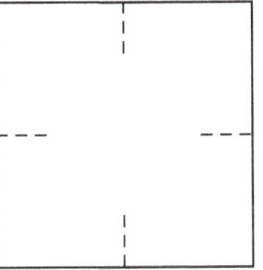

Make small marks by folding and unfolding in half.

Fold and unfold on the right.

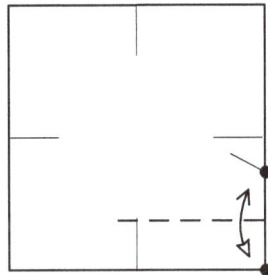

Fold and unfold. Rotate 90°.

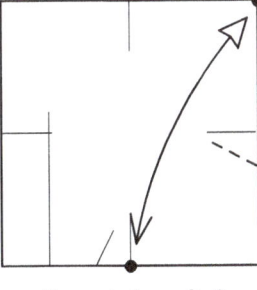

Repeat steps 2–3 three times.

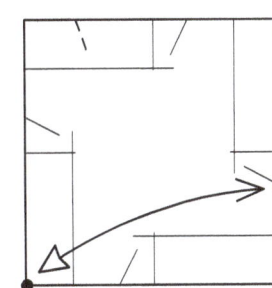

Fold and unfold at the top.

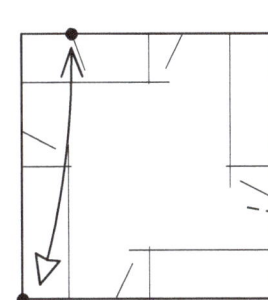

Fold and unfold on the right. Rotate 180°.

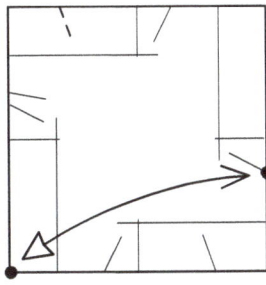

Repeat steps 5–6.

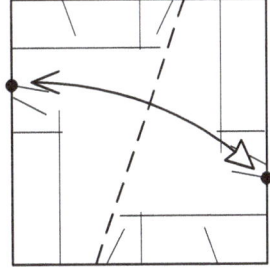

Fold and unfold.

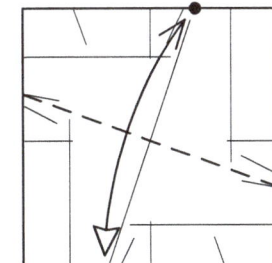

Fold and unfold.

Sunken Cube 37

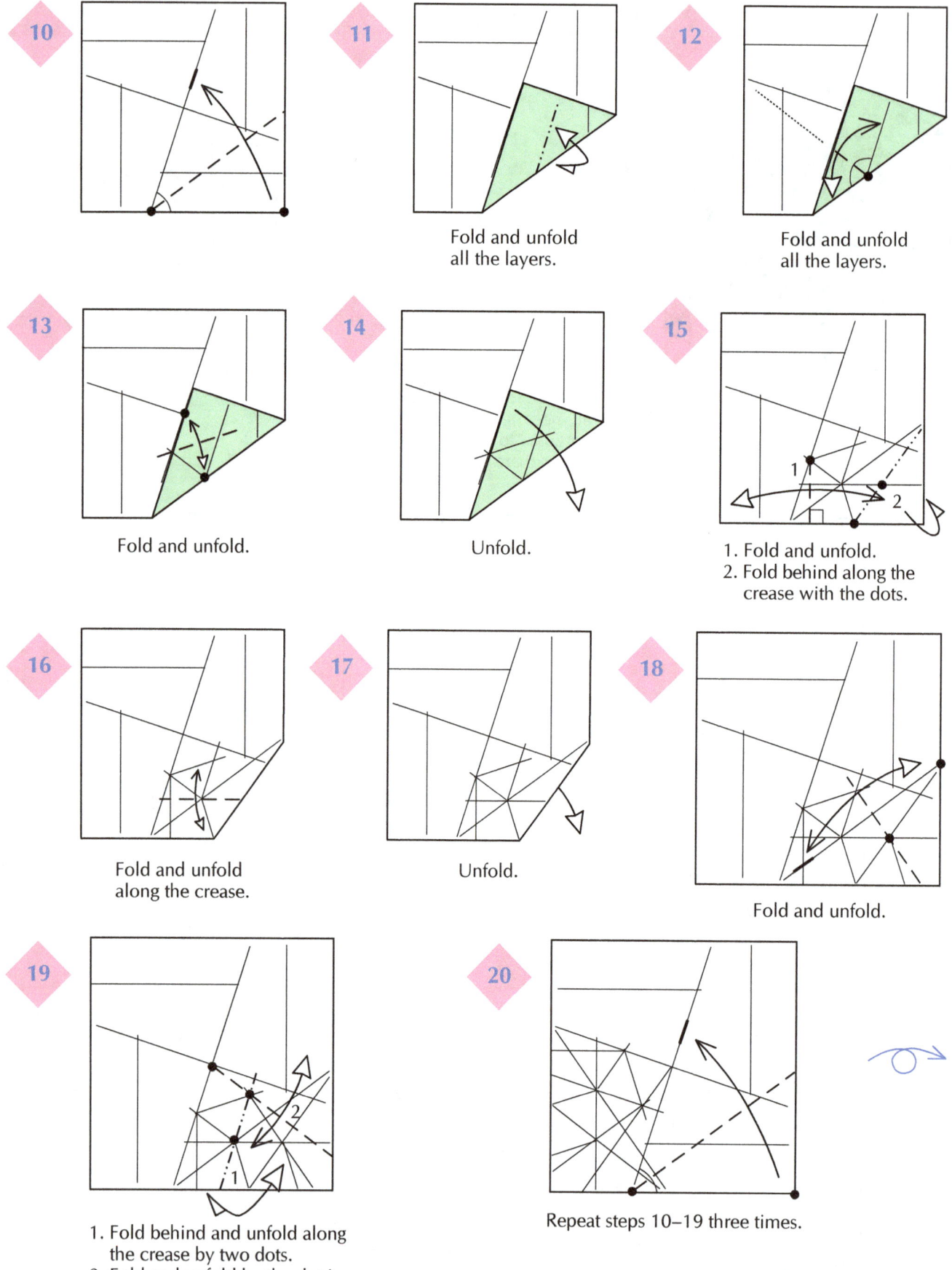

21

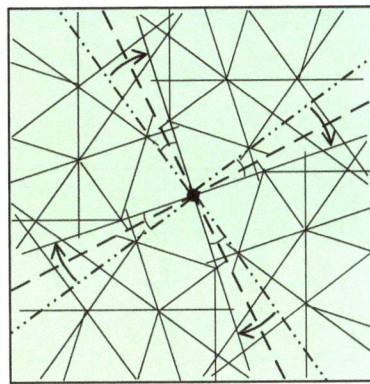

Bisect the angles. Mountain-fold along the creases. Puff out at the dot.

22

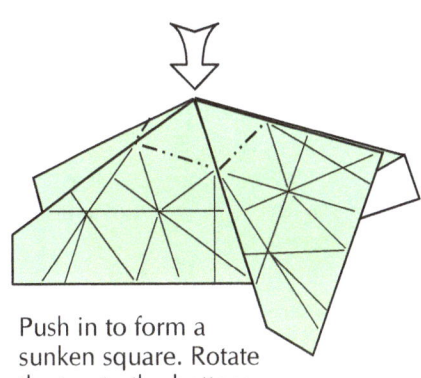

Push in to form a sunken square. Rotate the top to the bottom.

23

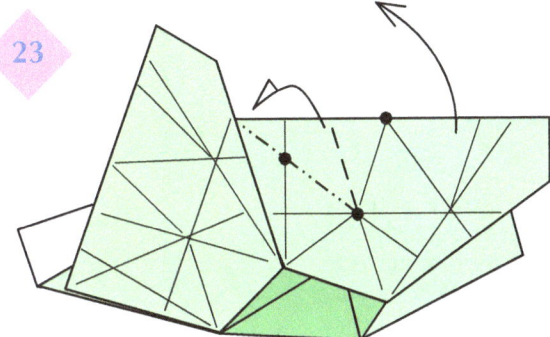

Push in at the lower dot. The other two dots will meet.

24

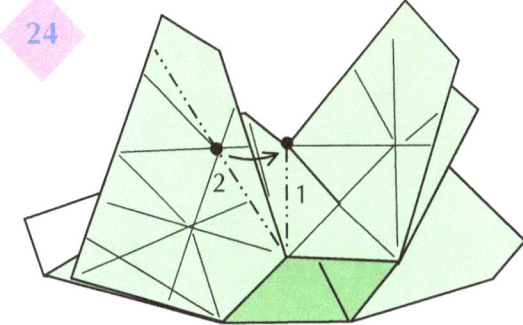

1. Fold and unfold along the crease.
2. Slide the paper so the dots meet.

25

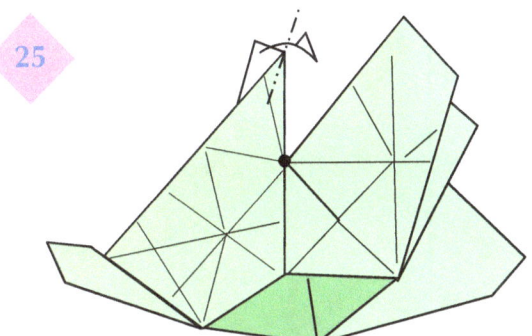

Fold the tab behind so the edge meets the dot.

26

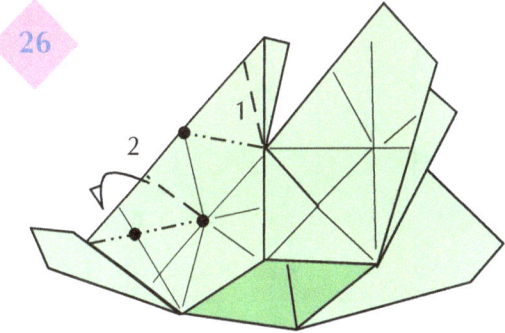

1. Fold and unfold along the creases.
2. Repeat steps 23–26 three times.

27

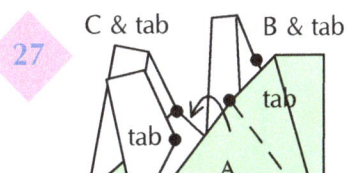
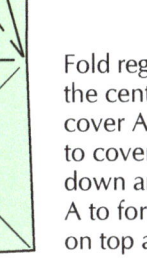

Fold region A down towards the center. Fold B down to cover A's tab. Fold C down to cover B's tab. Fold D down and tuck its tab under A to form a sunken square on top and close the model.

28

Sunken Cube

*Sunken Cube* 39

# Sunken Dodecahedron

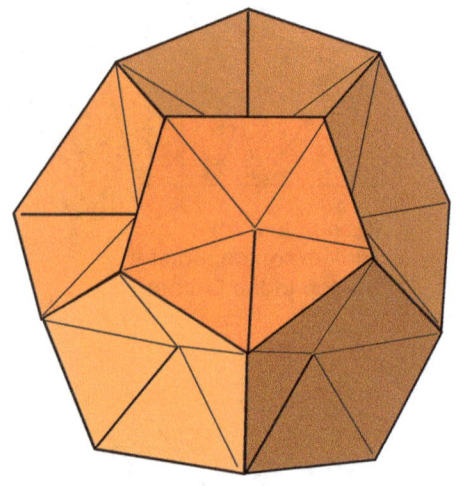
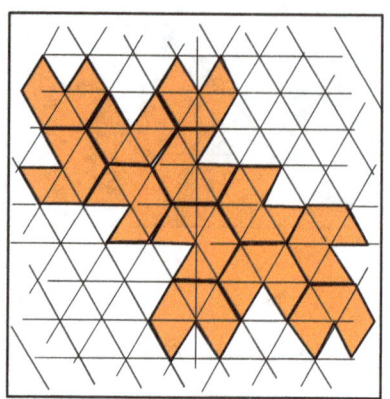

This sunken dodecahedron is one of several stellated icosahedra. It is composed of 60 equilateral triangular faces. After the 1/5 mark is found in step 3, much precreasing is used to make many triangles. This sunken polyhedron was actually much easier to design than the dodecahedron itself.

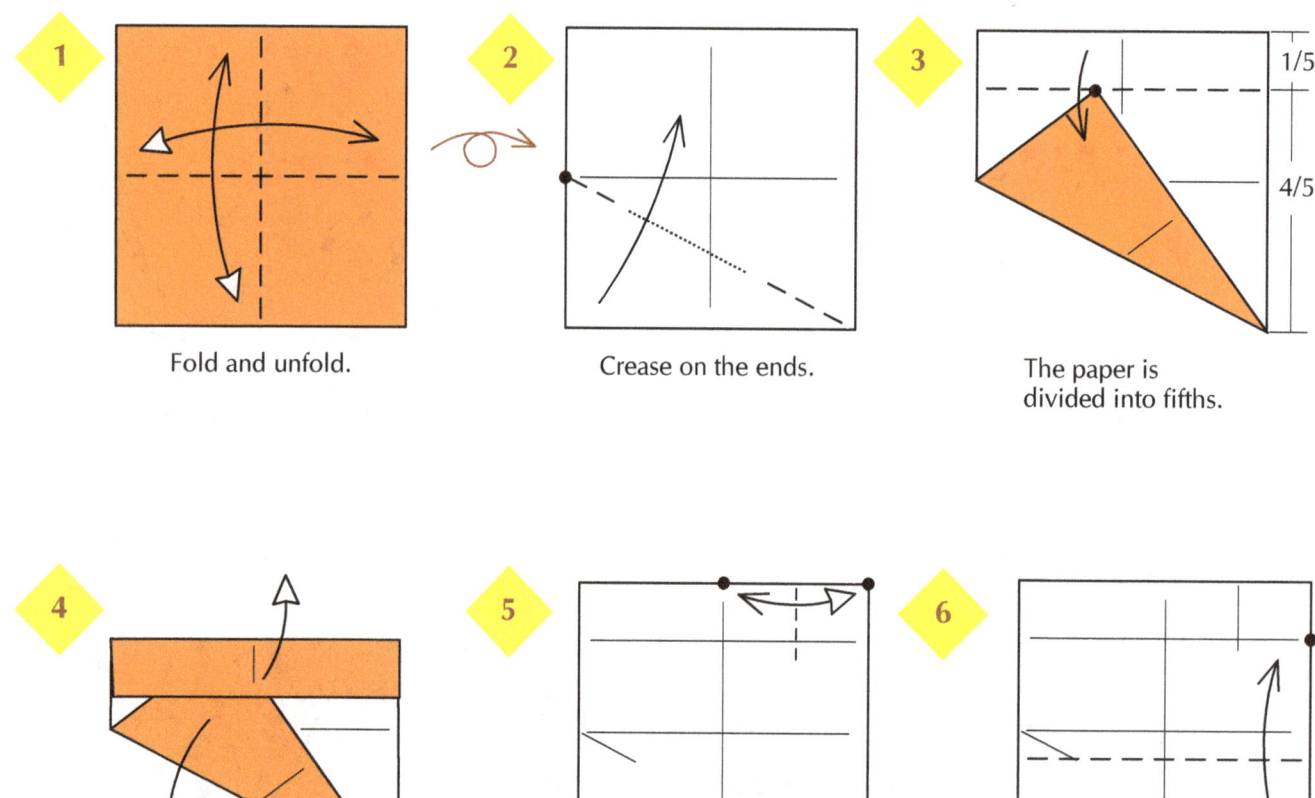

1. Fold and unfold.
2. Crease on the ends.
3. The paper is divided into fifths.
4. Unfold.
5. Fold and unfold.

40  3D Origami Platonic Solids & More

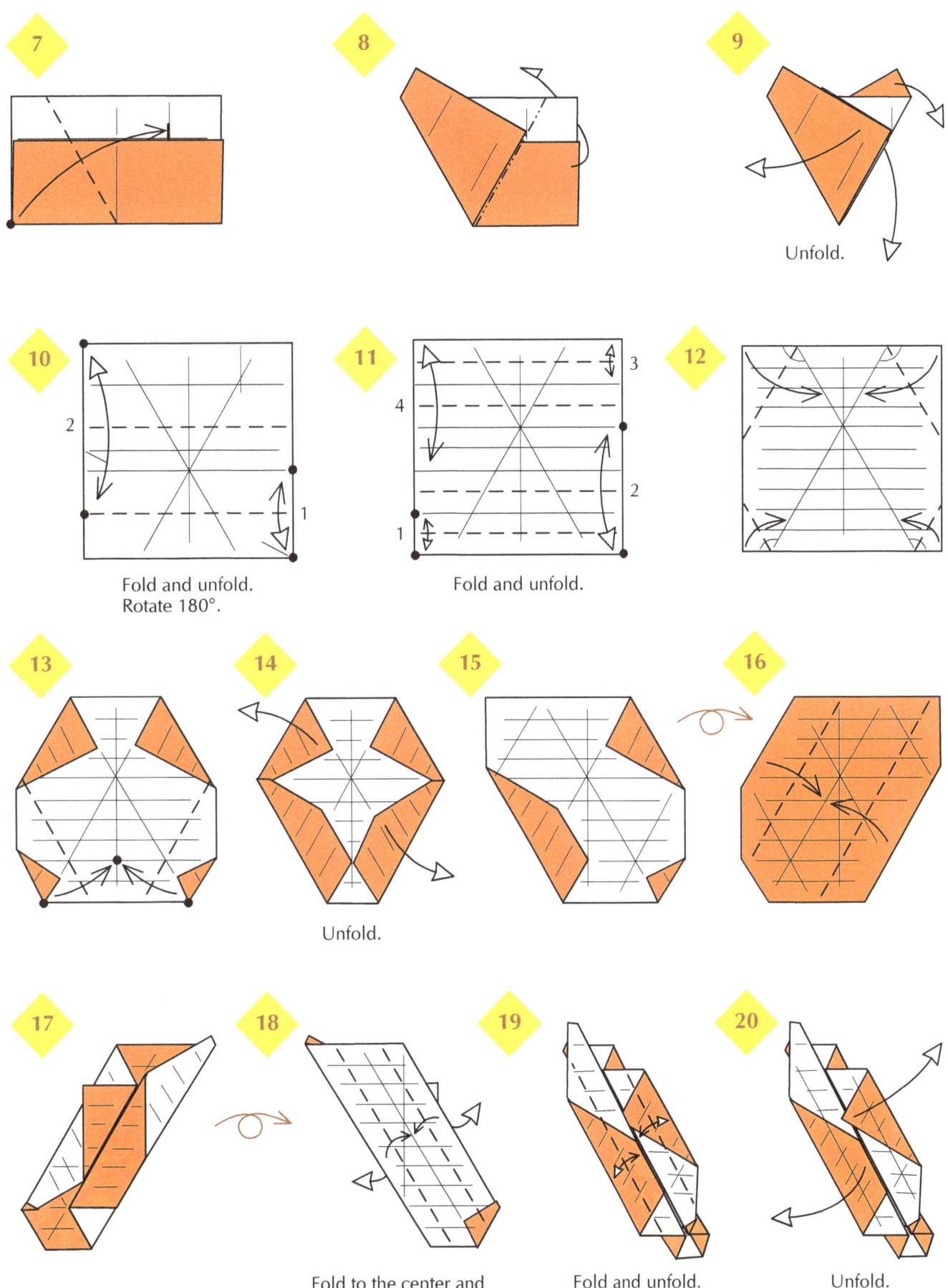

Sunken Dodecahedron 41

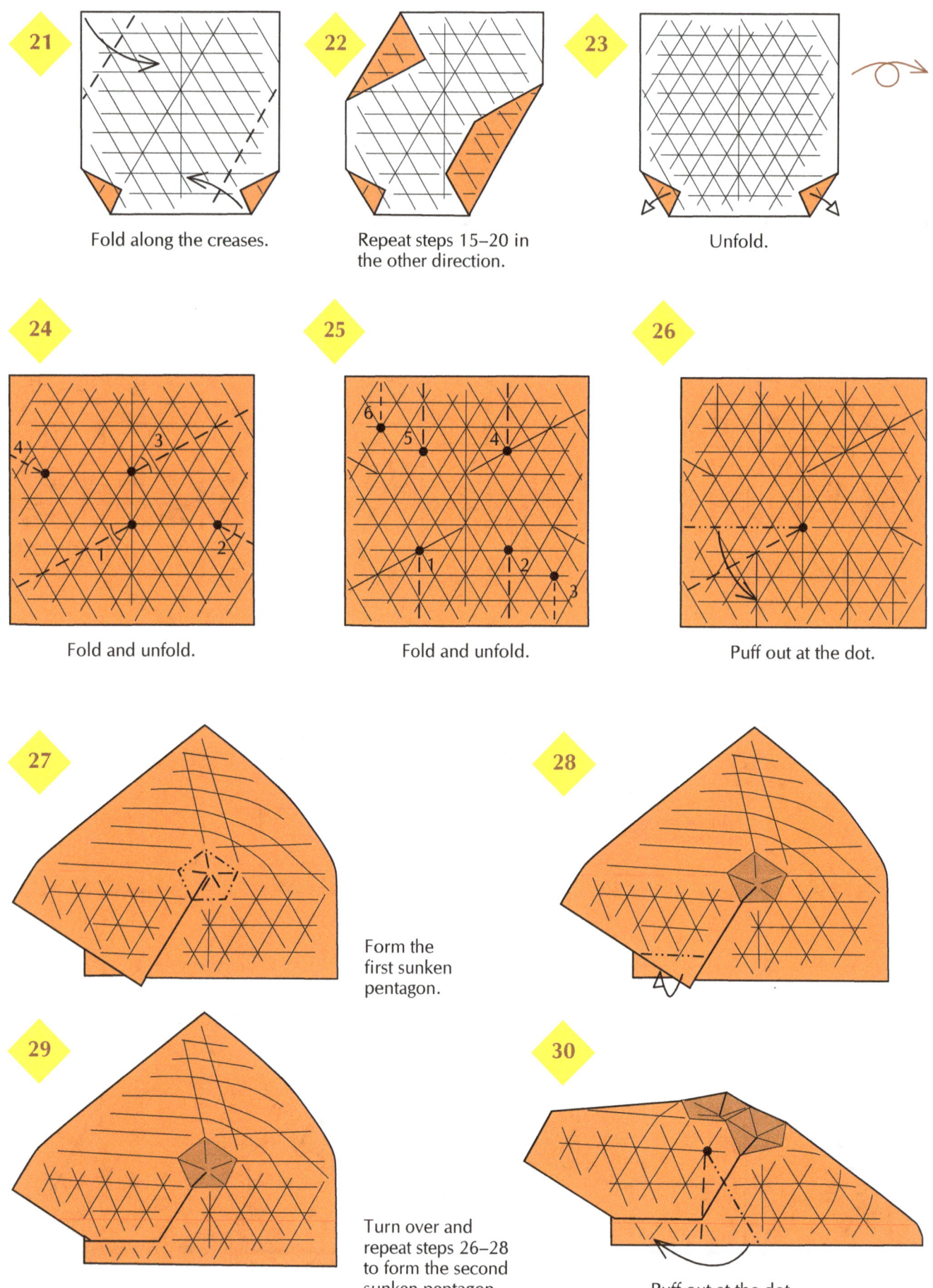

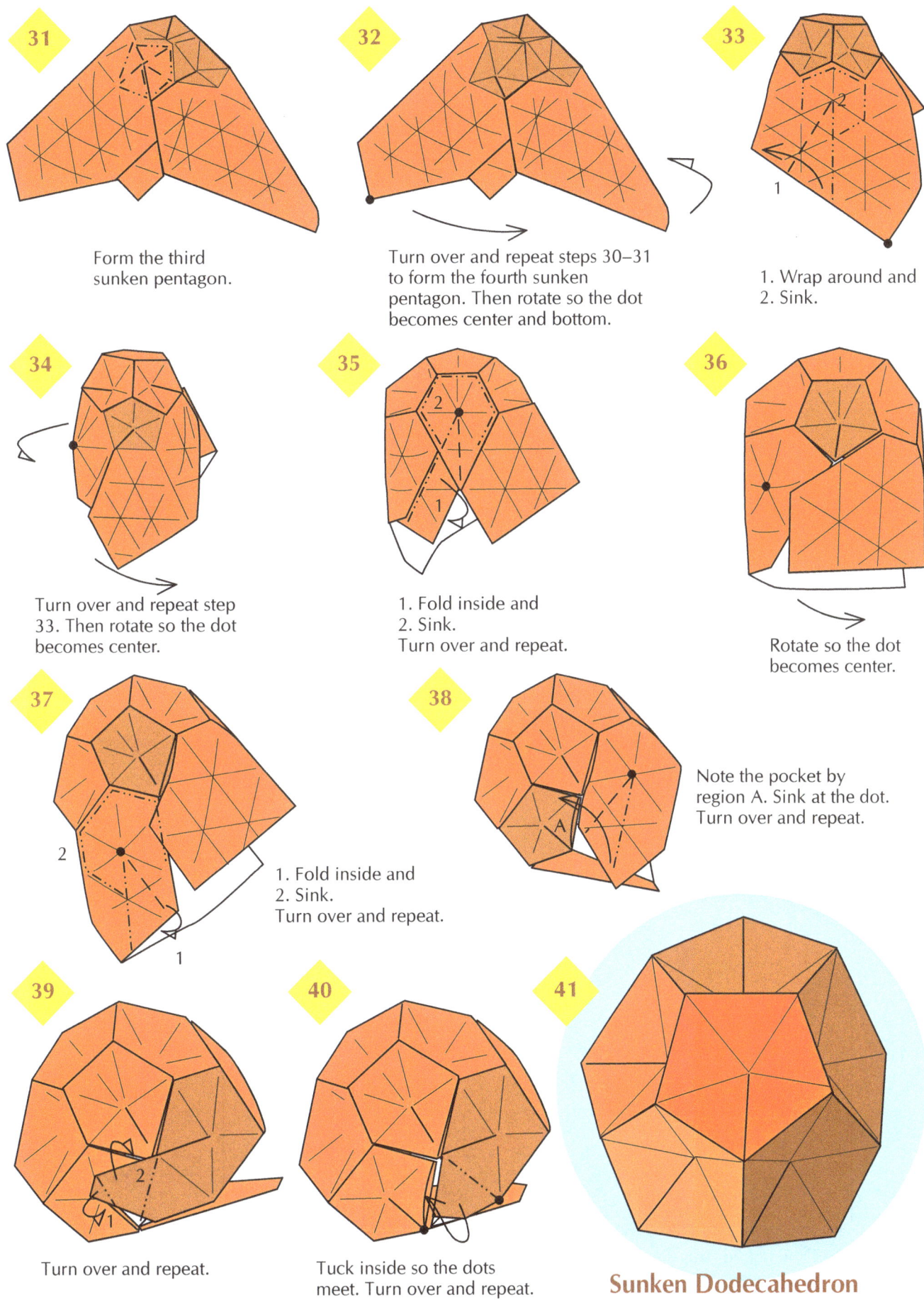

Sunken Dodecahedron

# Sunken Icosahedron

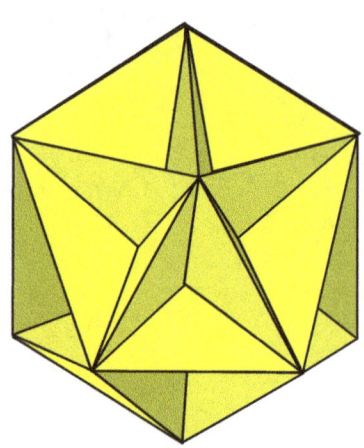
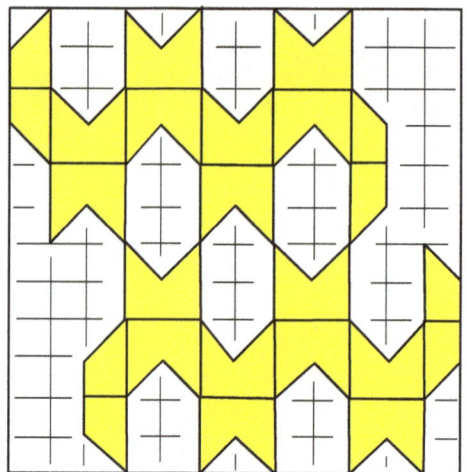

This complex shape is composed of 60 isosceles right triangular faces. It is formed by first making a fan. It has a four-star (very complex) rating because of the sequence from steps 20–33 as the fan is turned into a tower. But the folds before and after are not so difficult. The paper is divided into twelfths. This shape is complex and does not hold together as well as the other models in this collection, you can choose nonstandard methods (such as tape) to keep it together.

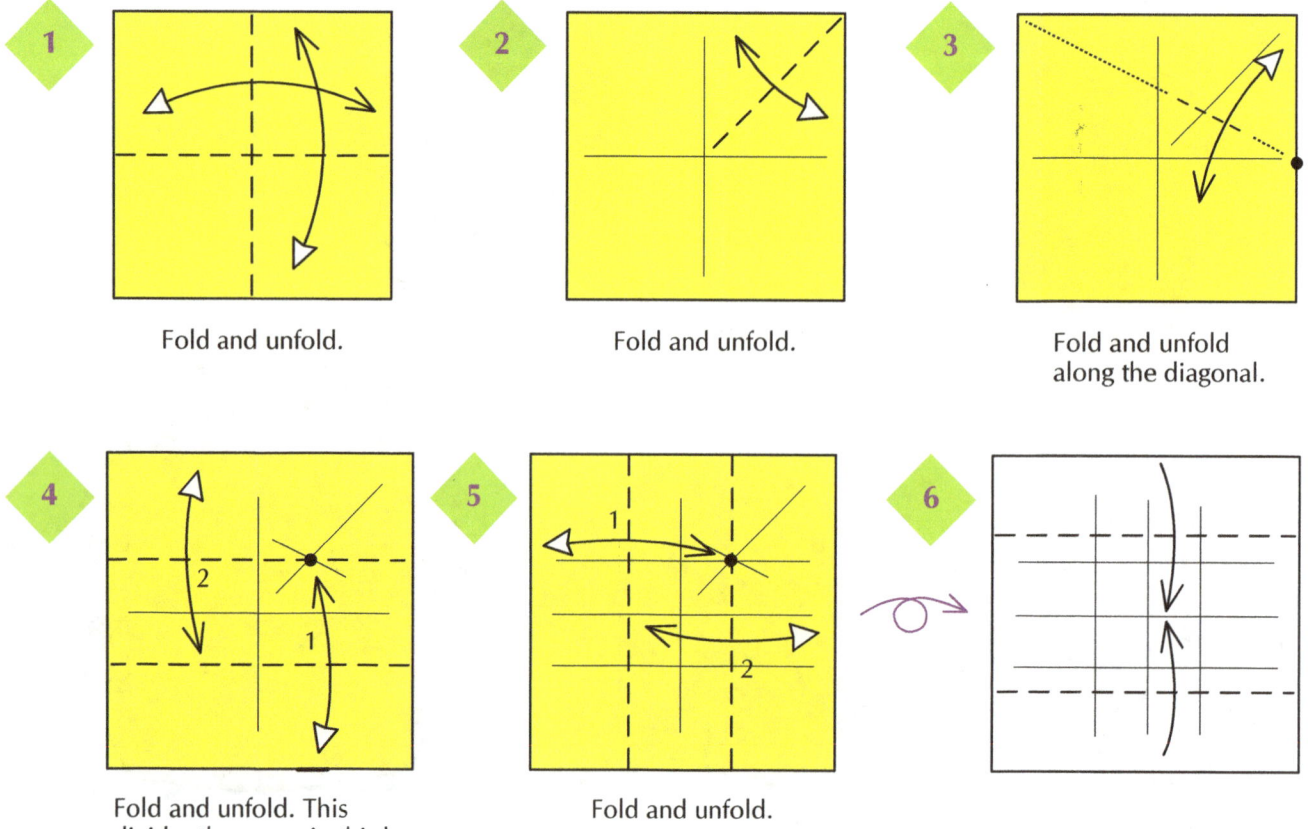

44   *3D Origami Platonic Solids & More*

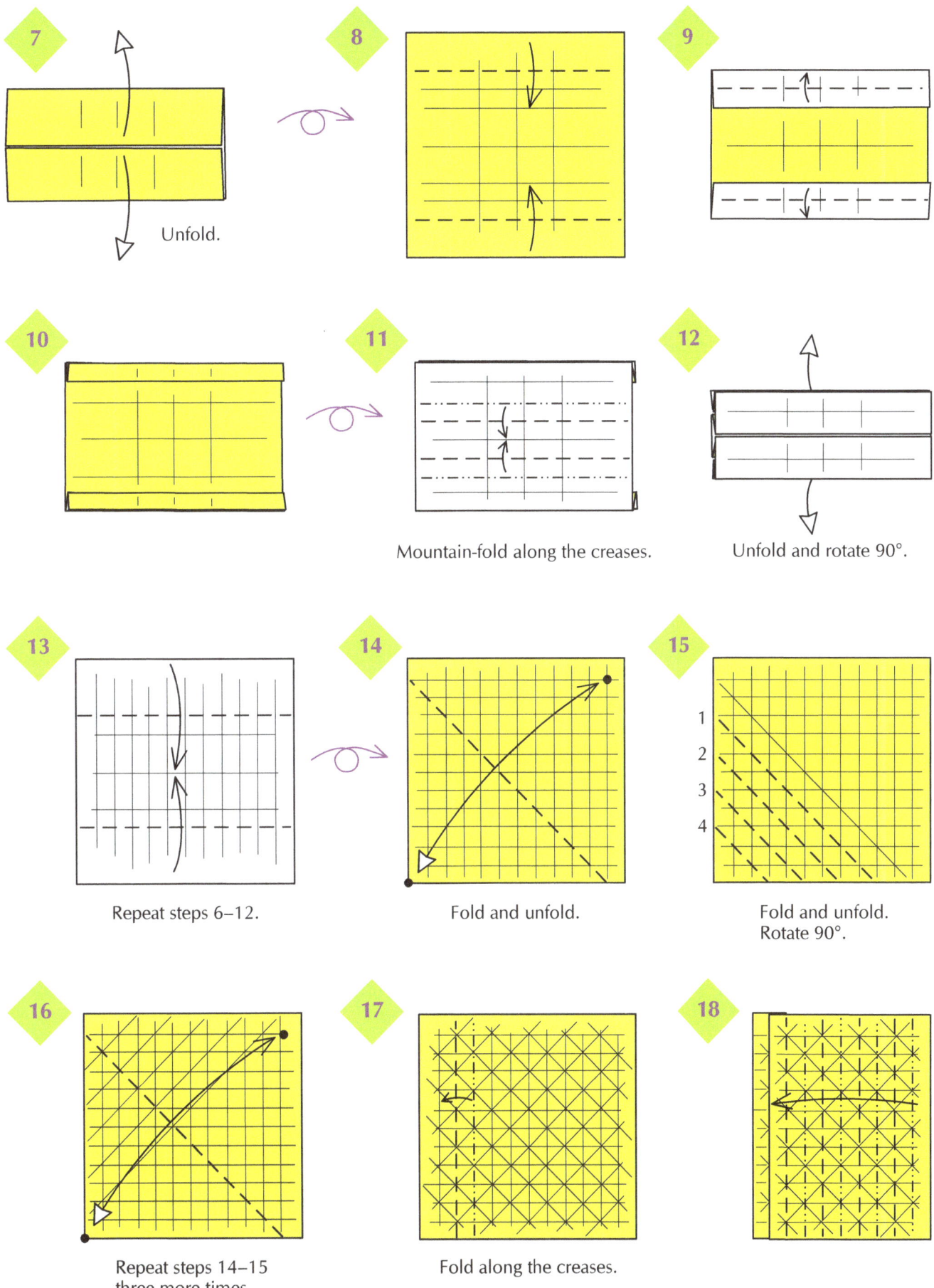

Sunken Icosahedron 45

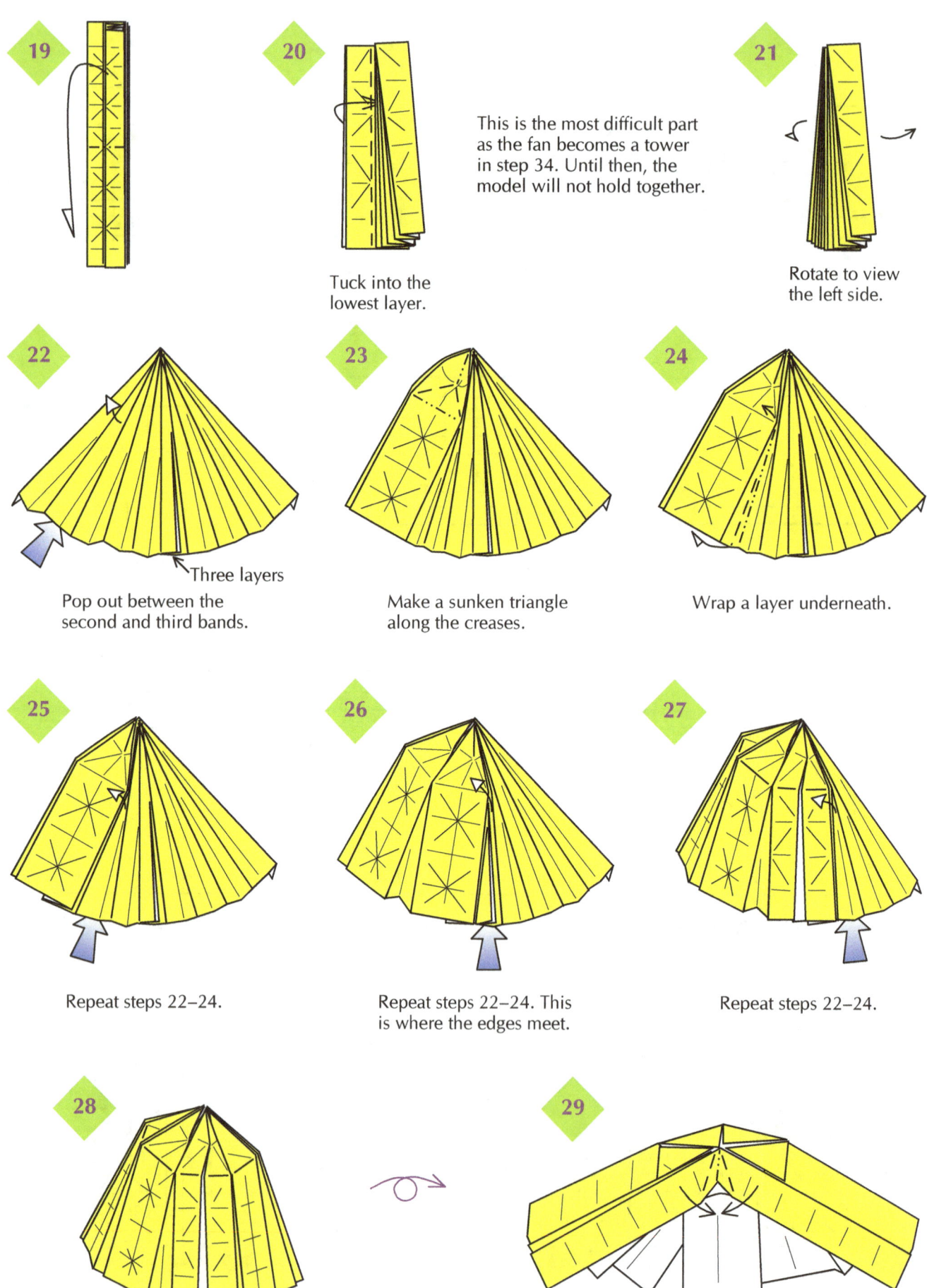

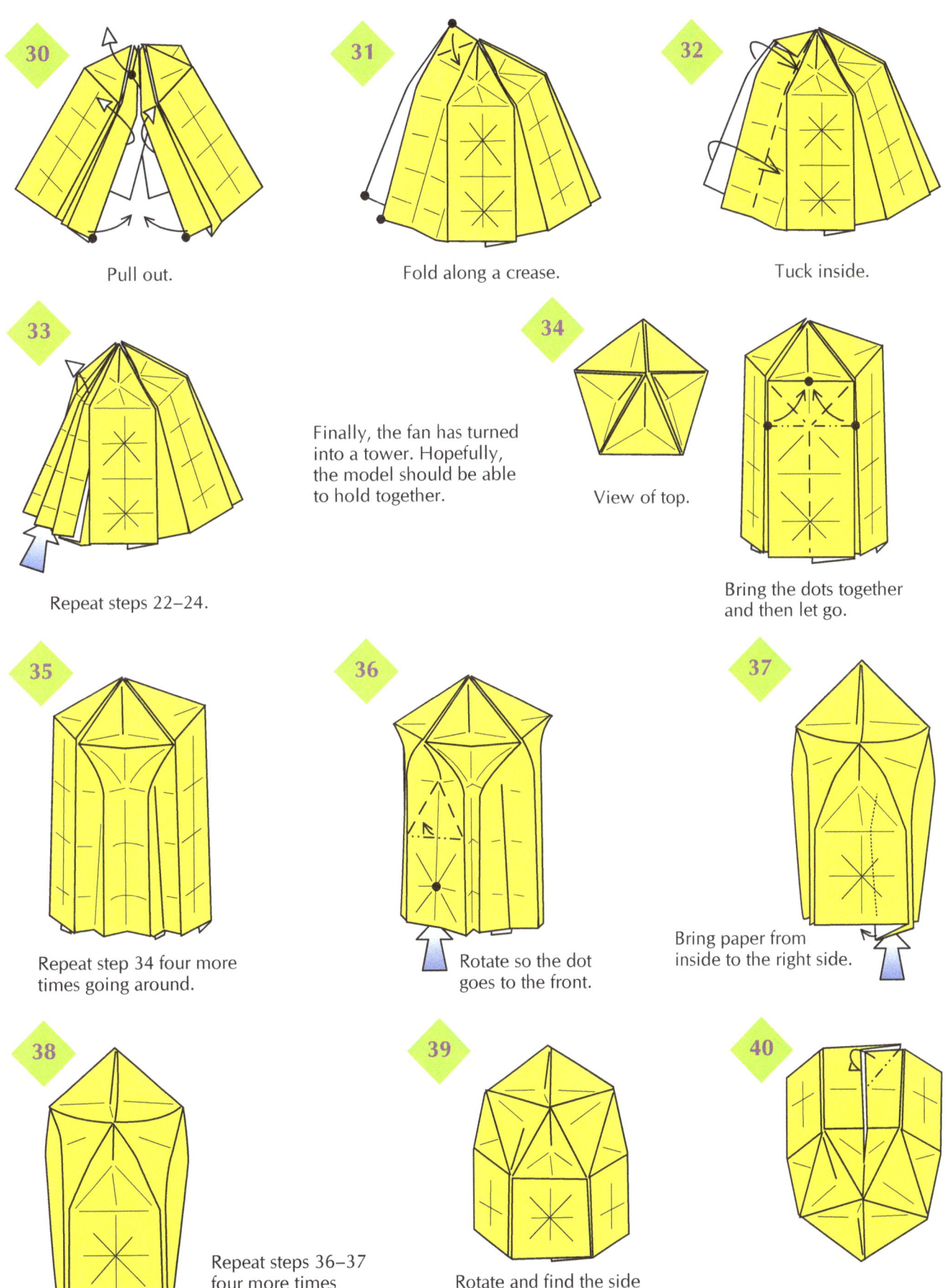

Sunken Icosahedron 47

**41**
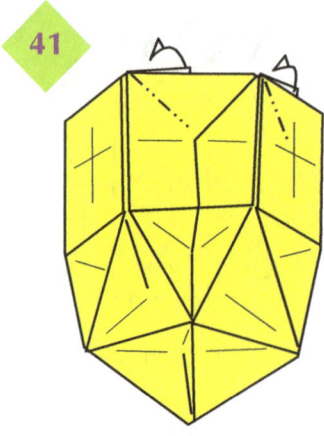
Fold all the loose edges going all around.

**42**
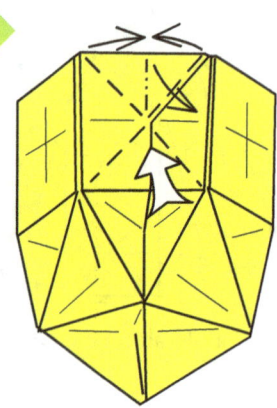
Form a sunken triangle bringing the extra paper to the front.

**43**
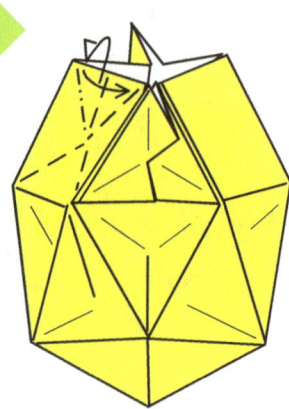
Form a sunken triangle while folding the extra paper inside.

**44**
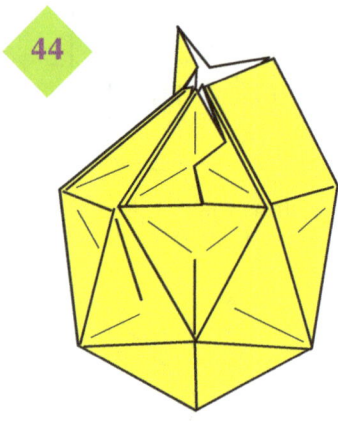
Repeat steps 43 on the right.

**45**
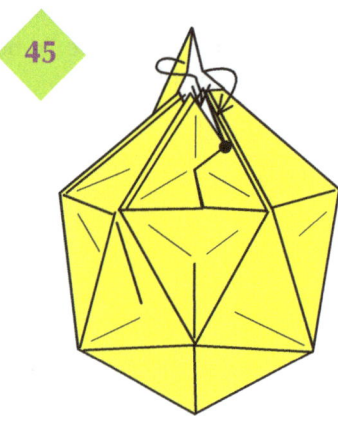
Form the last two triangles on the back while bringing the extra paper to the front inside the front triangle.

**46**
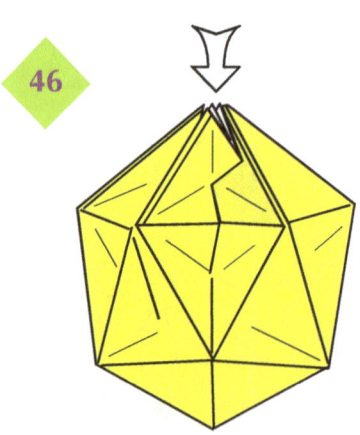
Bring the dark paper to the front to lock the folds. Also push down to keep the folds in place.

**47**
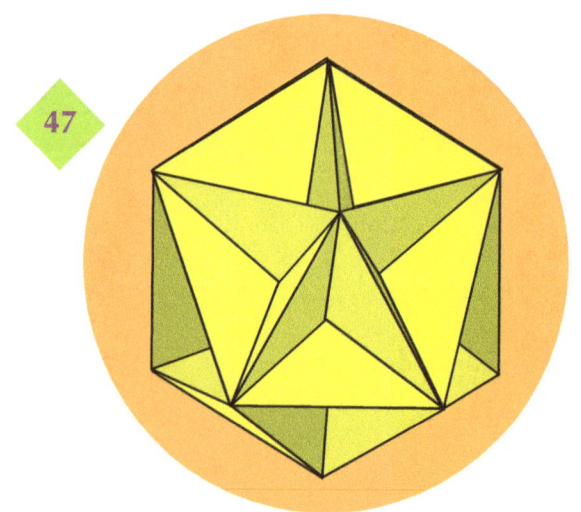

**Sunken Icosahedron**

48   3D Origami Platonic Solids & More

# Inside-Out Platonic Solids

Inside-out origami refers to models which show both sides of the paper for effect. To fold polyhedra with color patterns, the paper is first folded so both colors show on one side. Then a layout in 2D is placed. When folded, both sides are shown.

Consider the Three-Layered Cube. In figure 1, opposite edges are folded towards the center to show the colored side of the paper on the left and right, with a vertical white strip down the middle. The six squares are highlighted, showing each square with its color pattern. When folded into a cube, figure 2, the color pattern is realized.

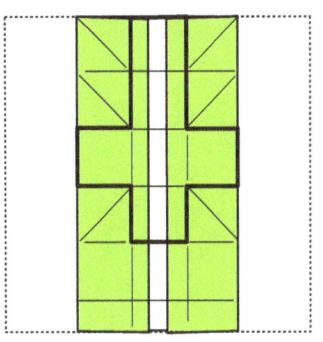

*Figure 1: Layout of cube in 2D showing the set-up for the color pattern.*

*Figure 2: Cube with color pattern.*

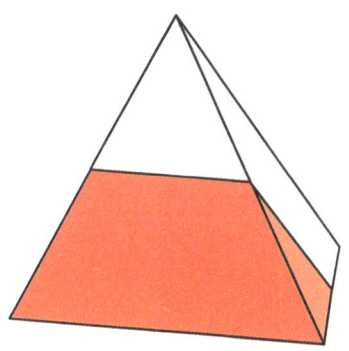

**Duo-Striped Tetrahedron**

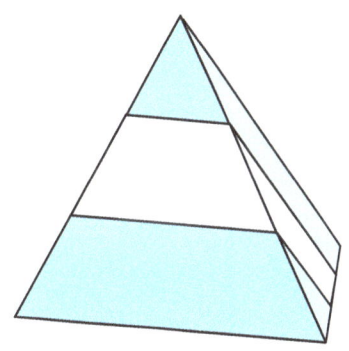

**Layered Tetrahedron**

**Three-Layered Cube**

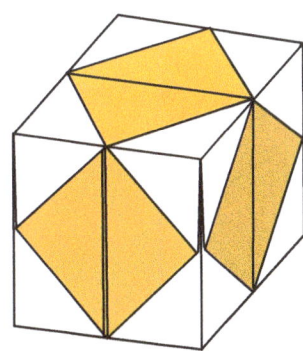

**Fancy Cube**

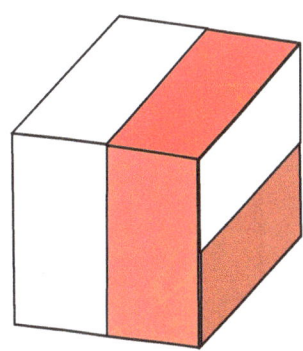

**Banded Cube**

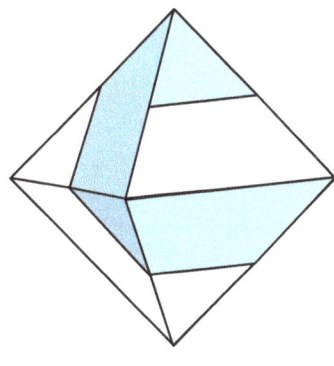

**Banded Octahedron**

*Inside-Out Platonic Solids* 49

# Duo-Striped Tetrahedron

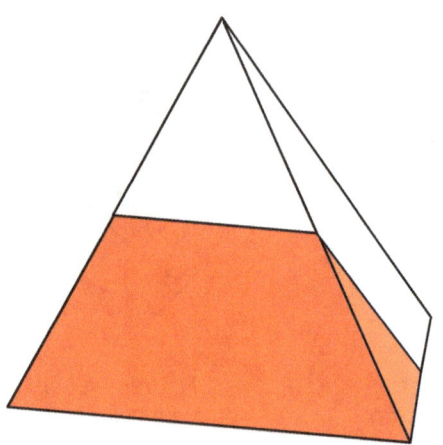
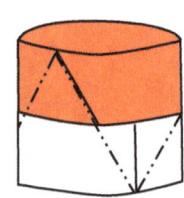
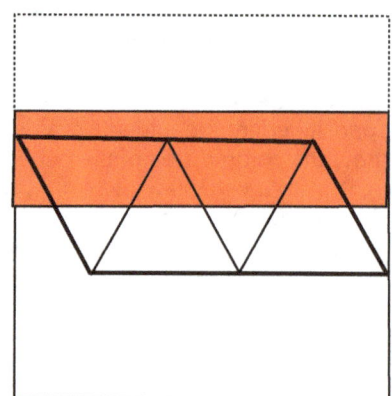

To fold this model, a striped cylinder is formed. With a few folds, the cylinder turns into the striped tetrahedron. The paper is divided into fifths.

1. Fold and unfold on the left and right.

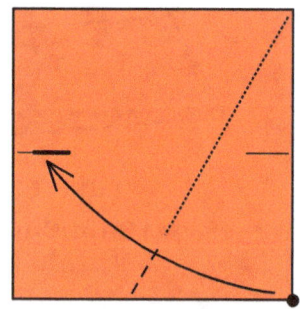

2. Crease at the bottom.

3. Unfold.

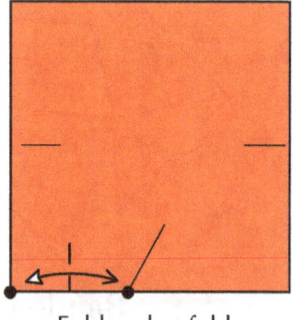

4. Fold and unfold. Rotate 180°.

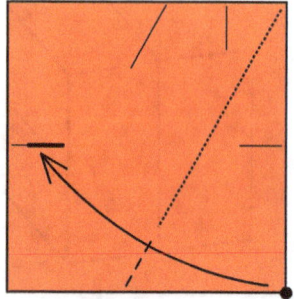

5. Repeat steps 2–4.

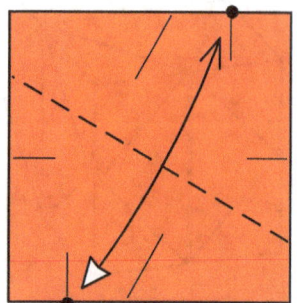

6. Fold and unfold.

50   *3D Origami Platonic Solids & More*

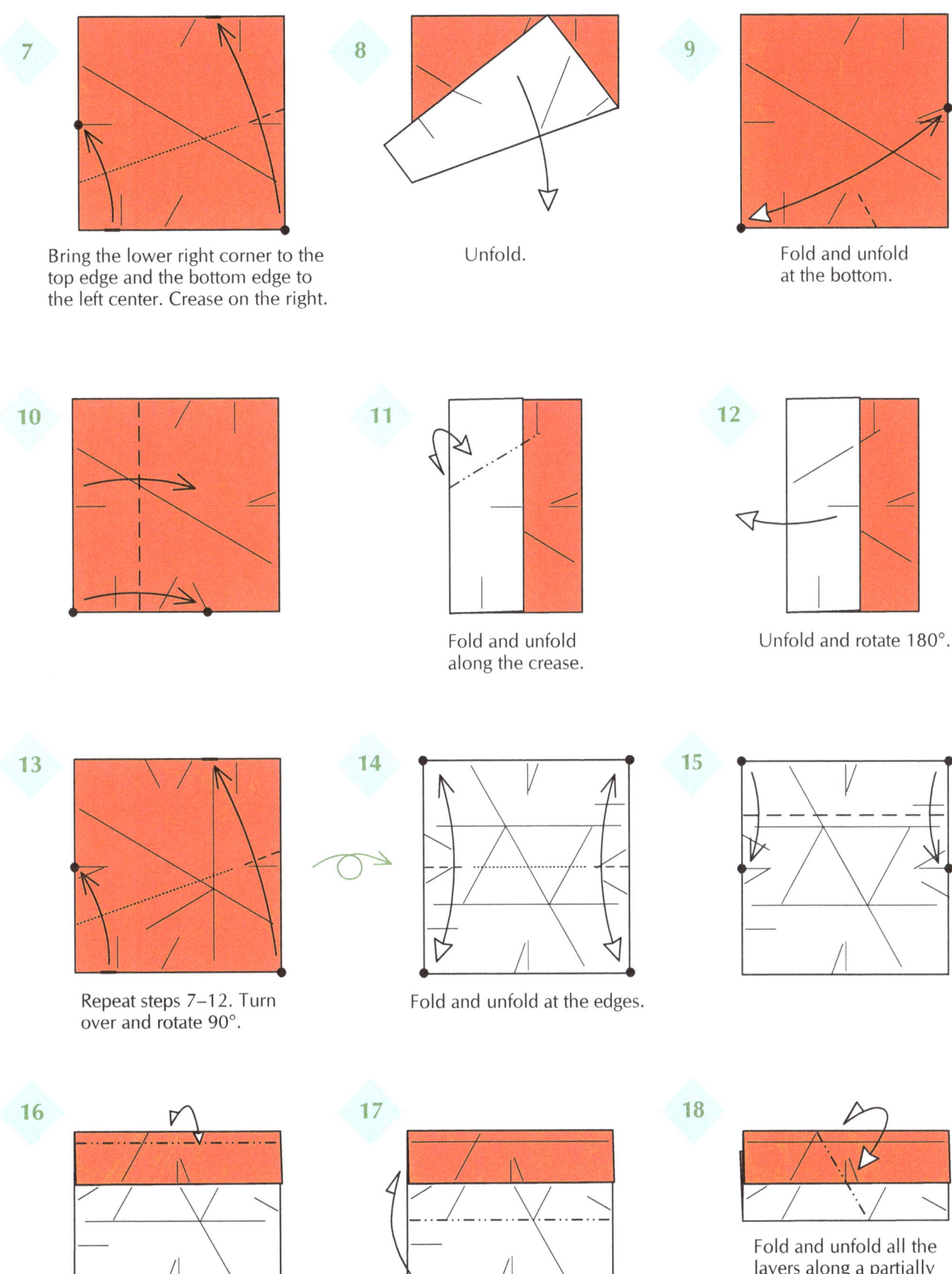

Duo-Striped Tetrahedron 51

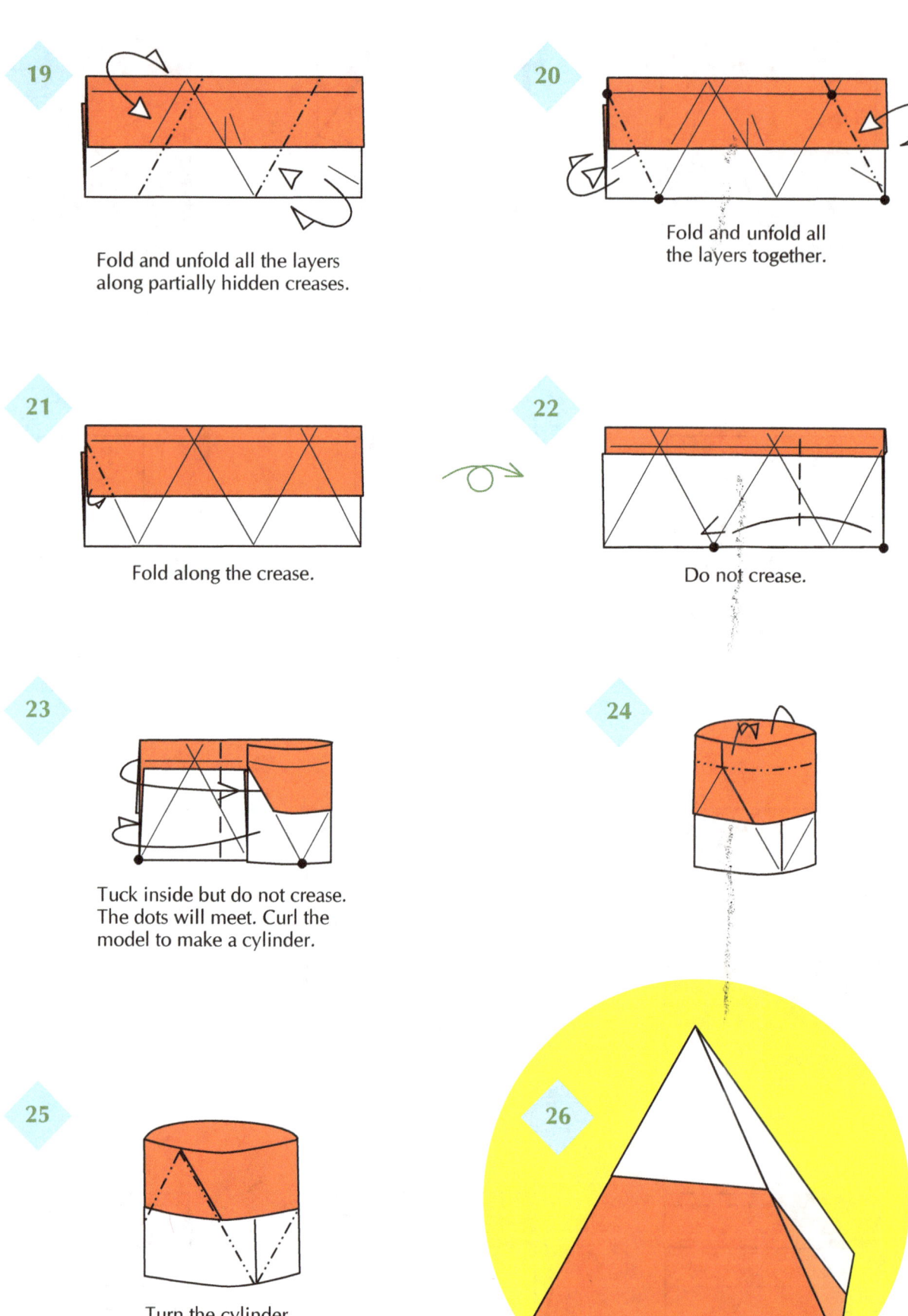

# Layered Tetrahedron

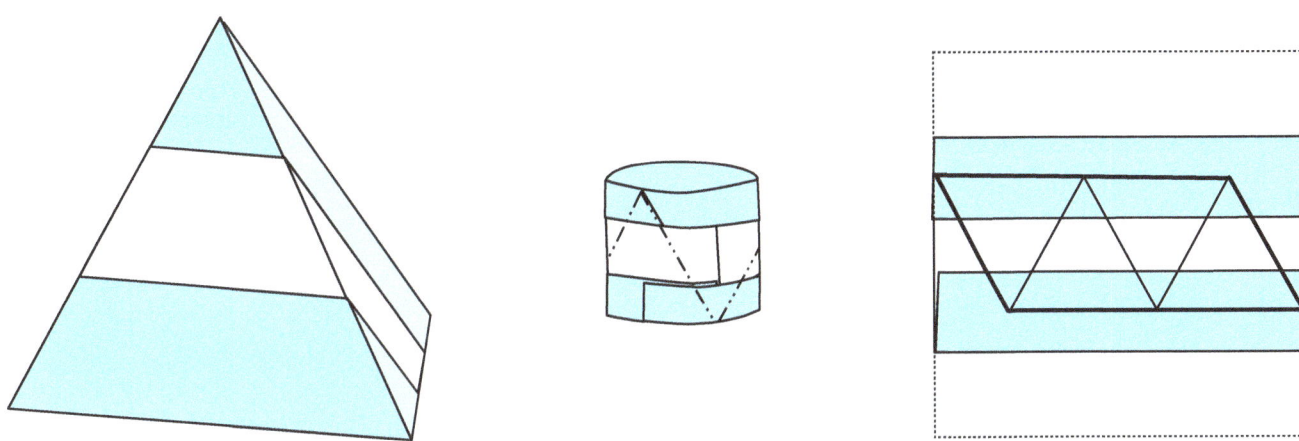

To fold this model, a striped cylinder is formed. With a few folds, the cylinder turns into the striped tetrahedron. The paper is divided into fifths.

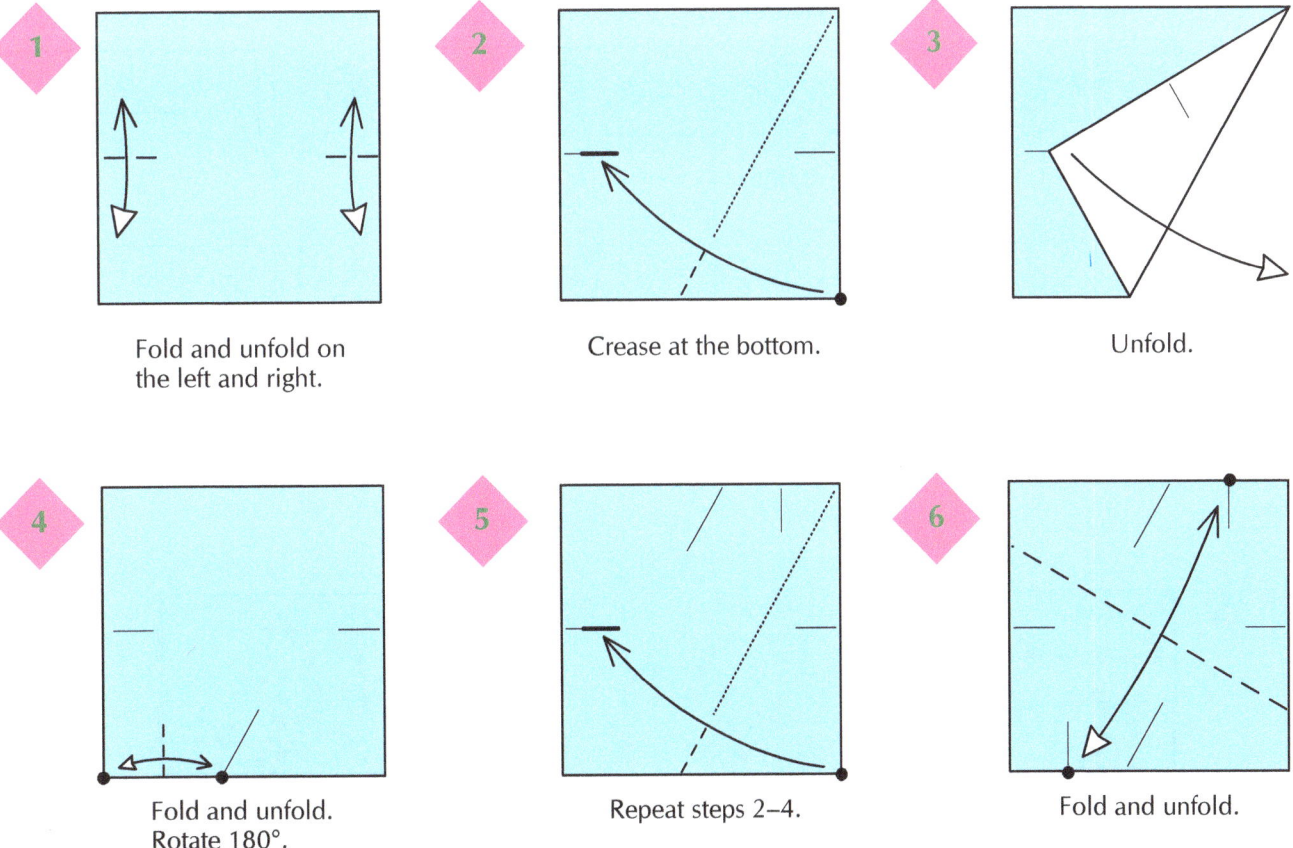

Layered Tetrahedron 53

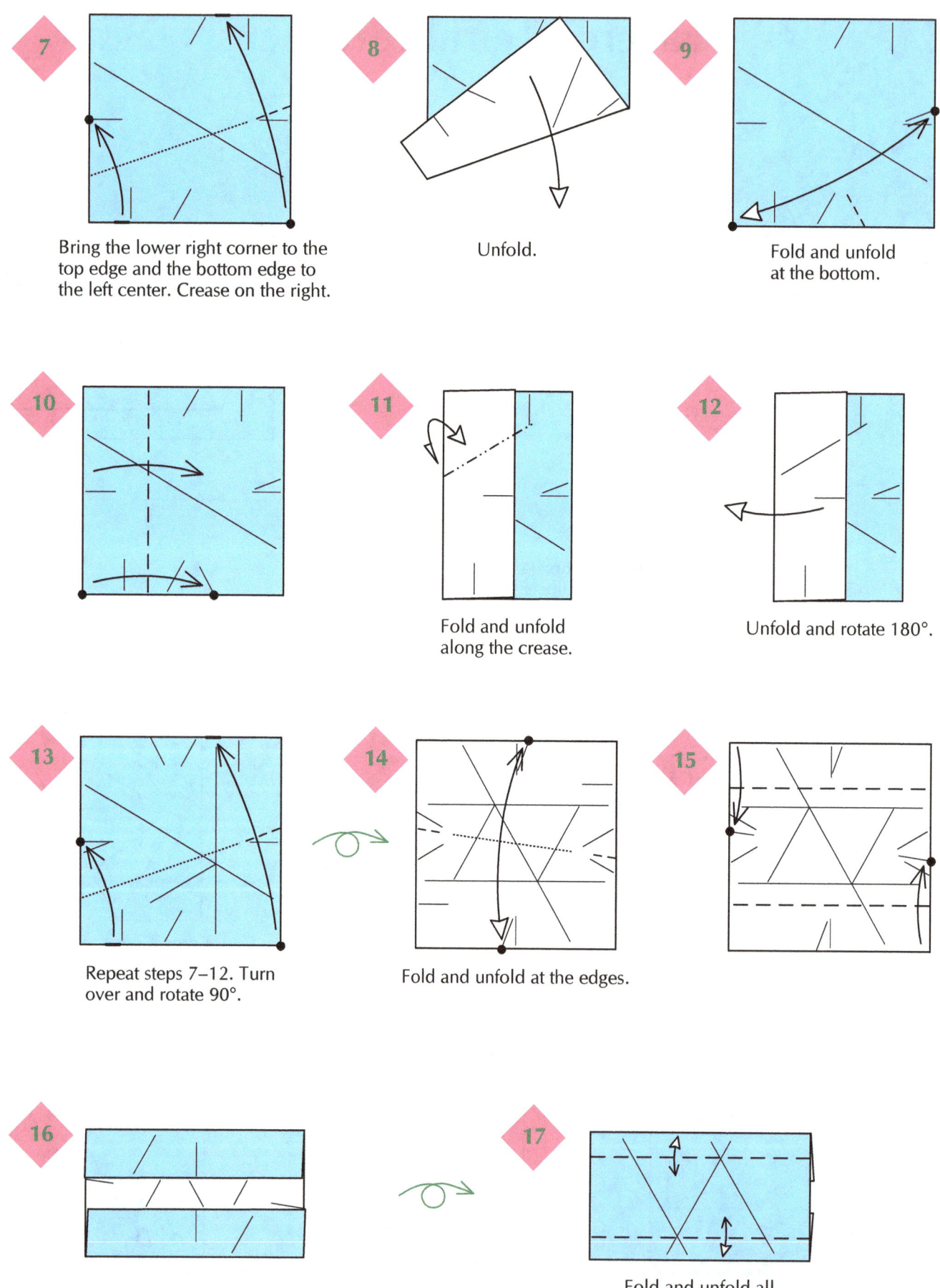

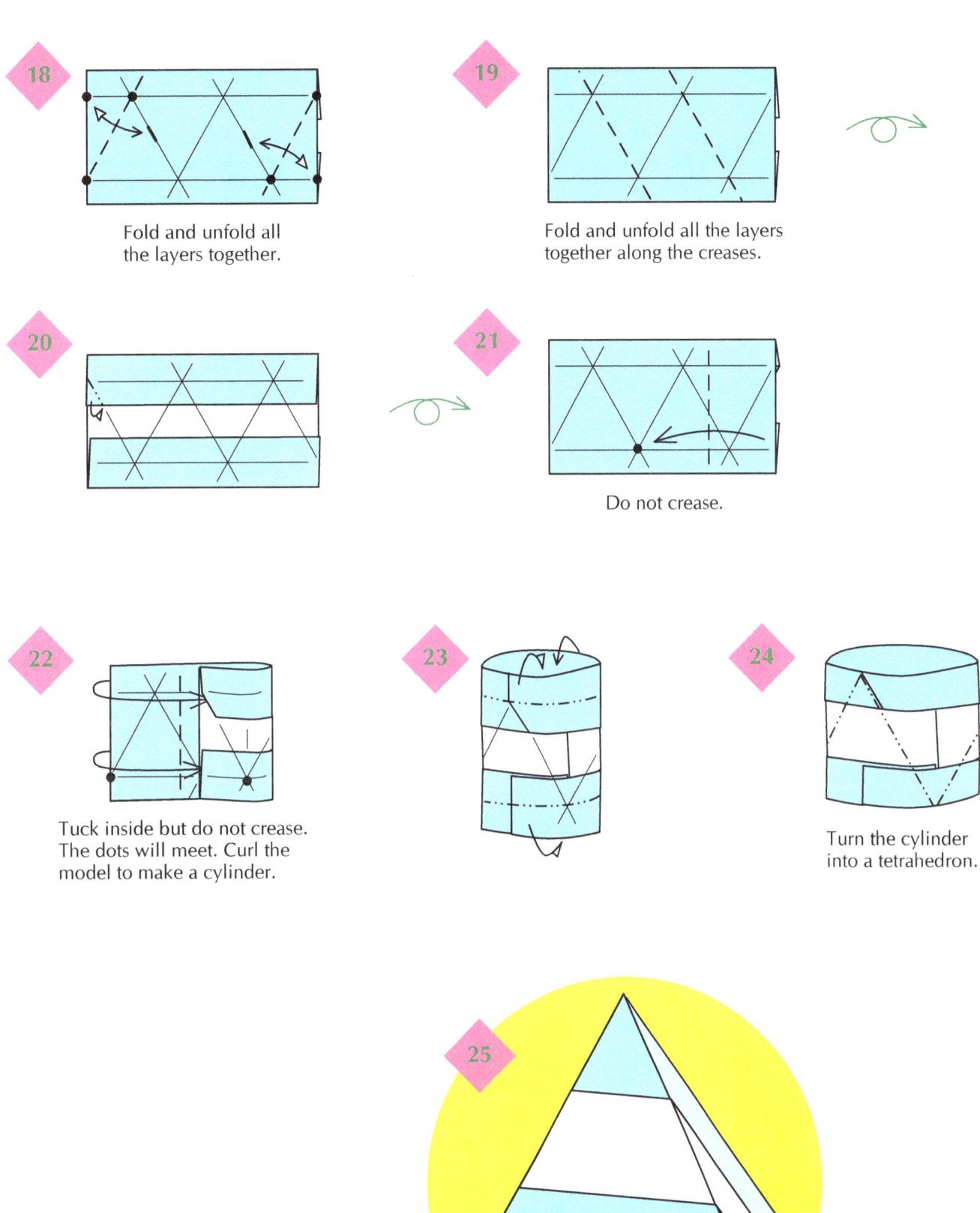

**Layered Tetrahedron**

# Three-Layered Cube

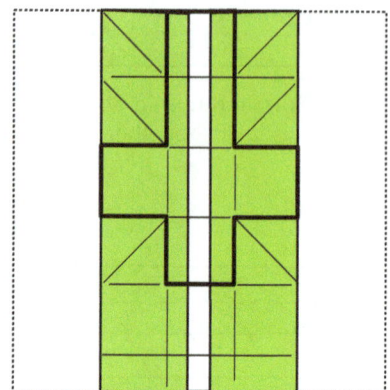

By folding opposite edges towards the center while leaving a white strip, a layout for the cube can be made that will result in this three-layered cube. The paper is divided into seventeenths. Even symmetry is used.

1

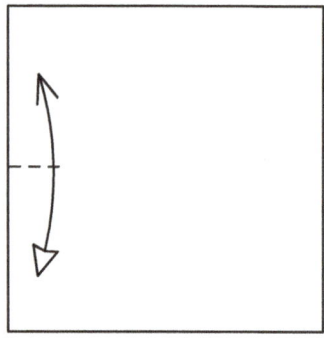

Fold and unfold on the left.

2

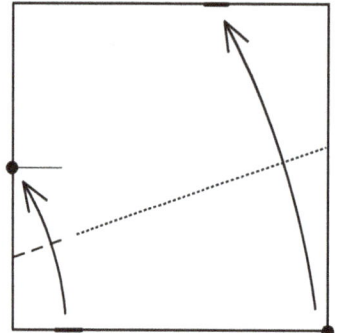

Bring the bottom right corner to the top and the bottom edge to the dot. Crease on the left.

3

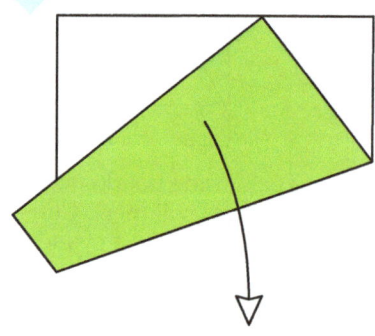

Unfold.

4

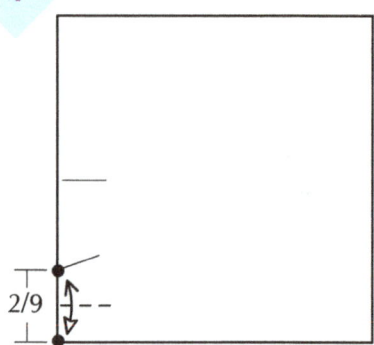

The 2/9 mark is found. Fold and unfold so the dots meet. Rotate 180°.

5

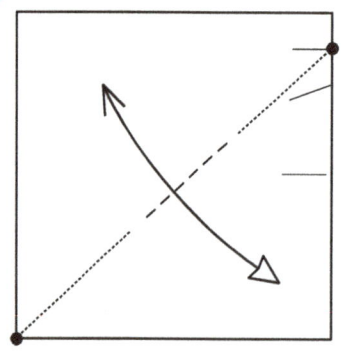

Fold and unfold in the center.

6

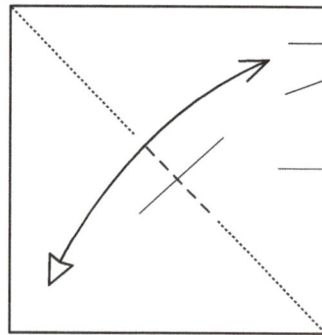

Fold and unfold in the center, along the diagonal.

56   *3D Origami Platonic Solids & More*

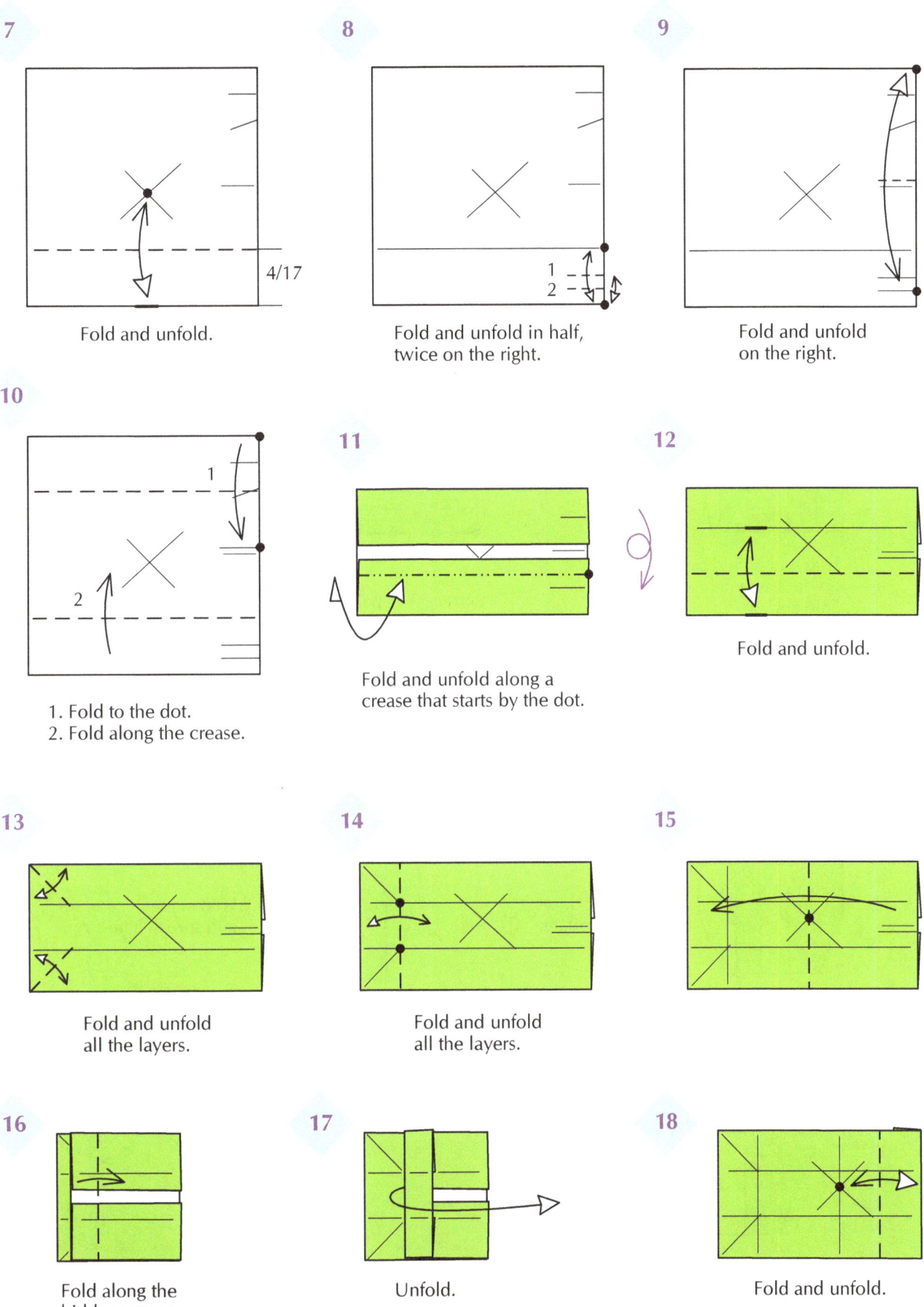

Three-Layered Cube 57

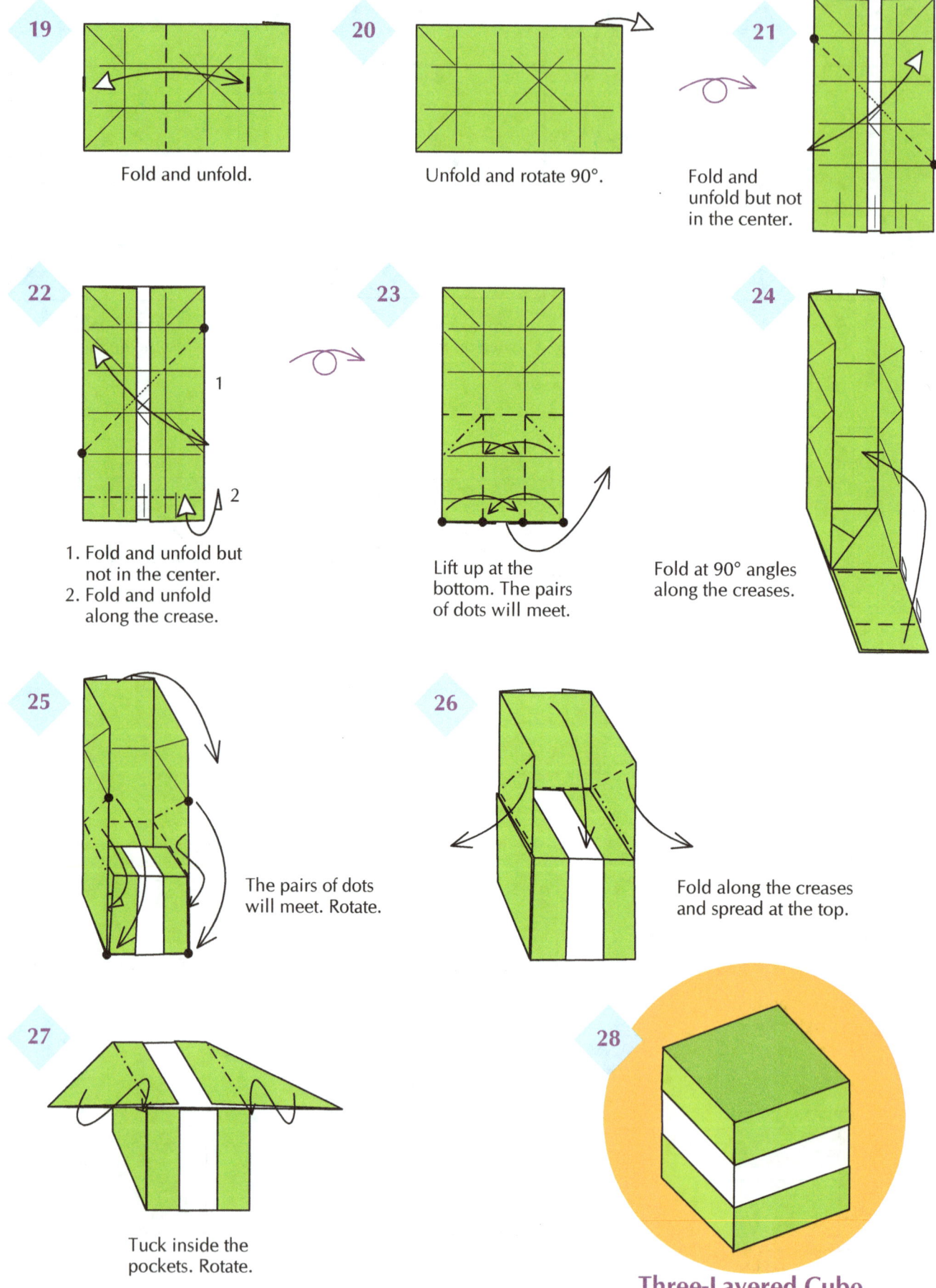

# Fancy Cube

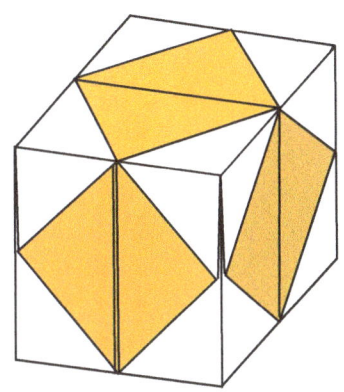

Each face of this cube has a diamond color pattern. The paper is divided into ninths. Square symmetry is used.

1

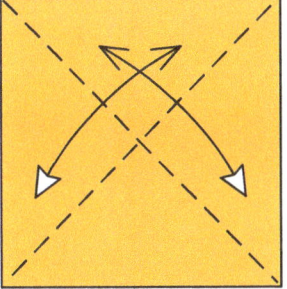

Fold and unfold along the diagonals.

2

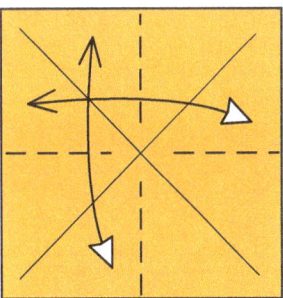

Fold and unfold but not in the center.

3

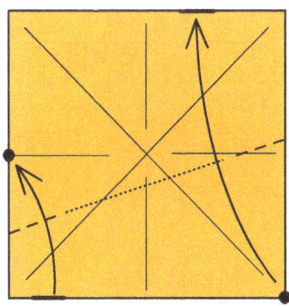

Bring the lower right corner to the top edge and the bottom edge to the left center. Crease on the left and right.

4

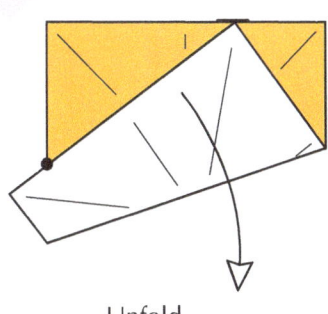

Unfold.

5

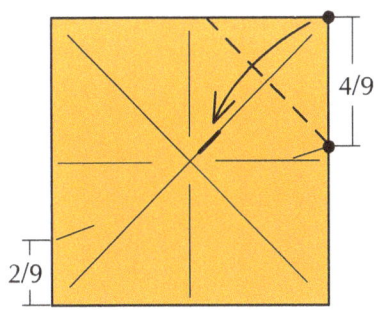

The 2/9 and 4/9 marks are found.

6

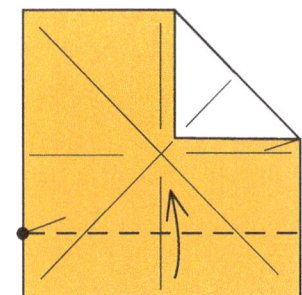

Fancy Cube 59

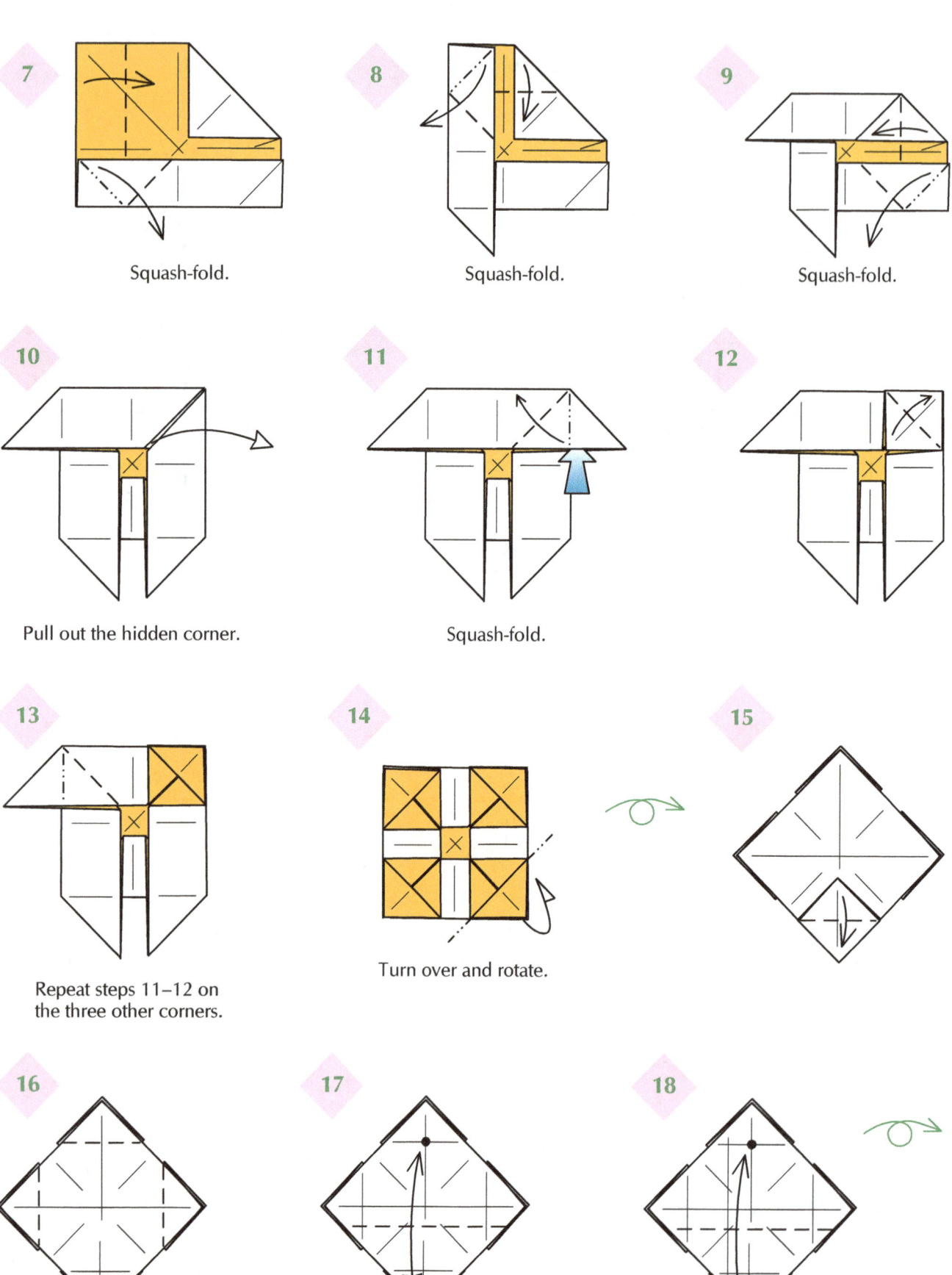

60  3D Origami Platonic Solids & More

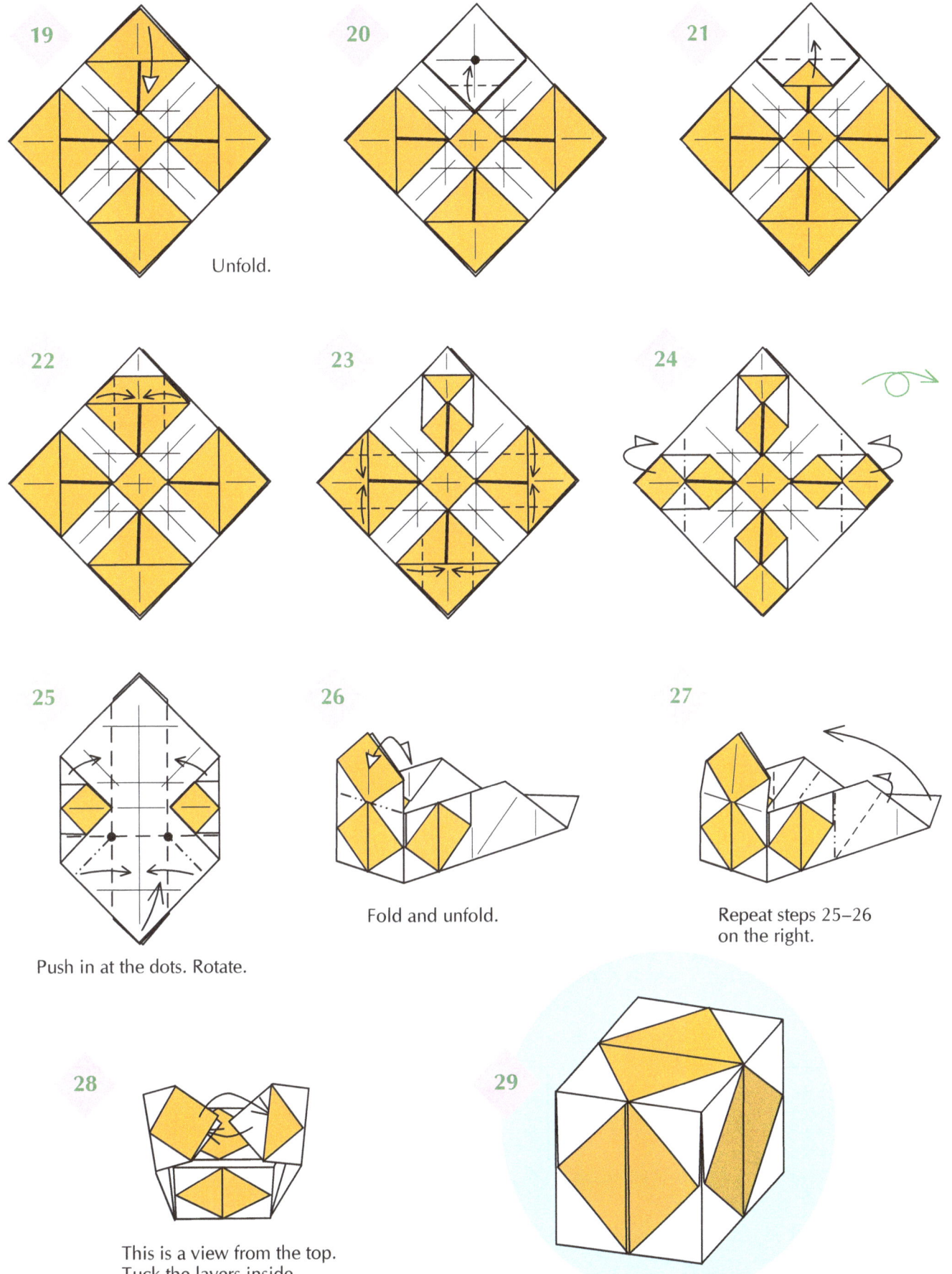

Unfold.

Push in at the dots. Rotate.

Fold and unfold.

Repeat steps 25–26 on the right.

This is a view from the top. Tuck the layers inside.

**Fancy Cube**

Fancy Cube

# Banded Cube

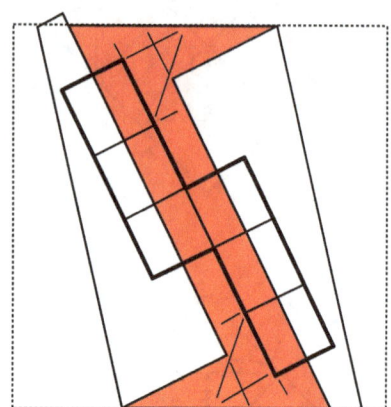

By folding two edges towards the center, a layout with stripes is formed. Placing the six square faces in two rows with three per row is an unusual way to contruct a cube. Odd symmetry is used.

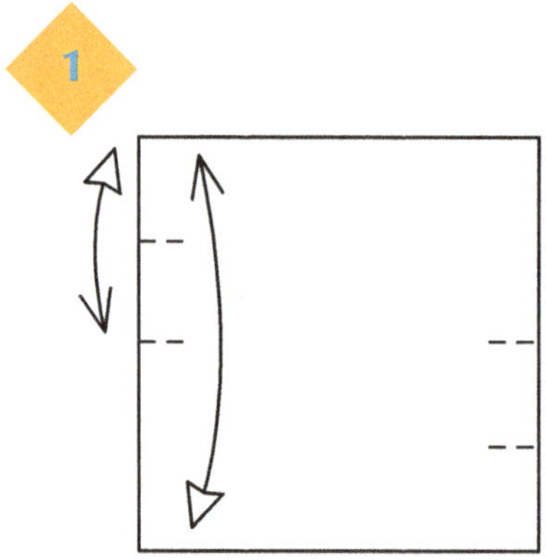

**1.** Make small marks by folding and unfolding in quarters.

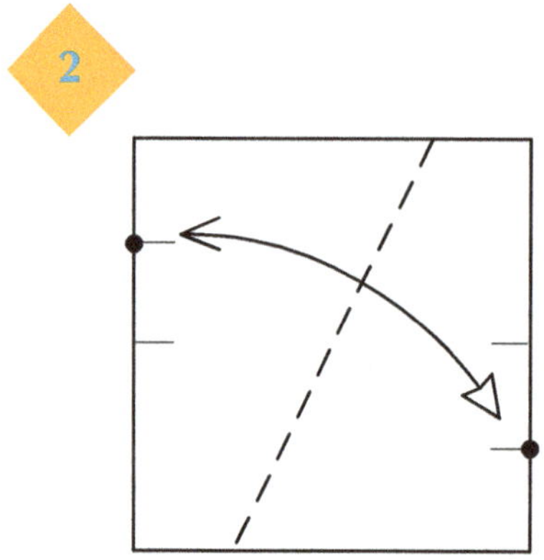

**2.** Fold and unfold.

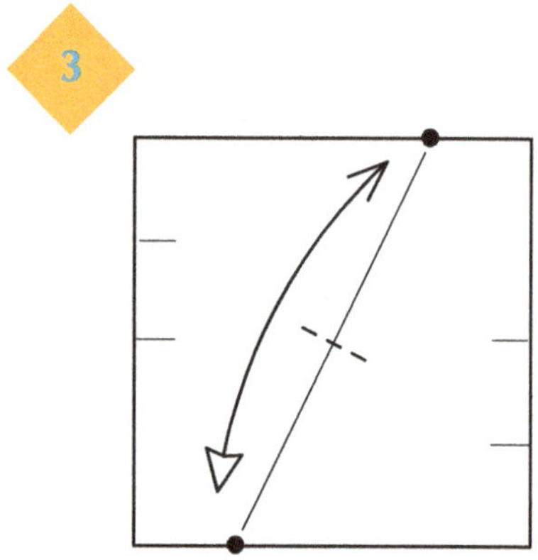

**3.** Fold and unfold in the center.

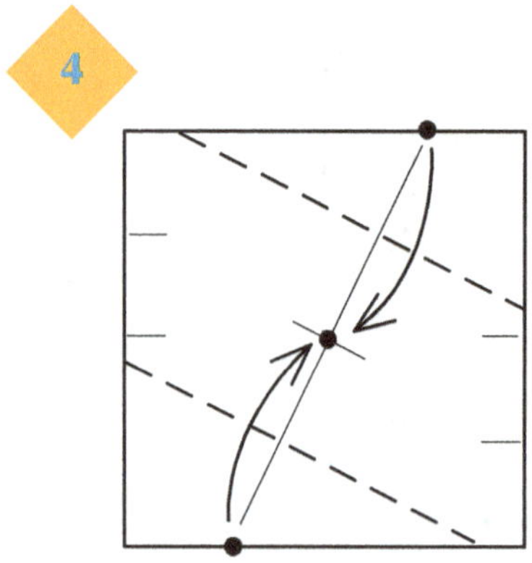

**4.**

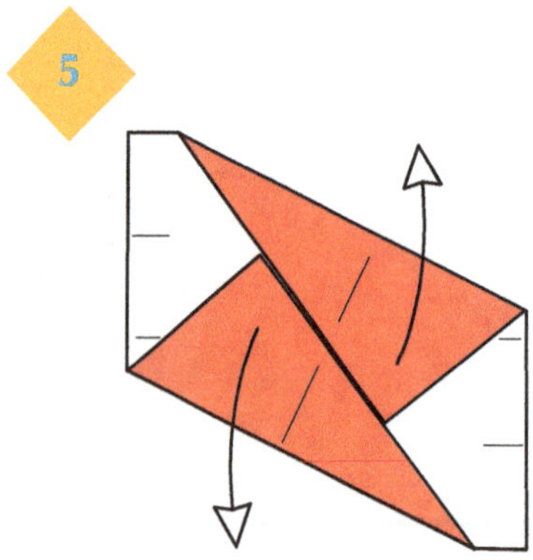

**5.** Unfold.

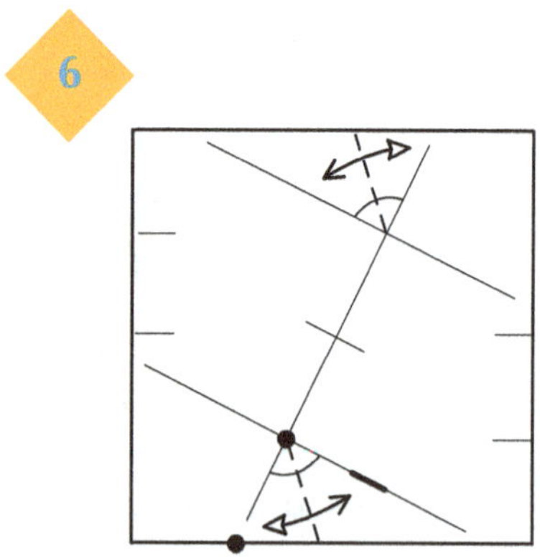

**6.** Fold and unfold.

62  3D Origami Platonic Solids & More

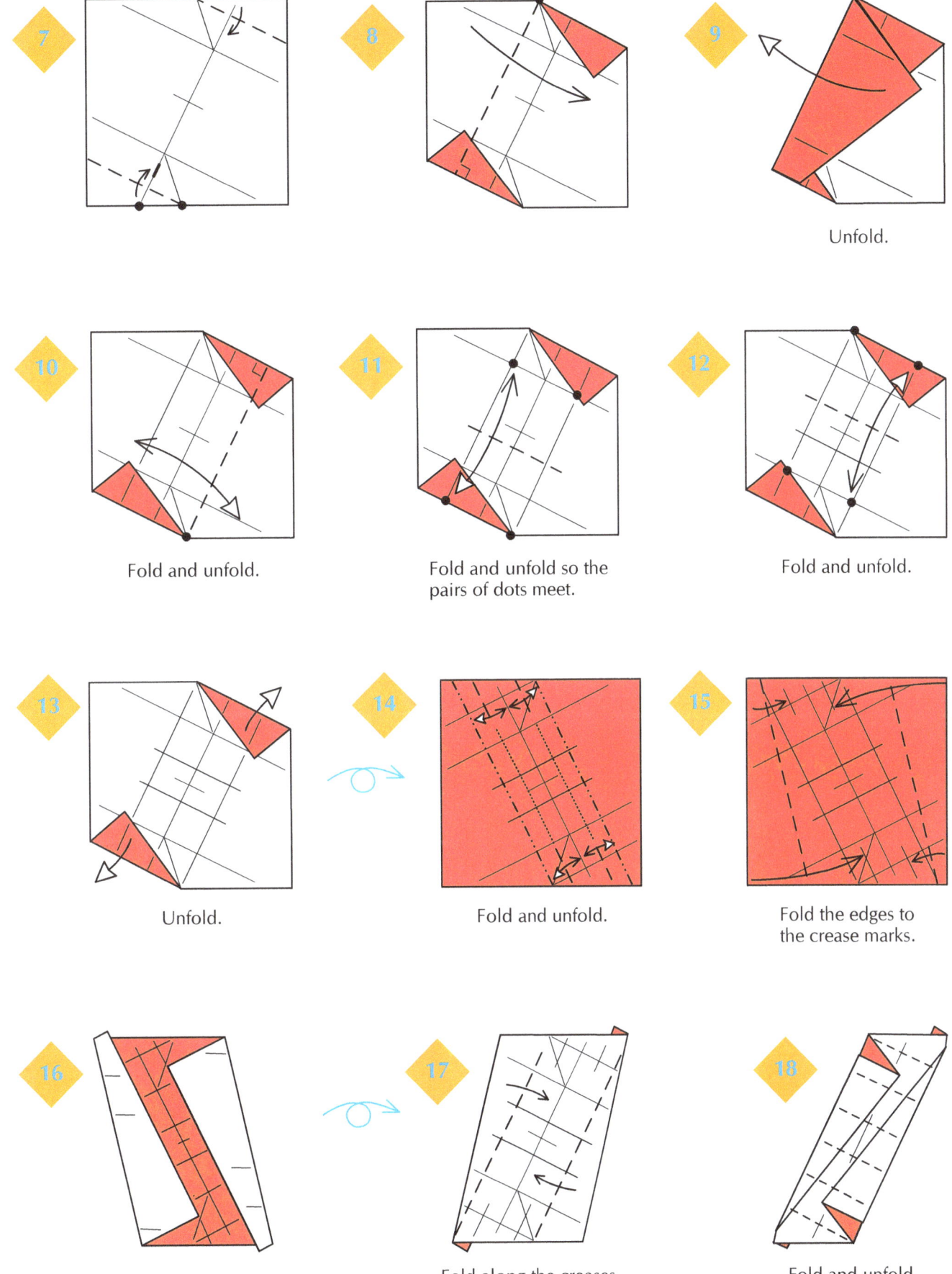

Banded Cube 63

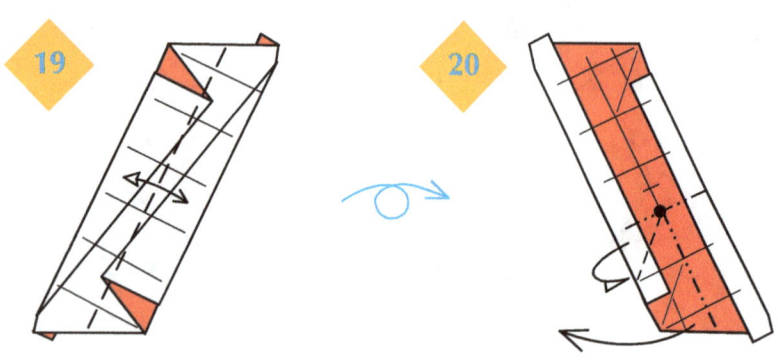

19. Fold and unfold.

20. Puff out at the dot.

21. Fold and unfold along the creases. Rotate.

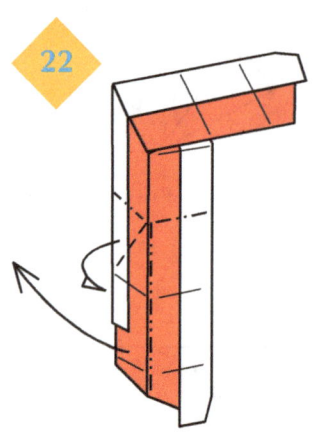
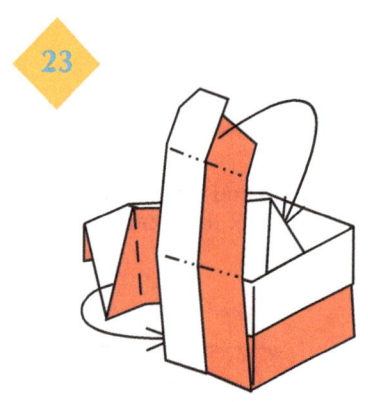

22. Repeat steps 20–21.

23. Tuck inside.

24. **Banded Cube**

64   *3D Origami Platonic Solids & More*

# Banded Octahedron

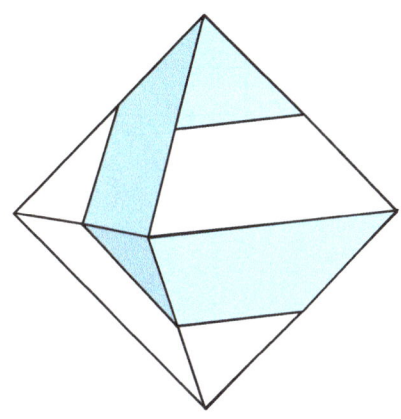

The layout shows two bands of four triangles each. This layout forms an octahedron. Odd symmetry is used.

**1**

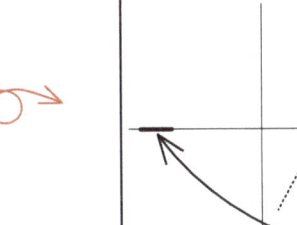

Fold and unfold.

**2**

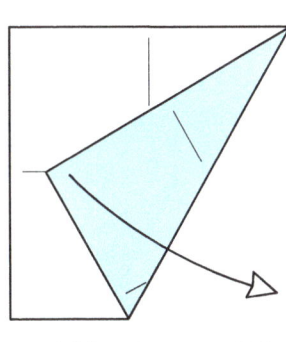

Fold at the bottom.

**3**

Unfold and rotate 180°.

**4**

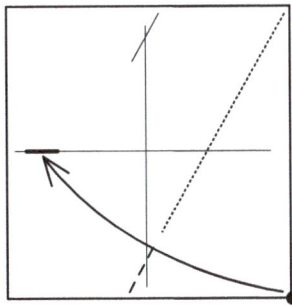

Repeat steps 2–3.

**5**

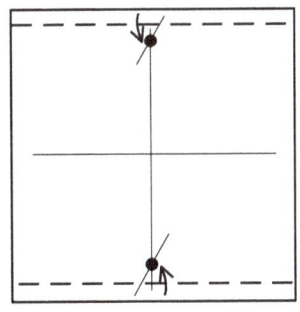

**6**

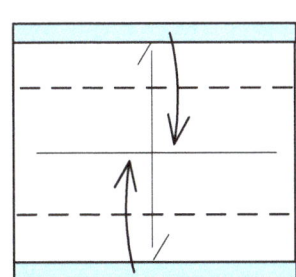

Banded Octahedron 65

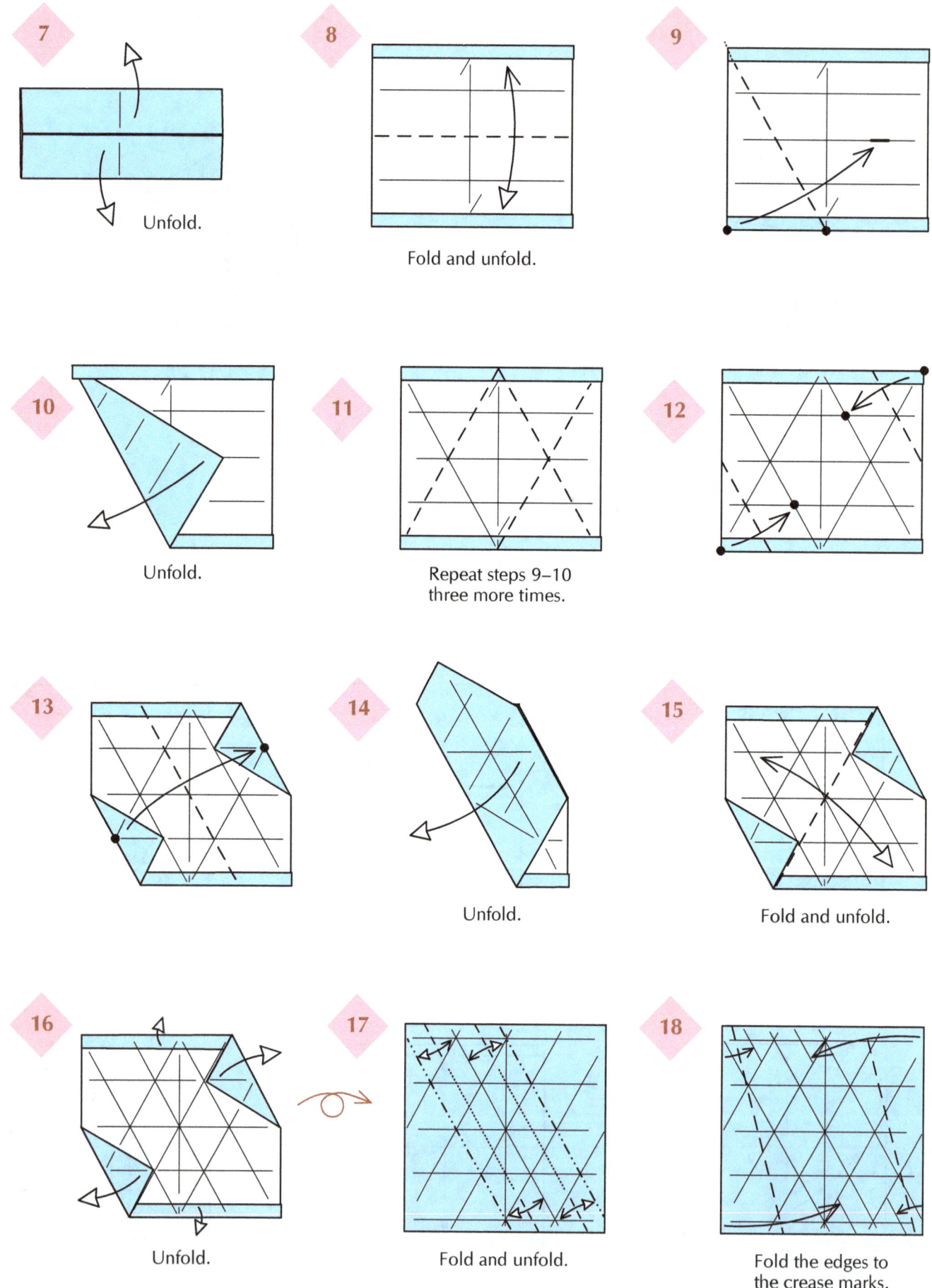

66  3D Origami Platonic Solids & More

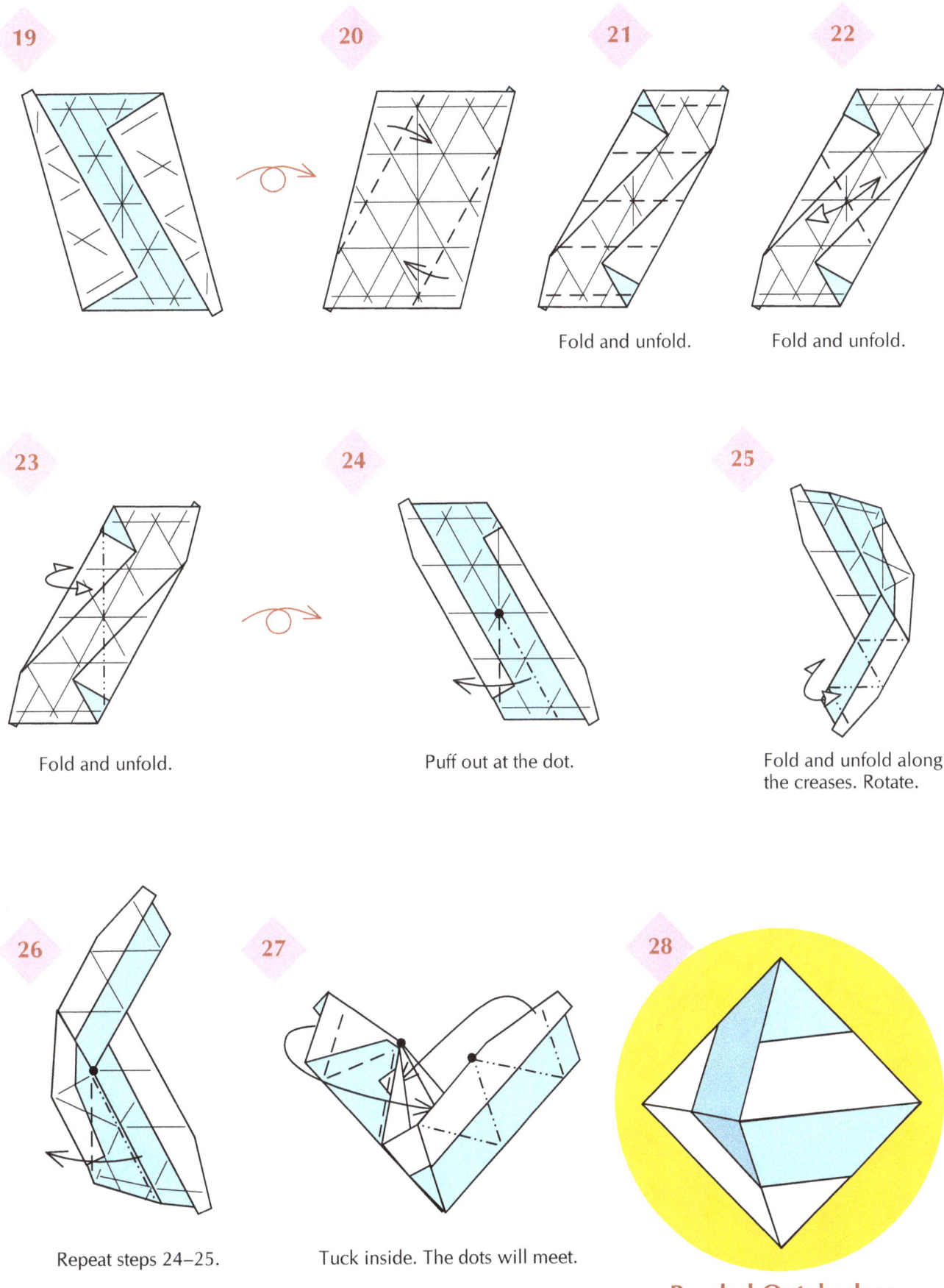

21. Fold and unfold.
22. Fold and unfold.
23. Fold and unfold.
24. Puff out at the dot.
25. Fold and unfold along the creases. Rotate.
26. Repeat steps 24–25.
27. Tuck inside. The dots will meet.

**Banded Octahedron**

*Banded Octahedron* 67

# Dimpled Polyhedra

These polyhedra are dimpled versions of some of the Archimedean solids. Archimedean solids are convex polyhedra where the faces are from two or more types of regular polygons and have identical vertices.

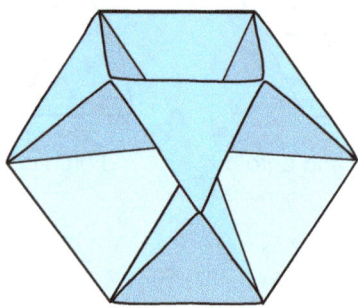

Octahemioctahedron

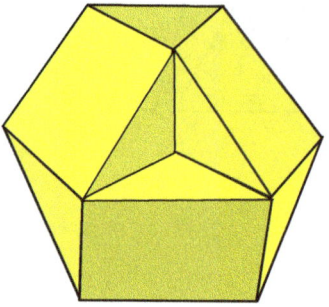

Cubehemioctahedron

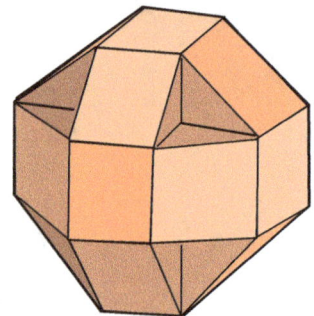

Dimpled Rhombicuboctahedron

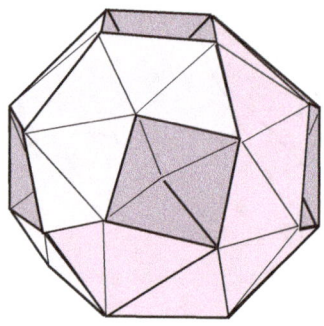

Dimpled Snub Cube

## Dimpled Rhombicuboctahedron

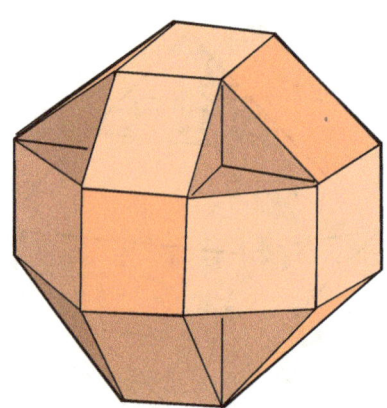
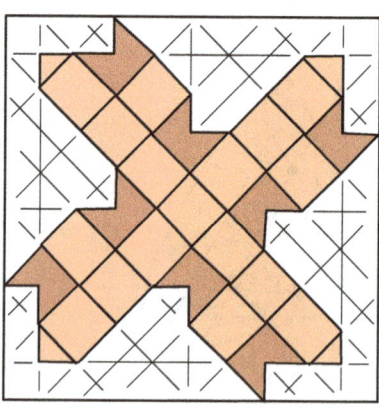

The rhombicuboctahedron has 18 square faces and 8 triagular faces. The dark regions of the crease pattern show the sunken sides. The paper is divided into tenths. Square symmetry is used.

68  *3D Origami Platonic Solids & More*

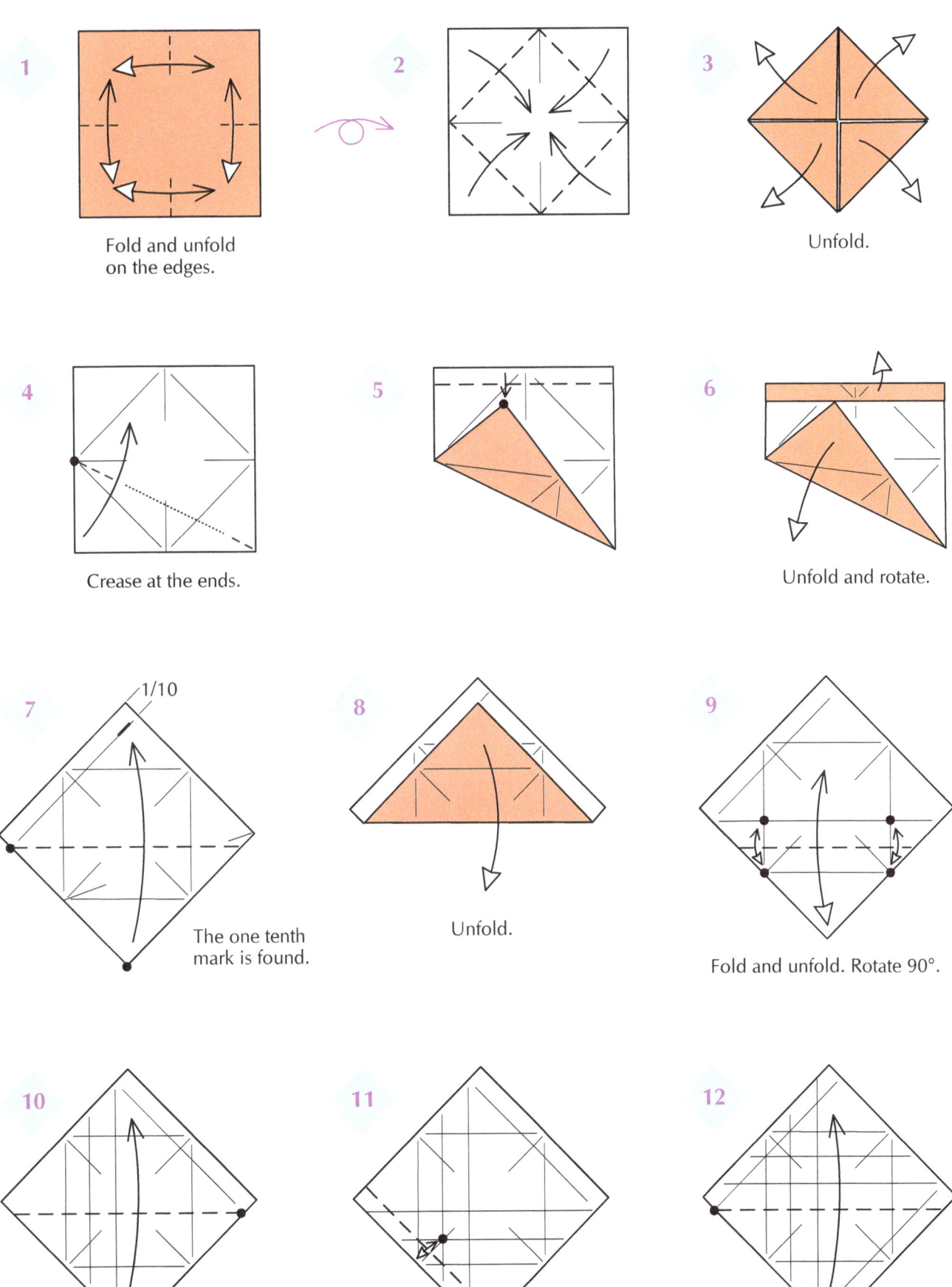

Dimpled Rhombicuboctahedron 69

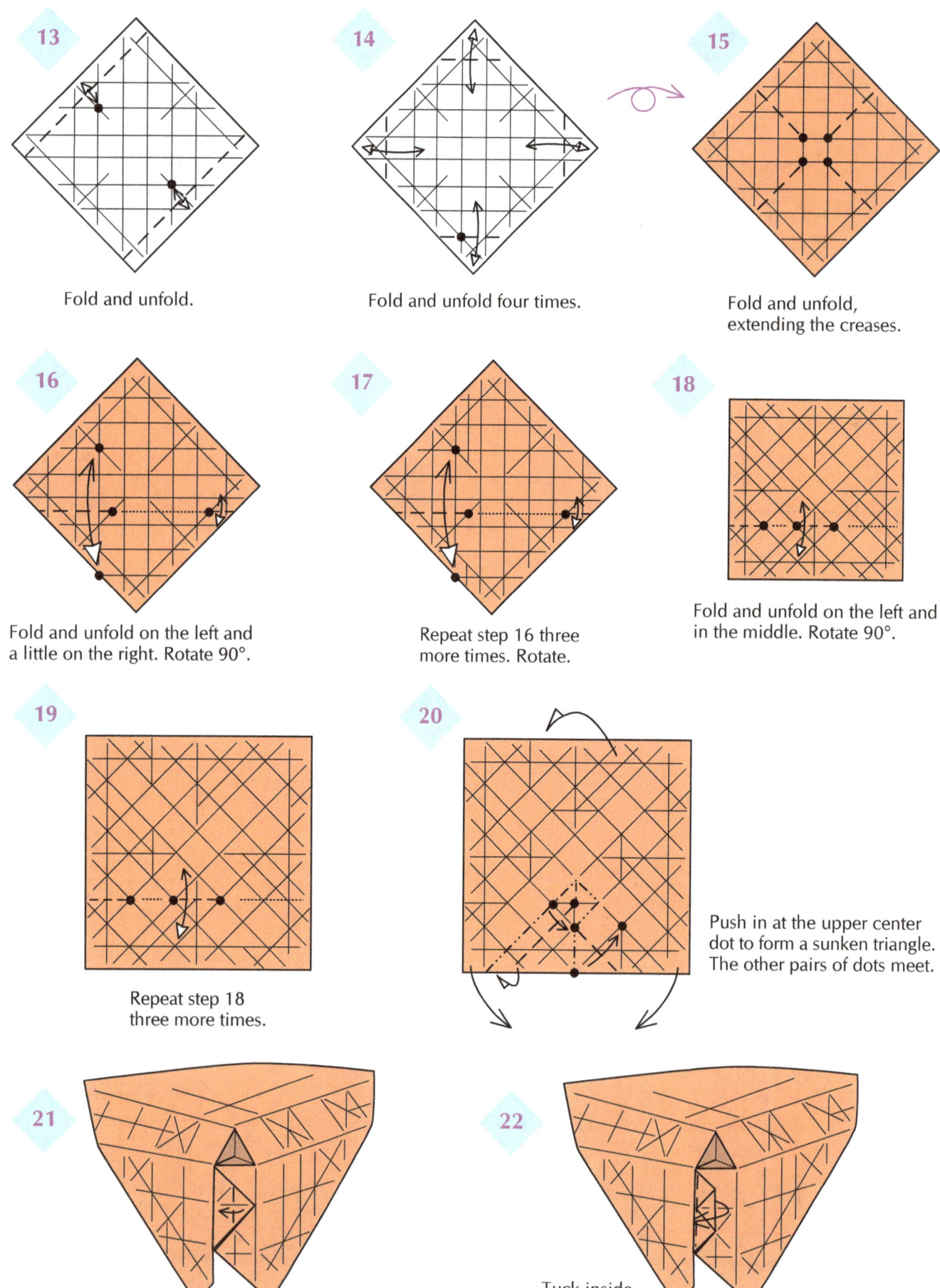

70   3D Origami Platonic Solids & More

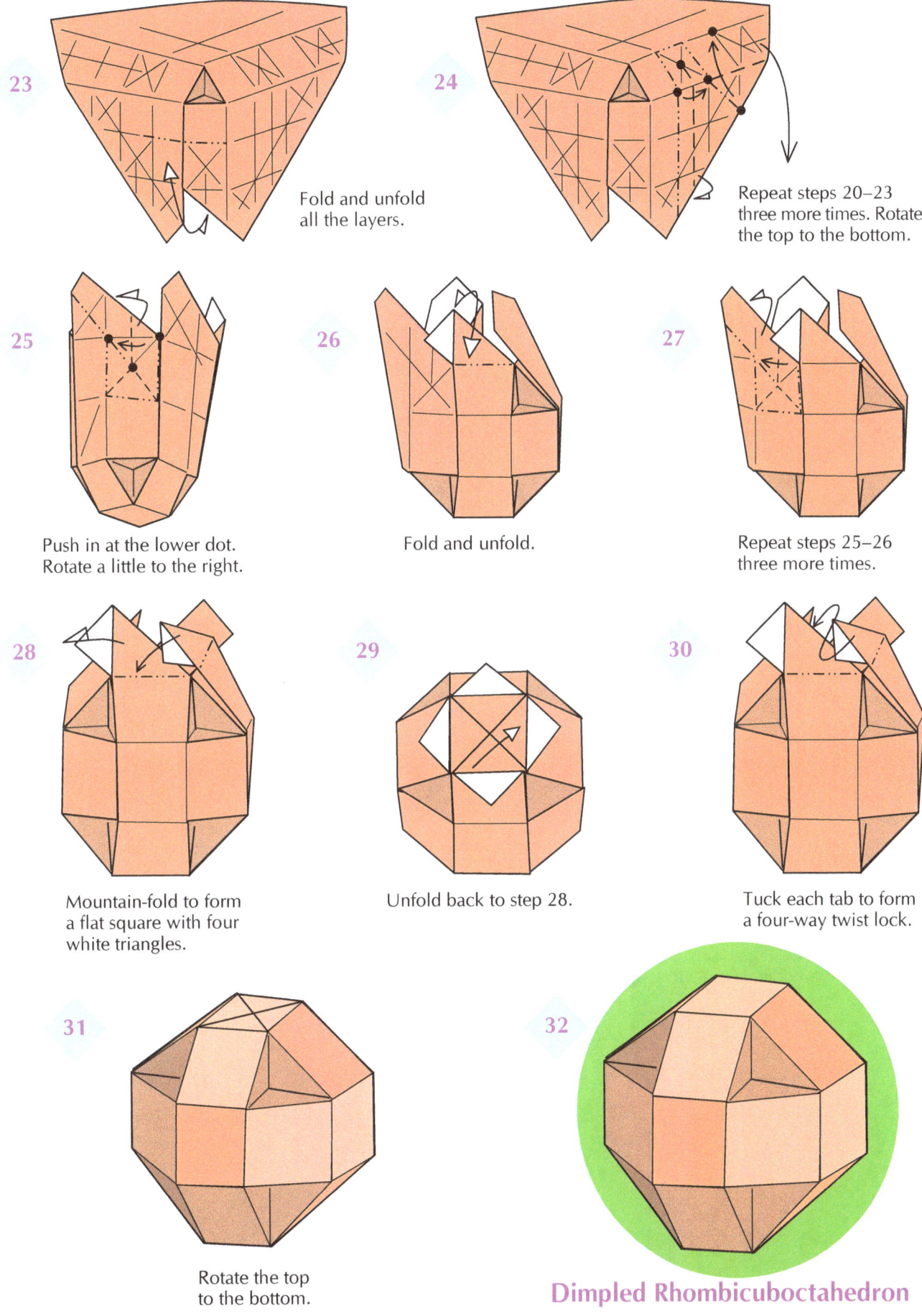

Dimpled Rhombicuboctahedron 71

# Cubehemioctahedron

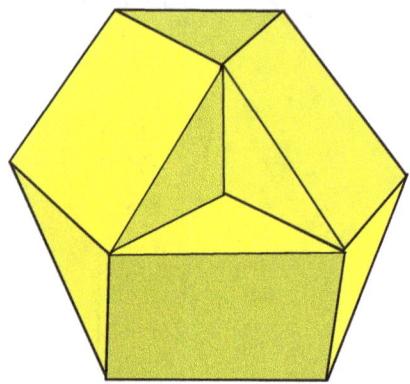
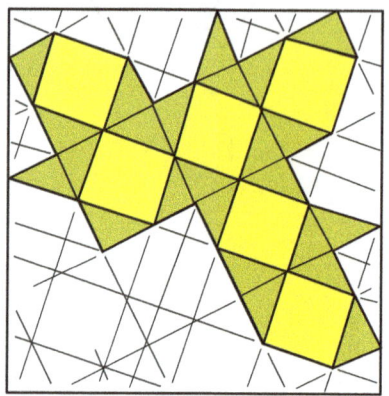

The cubehemioctahedron can be formed from a cube with sunken corners. This model uses 3/4 square symmetry. The darker paper in the crease pattern shows the sunken sides.

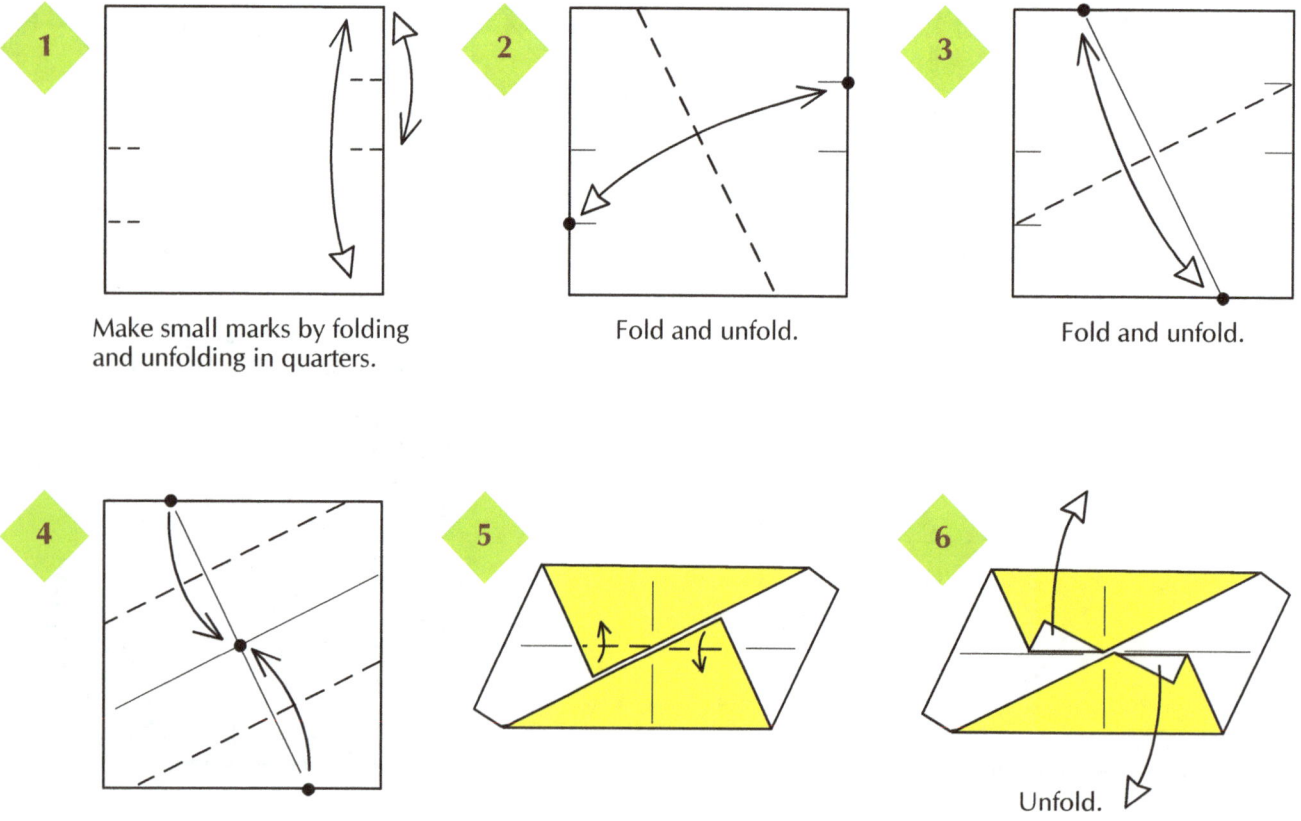

1. Make small marks by folding and unfolding in quarters.
2. Fold and unfold.
3. Fold and unfold.
4.
5.
6. Unfold.

72   3D Origami Platonic Solids & More

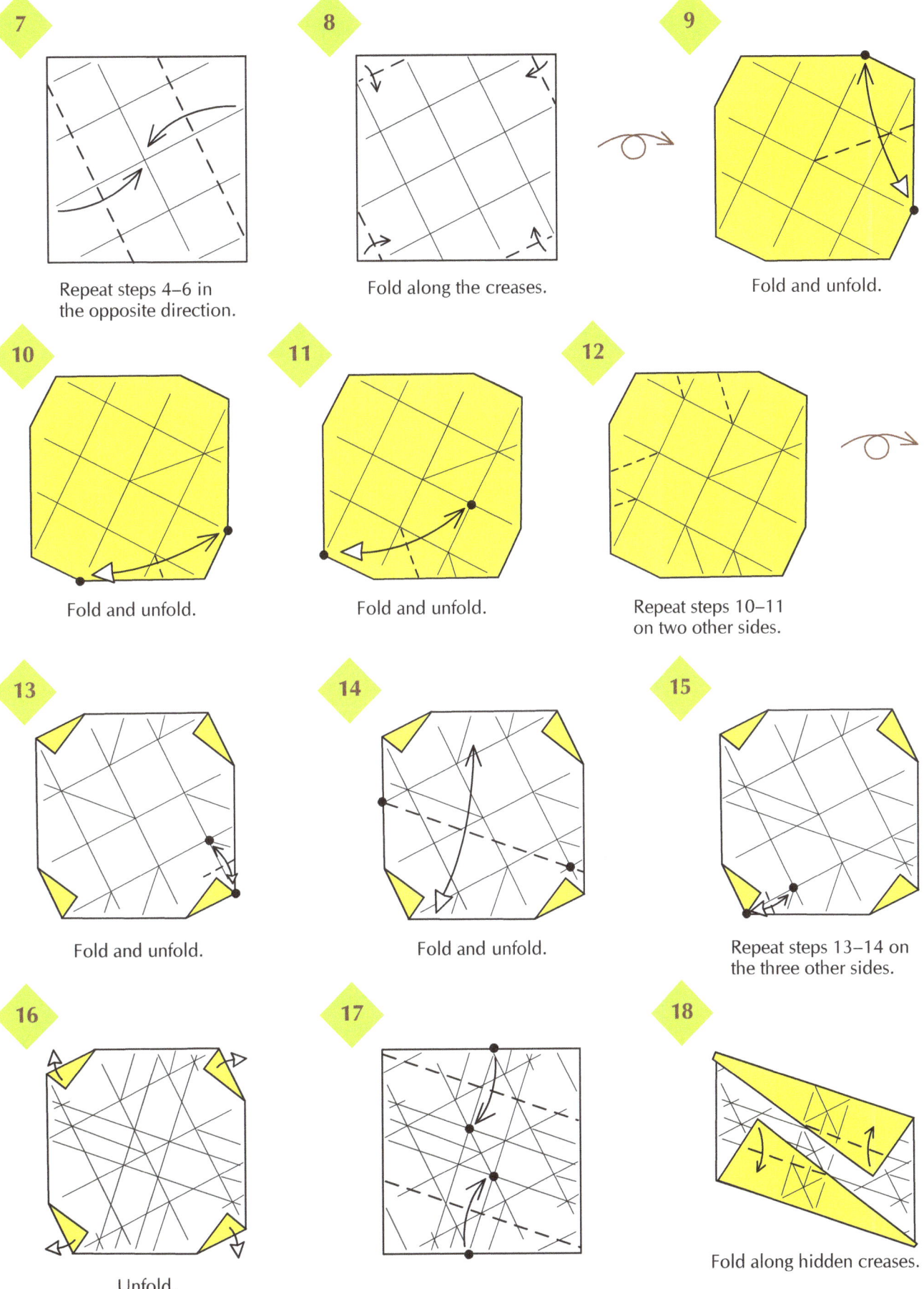

Cubehemioctahedron 73

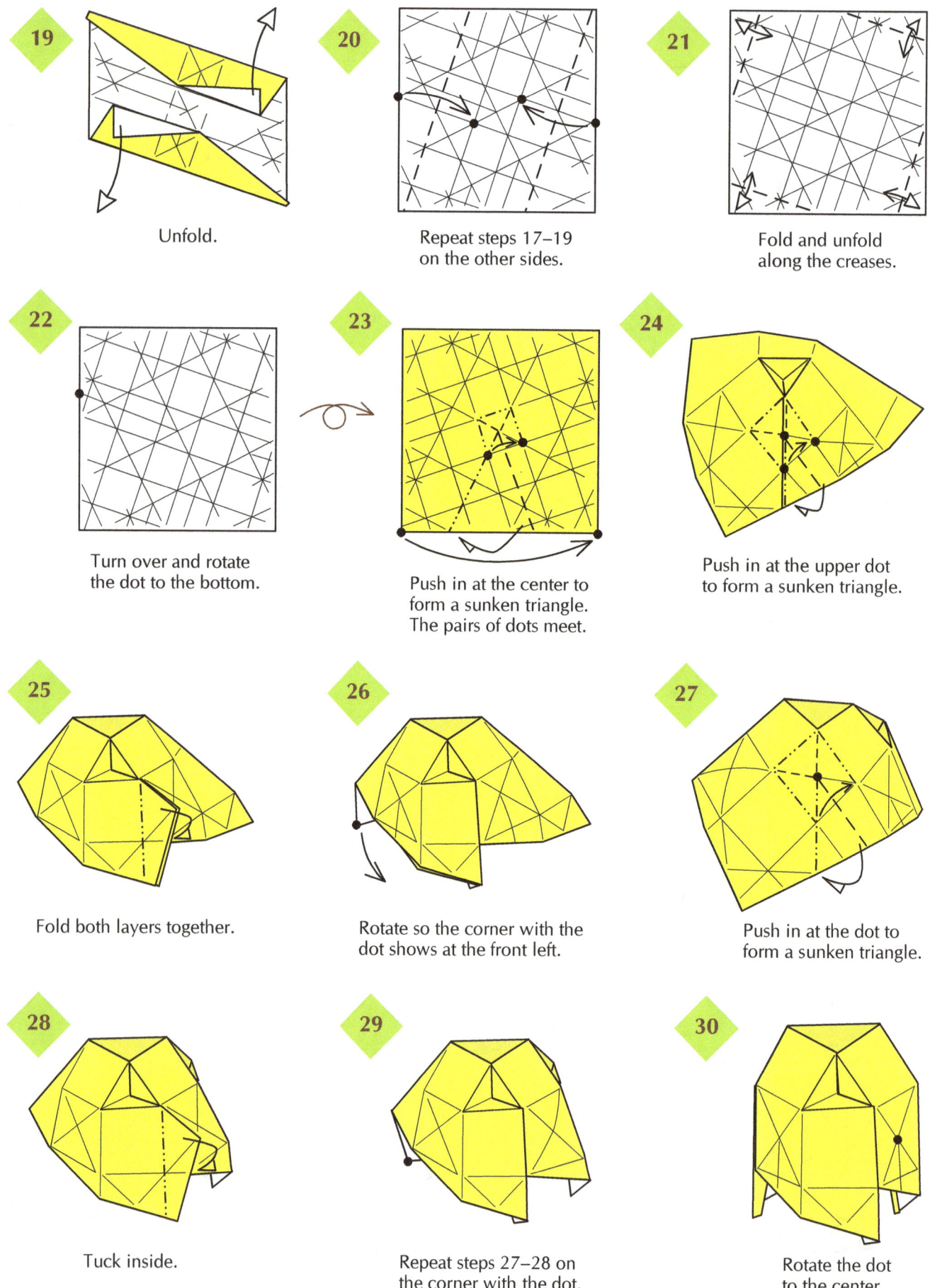

74   *3D Origami Platonic Solids & More*

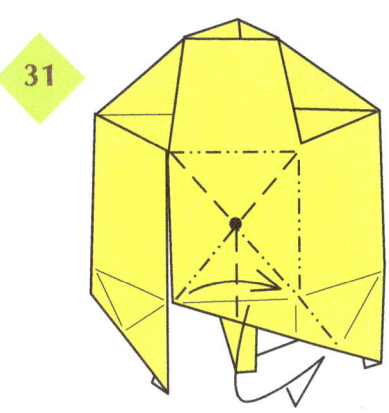

Push in at the dot to form a sunken triangle.

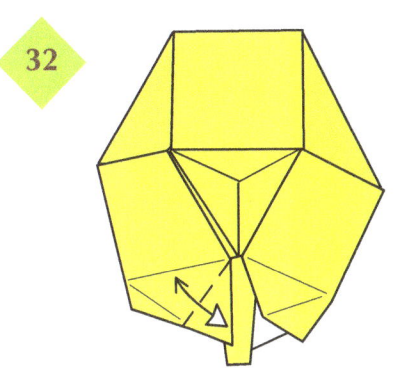

Fold and unfold along the crease.

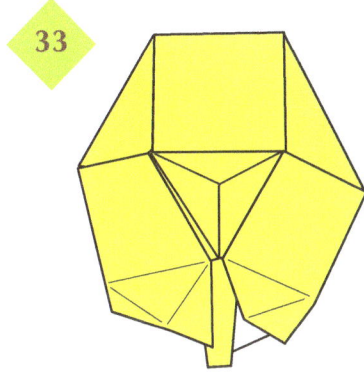

Repeat steps 31–32 two more times going around.

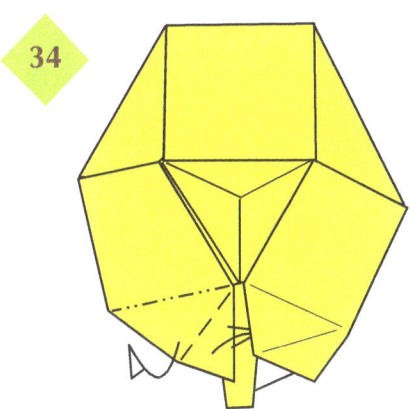

Begin to form the bottom sunken triangle by folding toward the inside center and tucking.

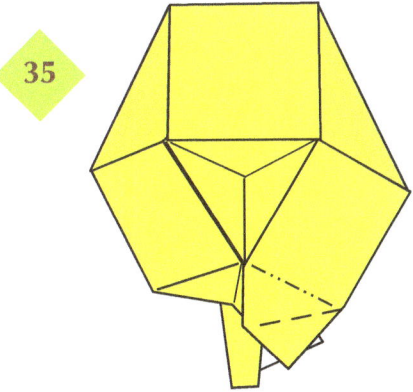

Repeat step 34 two more times to complete the bottom sunken triangle.

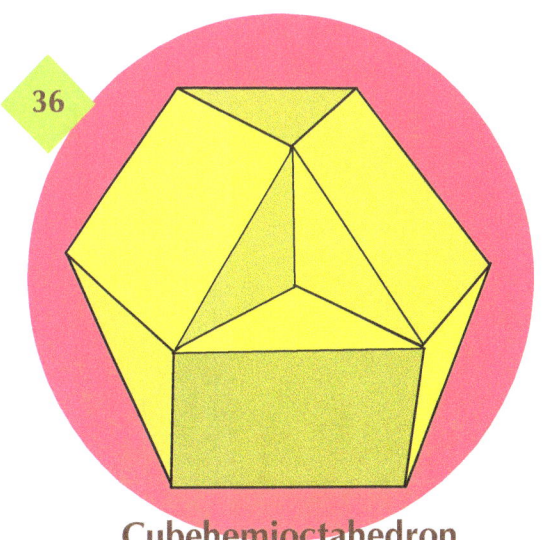

**Cubehemioctahedron**

*Cubehemioctahedron* 75

# Octahemioctahedron

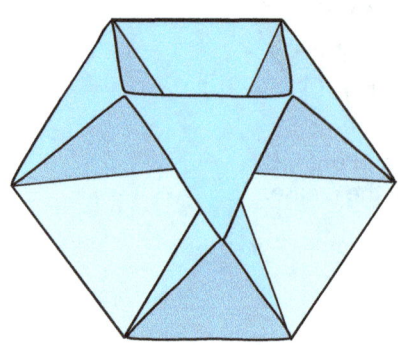
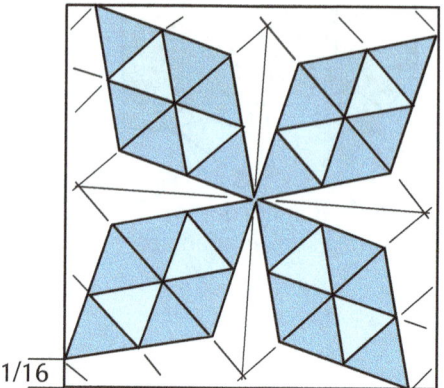

1/16

The octahemioctahedron can be formed from an octahedron with sunken vertices. The structure is similar to that of Octahedron (2) but the tab is 1/16 instead of 1/8. This makes for a larger model. The darker regions represent the sunken sides.

**1** Make small marks by folding and unfolding in half.

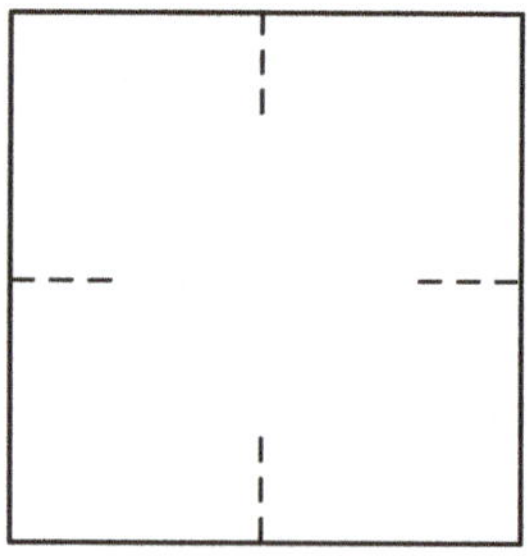

**2** Fold and unfold on the left. Rotate 90°.

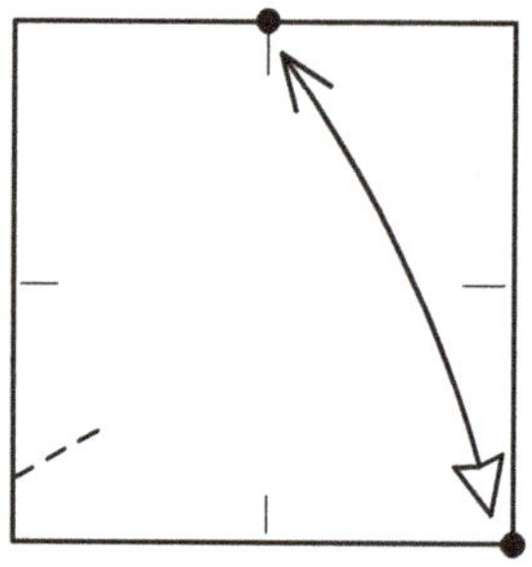

**3** Repeat step 2 three more times.

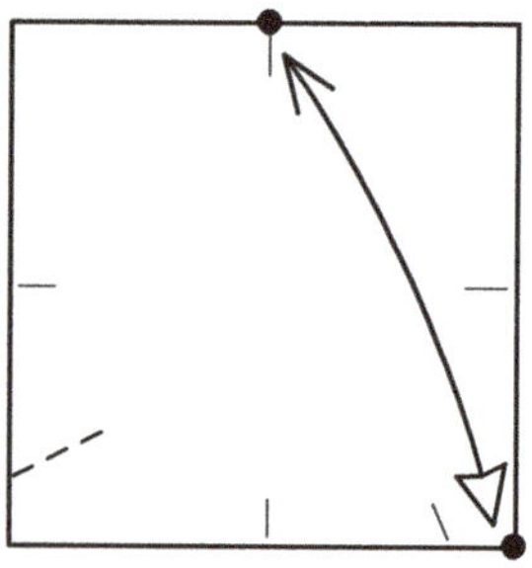

**4**

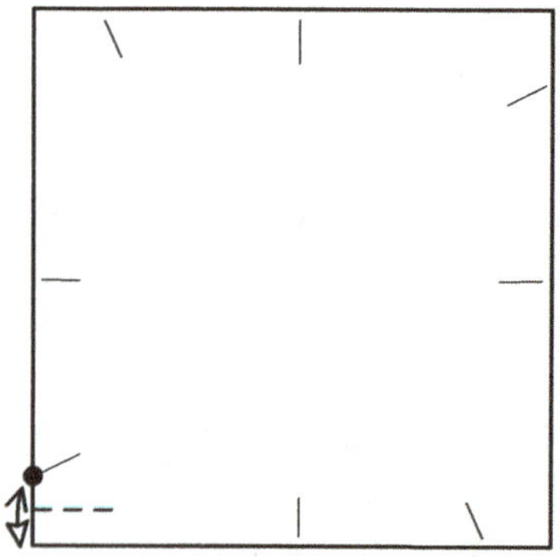

**5** 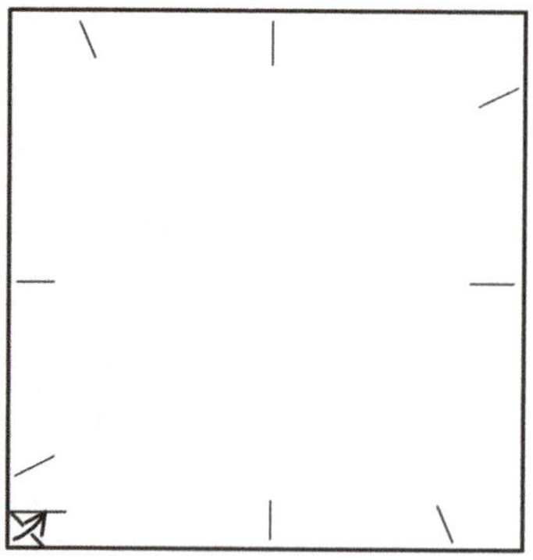 Rotate 90°.

**6** Repeat steps 4–5 three more times.

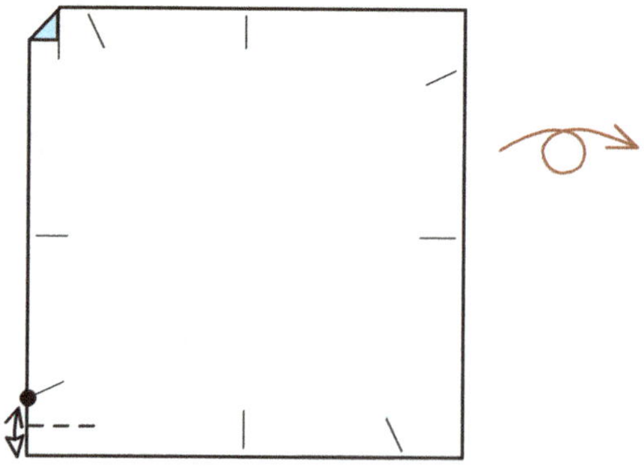

76   3D Origami Platonic Solids & More

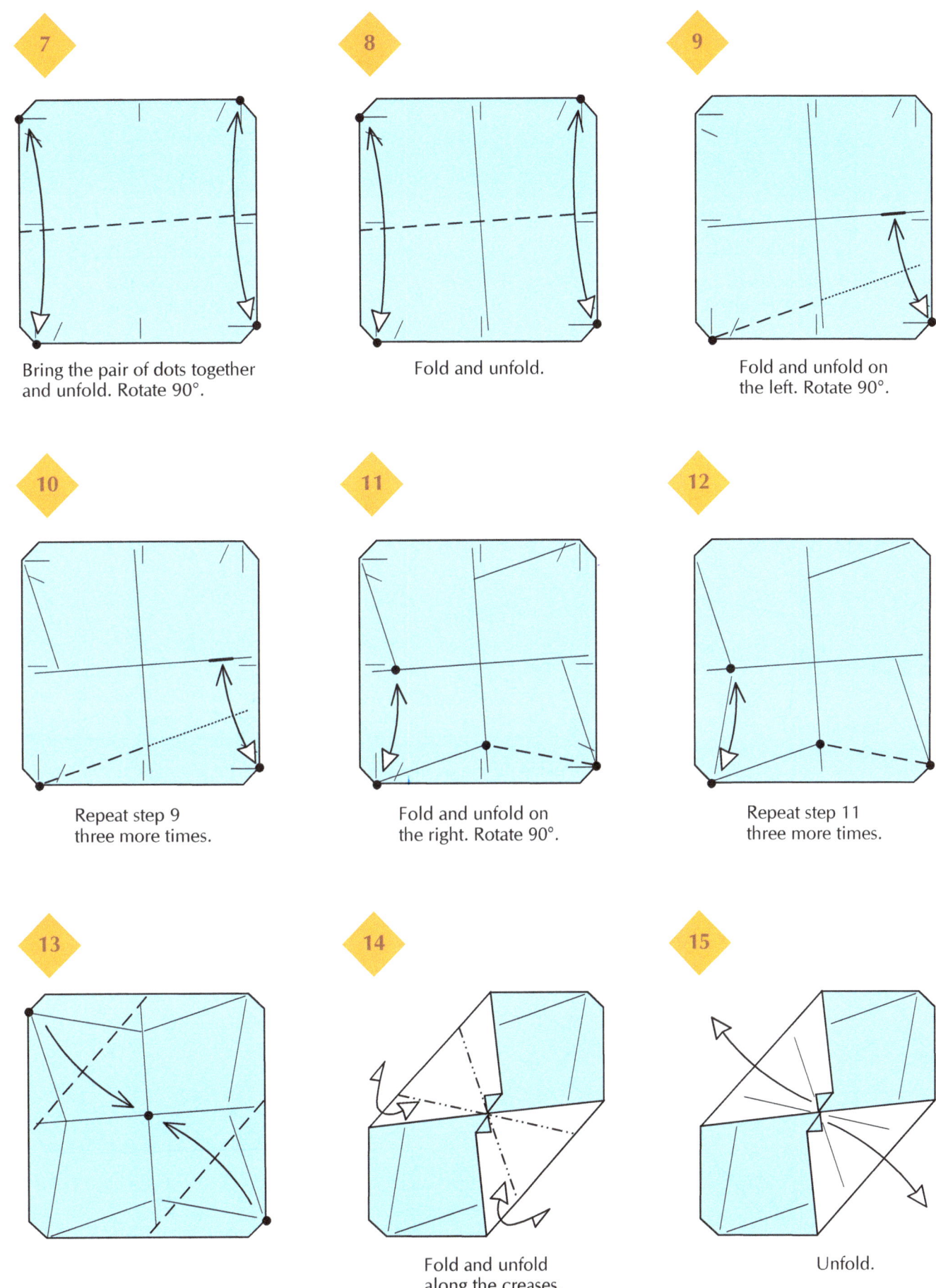

Octahemioctahedron 77

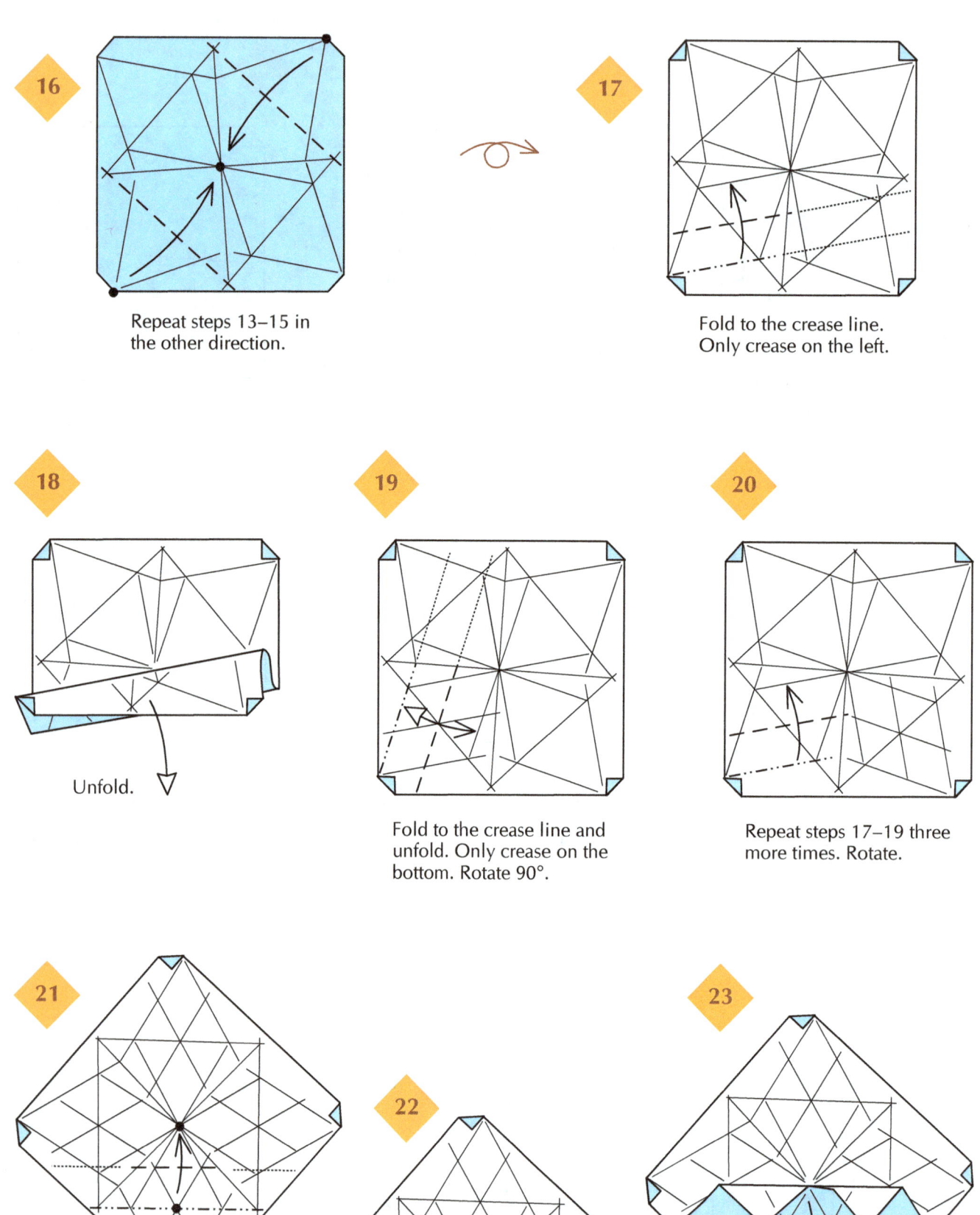

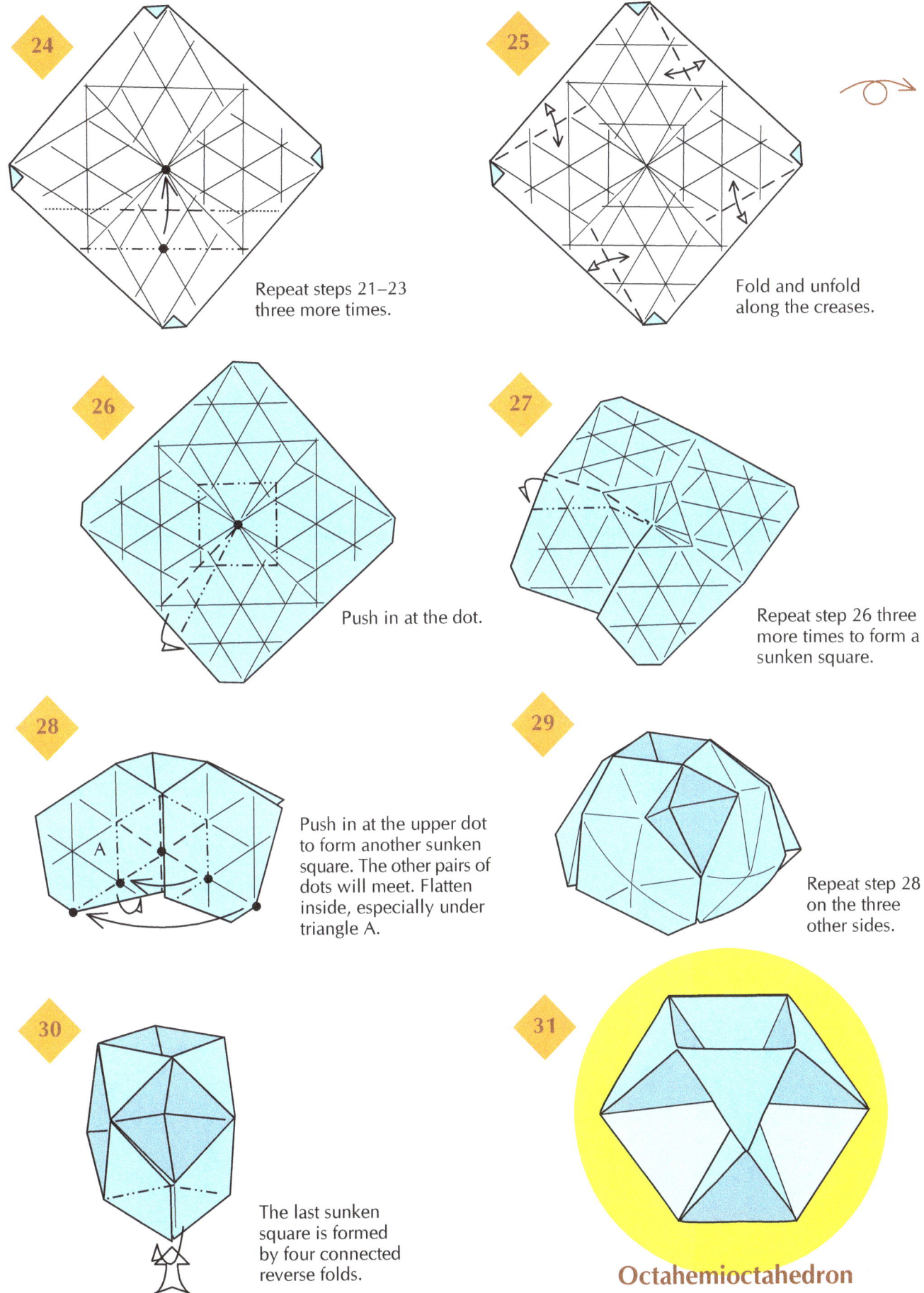

24. Repeat steps 21–23 three more times.

25. Fold and unfold along the creases.

26. Push in at the dot.

27. Repeat step 26 three more times to form a sunken square.

28. Push in at the upper dot to form another sunken square. The other pairs of dots will meet. Flatten inside, especially under triangle A.

29. Repeat step 28 on the three other sides.

30. The last sunken square is formed by four connected reverse folds.

31. **Octahemioctahedron**

# Dimpled Snub Cube

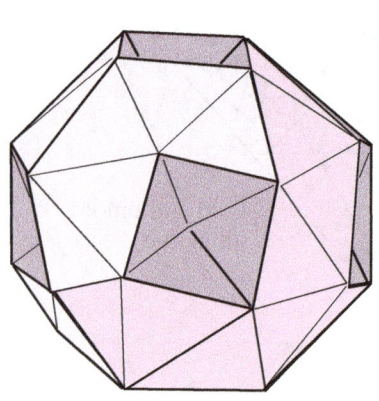

The snub cube is one of thirteen Archimedean Solids. It comes in a left and right handed form. This polyhedron has six dimpled square sides and 32 equilateral triangles. Square symmetry is used. The darker areas refer to the sunken squares.

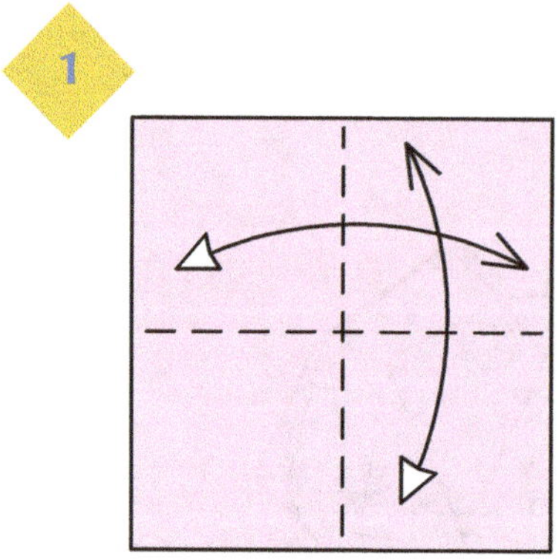

1. Fold and unfold.

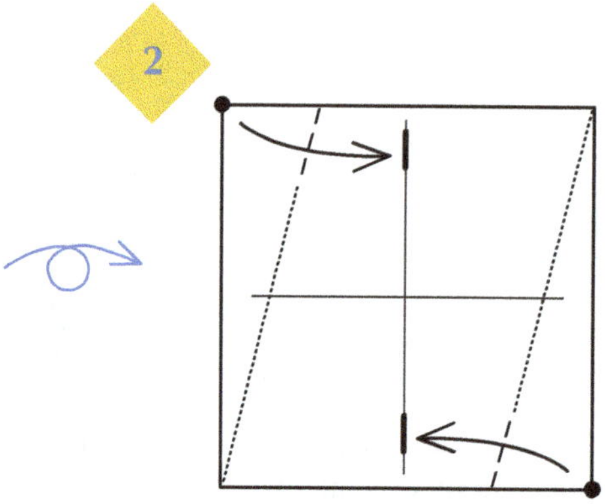

2. Bring the corners to the lines. Crease at the top and bottom.

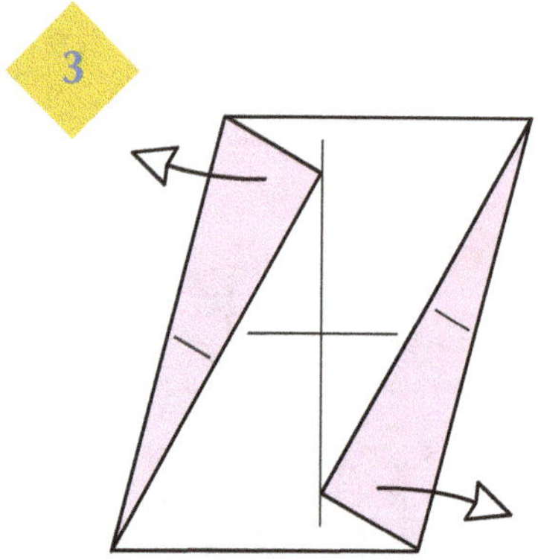

3. Unfold.

4. Fold and unfold at the top and bottom.

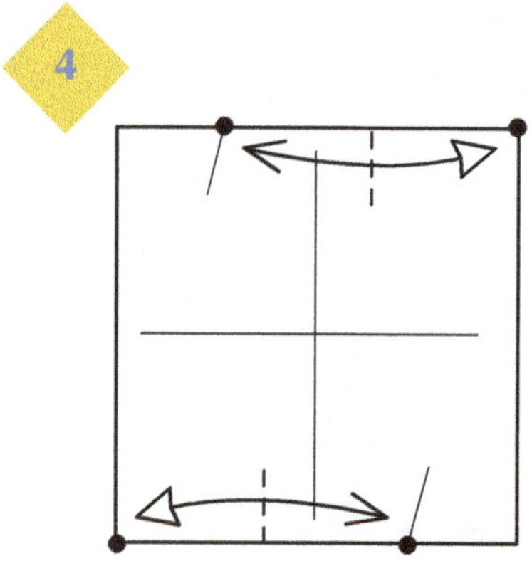

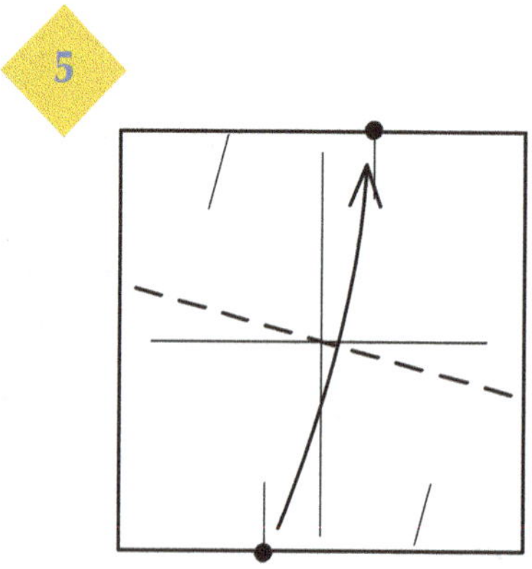

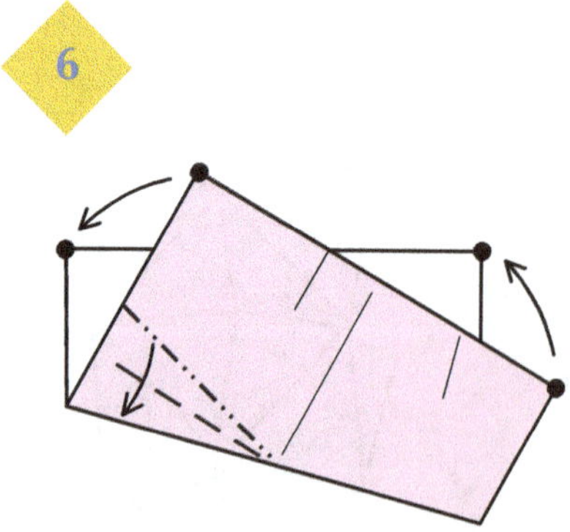

5.

6. Valley-fold along the crease. Turn over and repeat.

80   3D Origami Platonic Solids & More

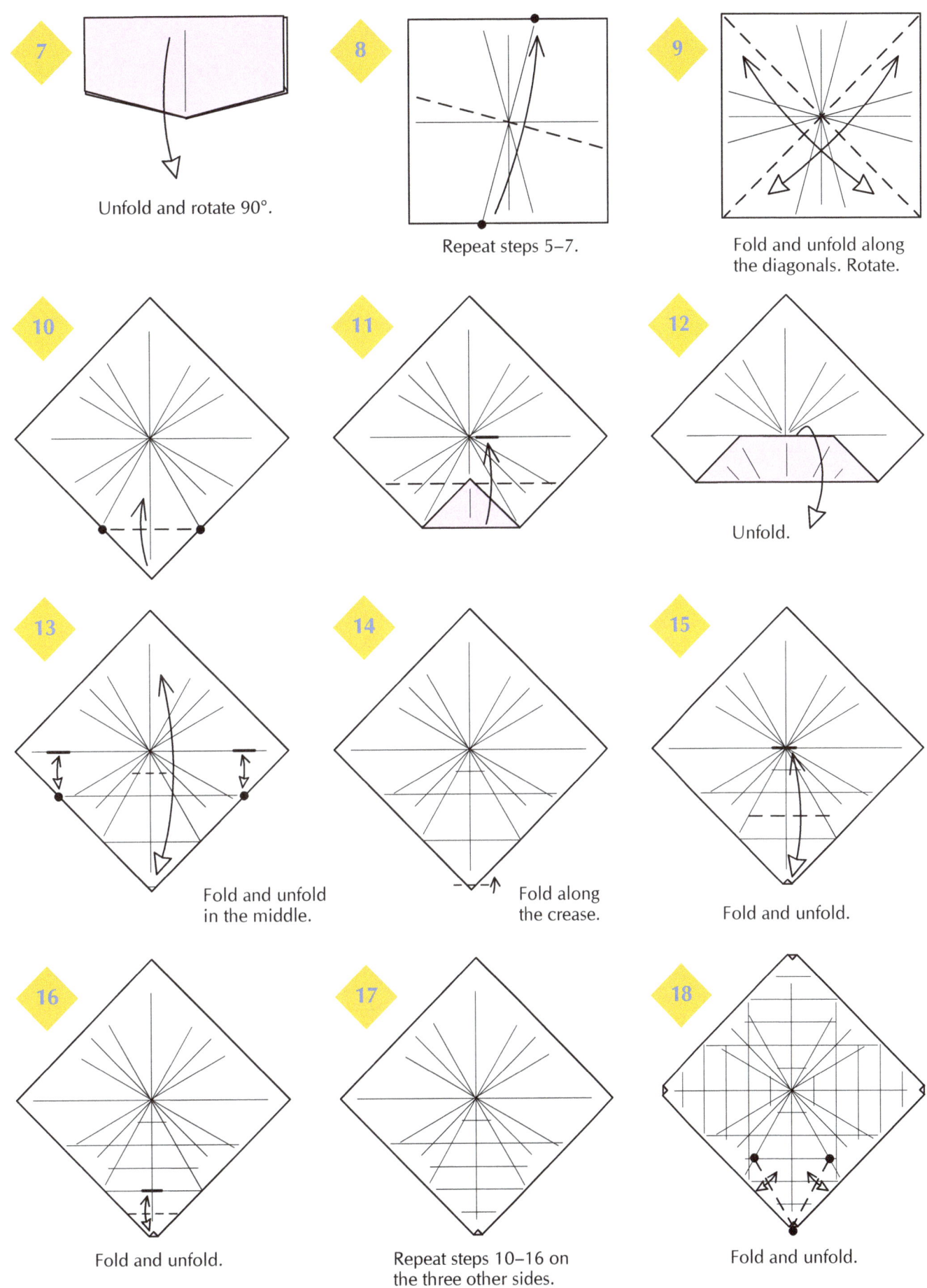

Dimpled Snub Cube 81

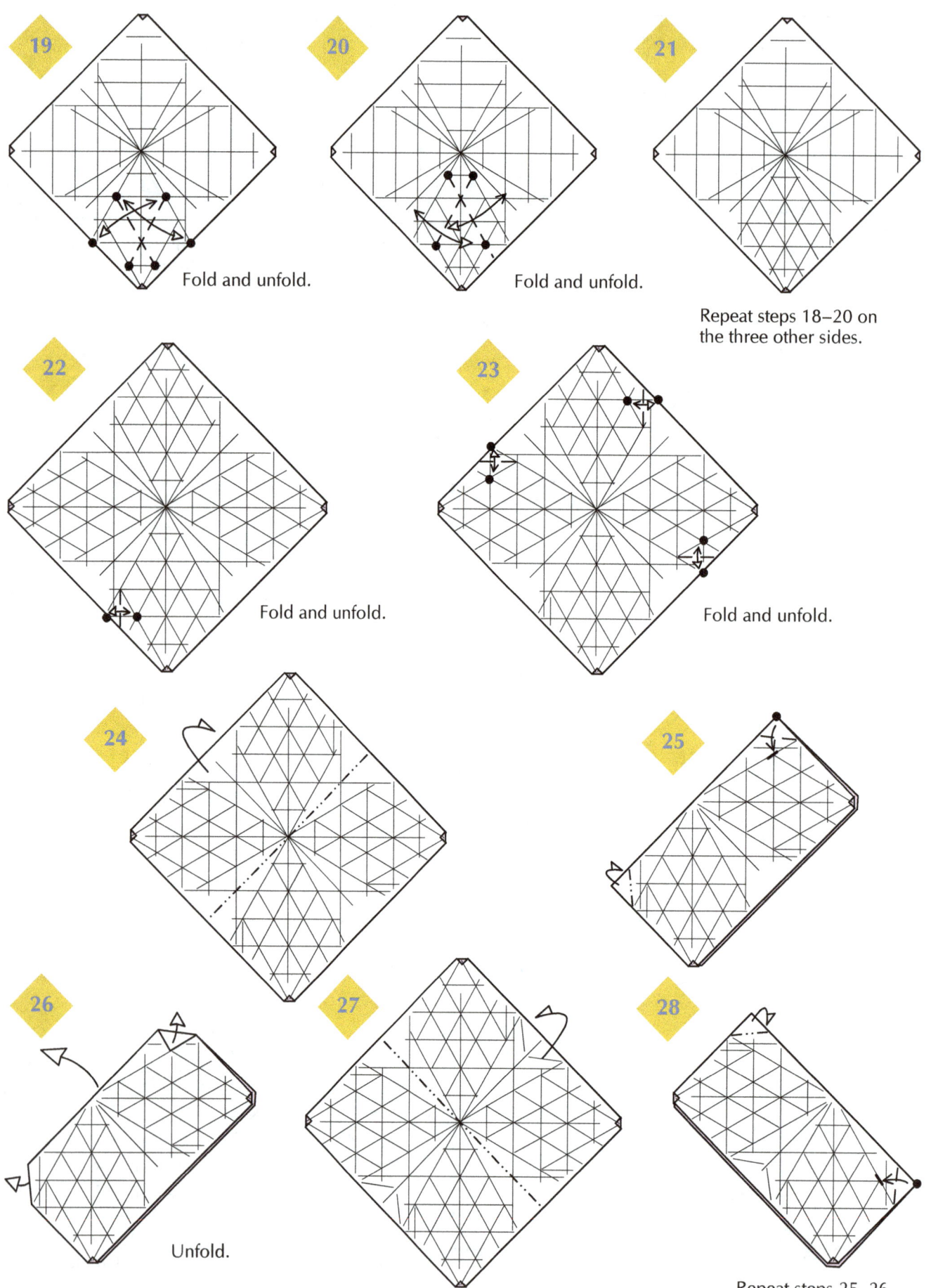

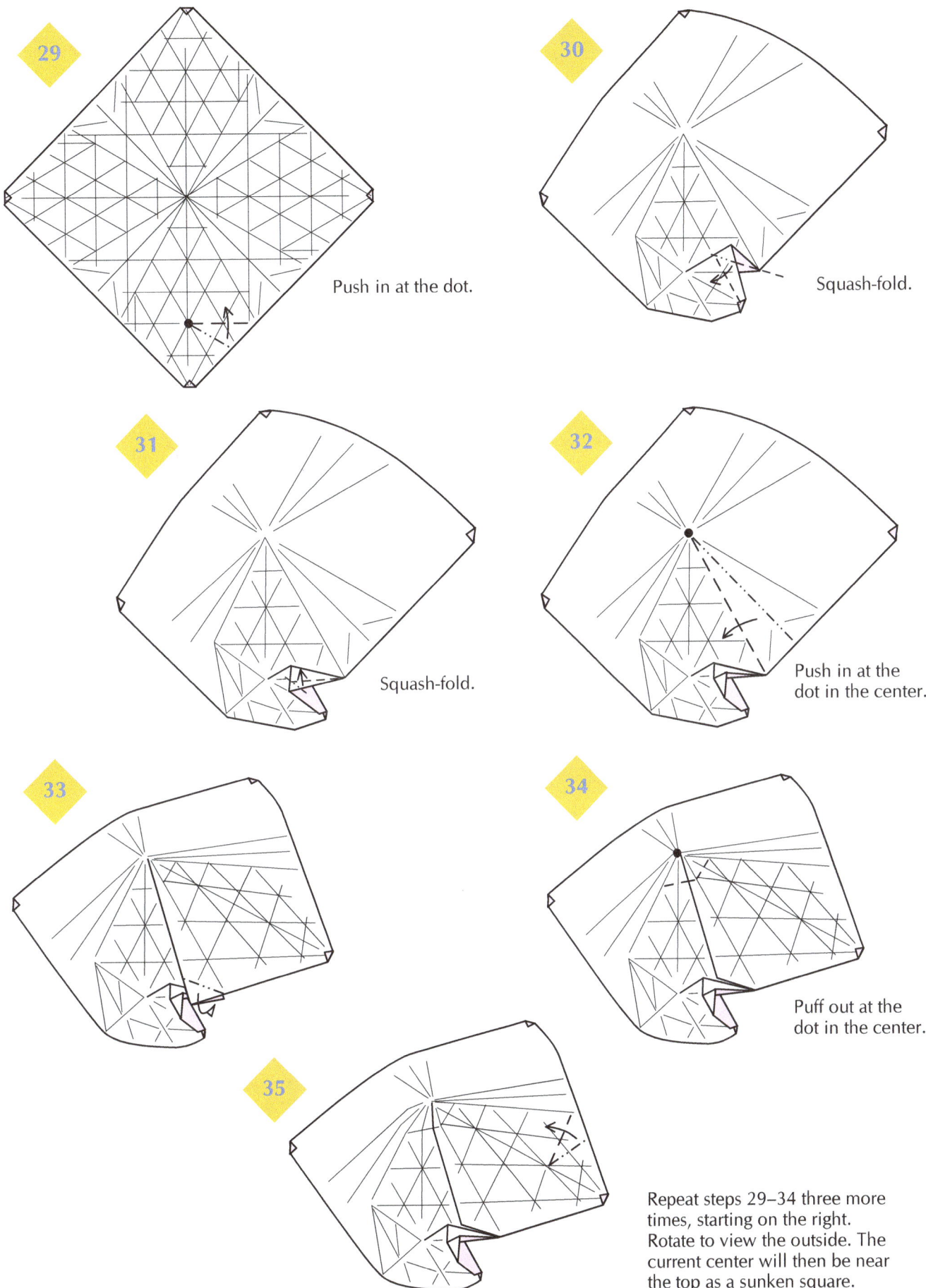

29. Push in at the dot.

30. Squash-fold.

31. Squash-fold.

32. Push in at the dot in the center.

33.

34. Puff out at the dot in the center.

35. Repeat steps 29–34 three more times, starting on the right. Rotate to view the outside. The current center will then be near the top as a sunken square.

*Dimpled Snub Cube* 83

**36**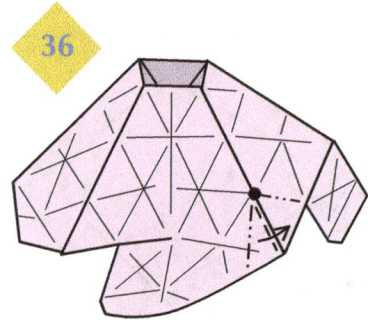
Puff out at the dot.

**37**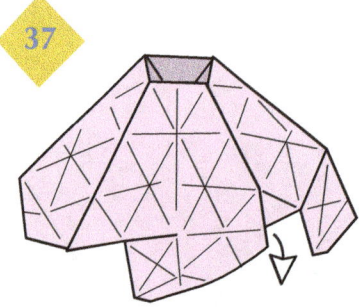
Unfold.

**38**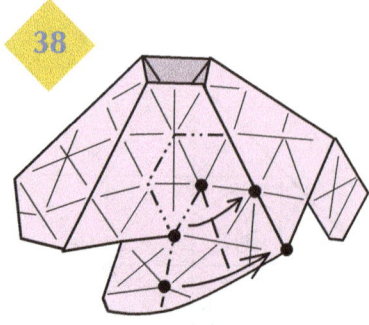
Push in at the upper dot to form a sunken square.

**39**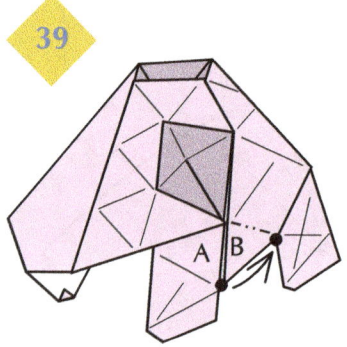
Repeat step 36 on the hidden layers so triangle A will cover triangle B.

**40**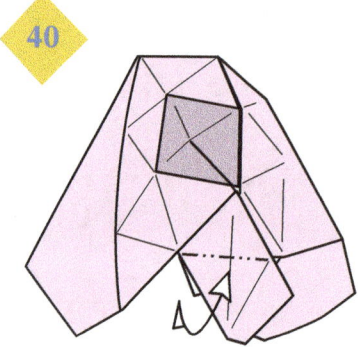
Fold and unfold.

**41**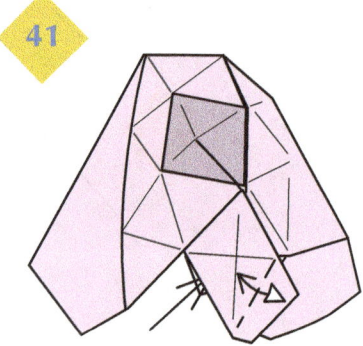
Fold and unfold. Note the pocket.

**42**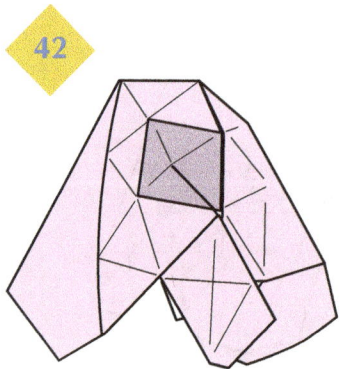
Repeat steps 36–41 three more times.

**43**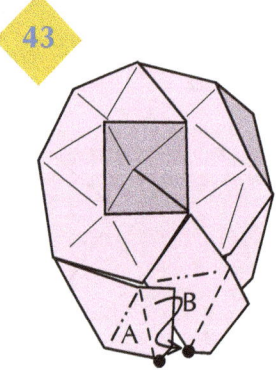
Triangles A and B are two of the four that will form the bottom sunken square. Tuck each of the flaps inside the pockets to close the model.

**44**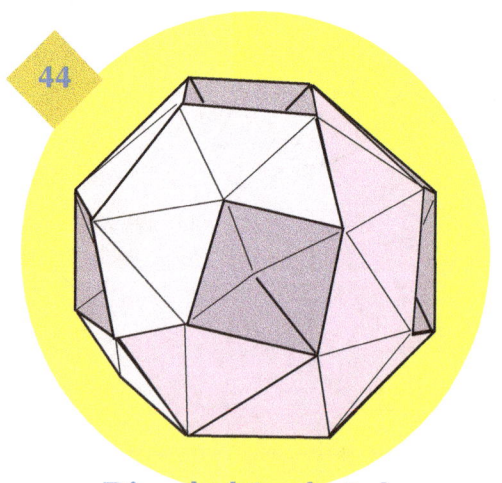

**Dimpled Snub Cube**

84   3D Origami Platonic Solids & More

# Octahedra

Octahedra are polyhedra with eight faces. This collection includes a dipyramid, trapezohedron, prism, and antiprism.

Dipyramids, or diamonds, are composed of a pair of identical pyramids joined at the base. All the faces are triangles.

A trapezohedron, or antidiamond, is composed of congruent kites where three angles are identical. All the faces are symmetrically staggered.

A prism is a polyhedron where two congruent polygons are connected by parallelograms.

An antiprism is a polyhedron where two congruent polygons are connected by a band of alternating triangles.

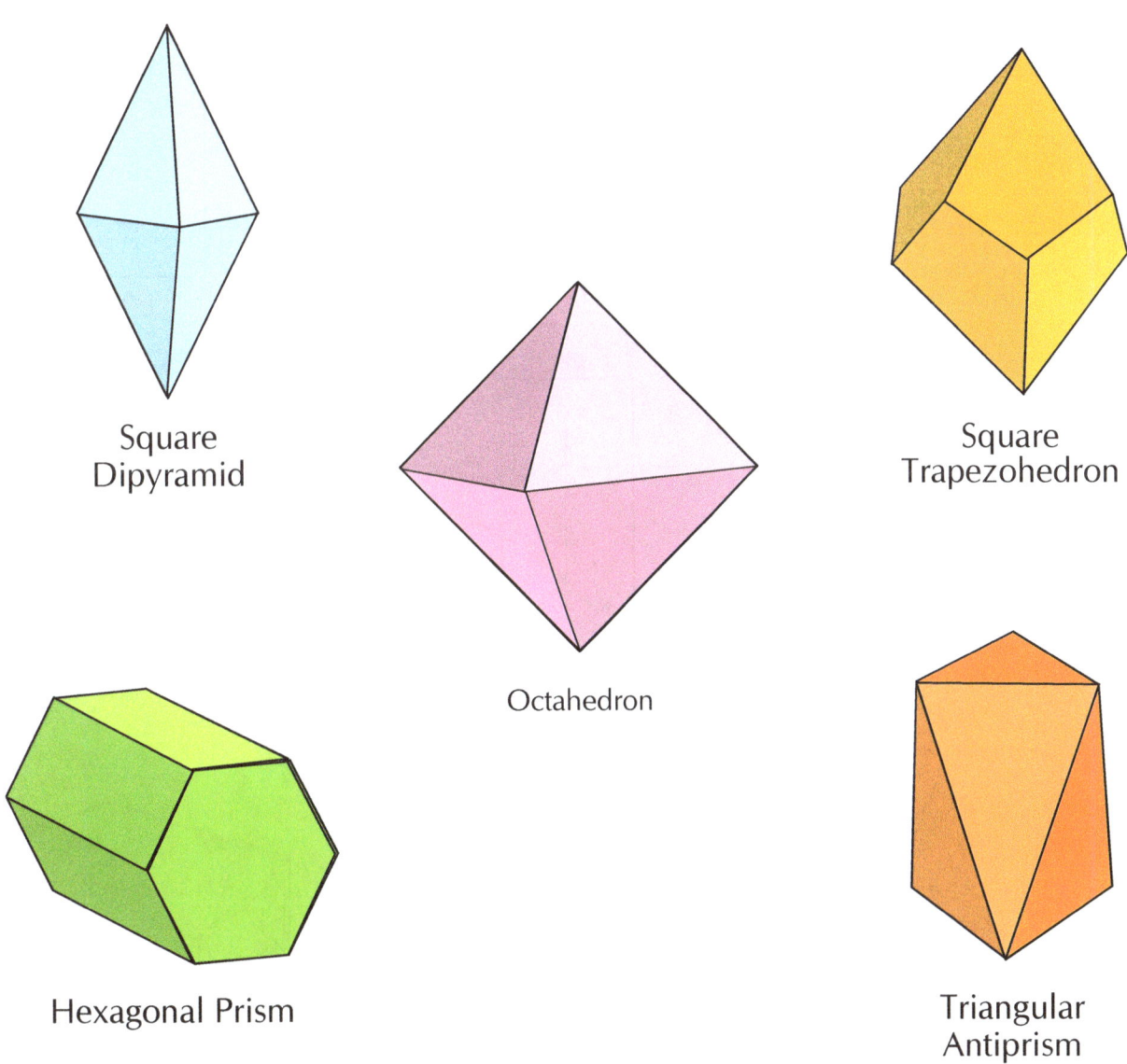

Square Dipyramid

Octahedron

Square Trapezohedron

Hexagonal Prism

Triangular Antiprism

*Octahedra* 85

# Square Dipyramid

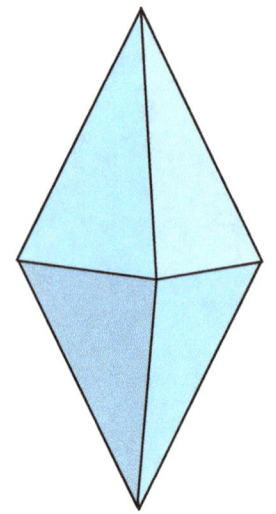

A square dipyramid is composed of eight identical isosceles triangles. For this model, the angles of each face are 36°, 72°, and 72°. Odd symmetry is used.

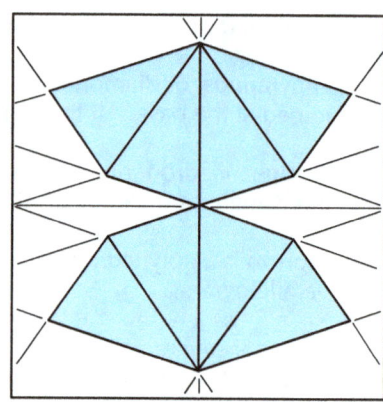

 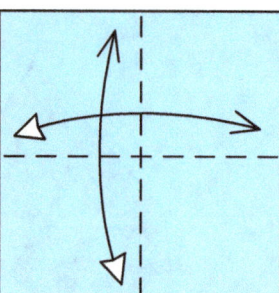

Fold and unfold.

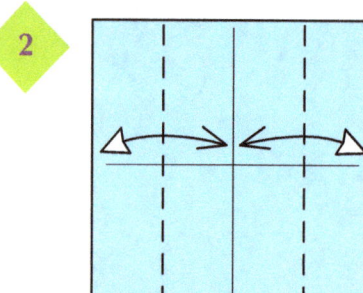

Fold and unfold in the center and on the edges.

Fold and unfold at the top.

 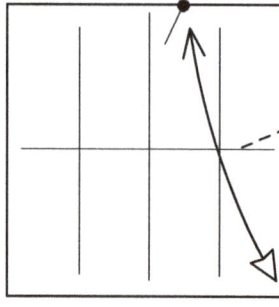

Fold and unfold on the right.

Fold and unfold on the bottom. Rotate 180°.

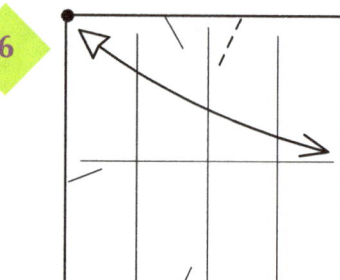

Repeat steps 3–5.

 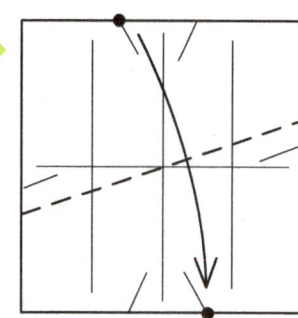

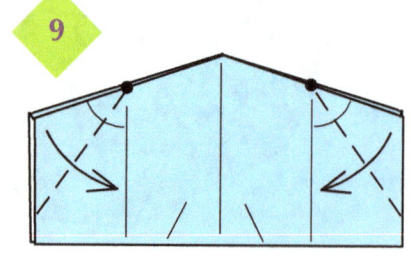

Valley-fold along the crease. The dots will meet. Turn over and repeat.

Bisect the angles and repeat behind.

86  3D Origami Platonic Solids & More

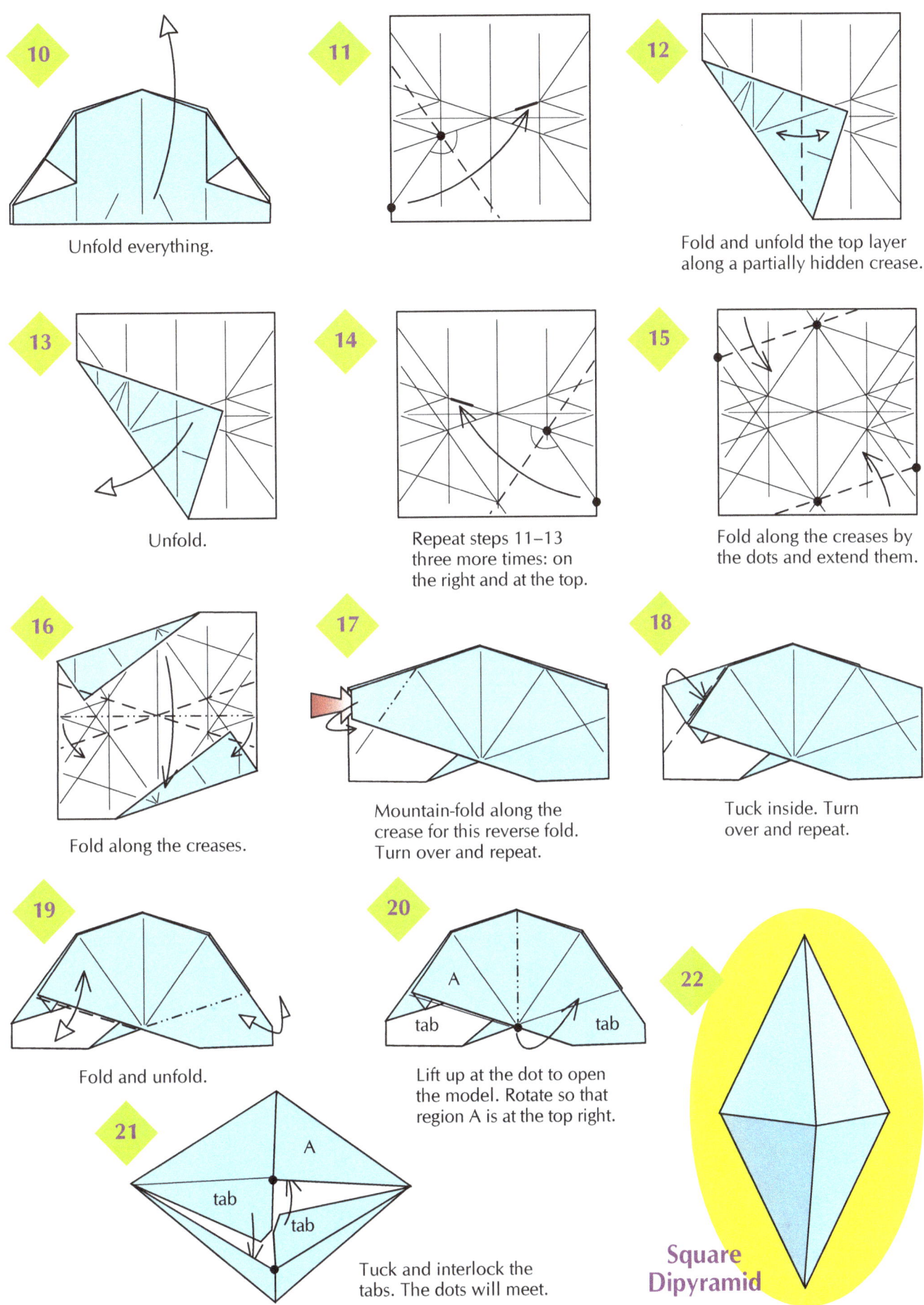

Square Dipyramid 87

# Square Trapezodedron

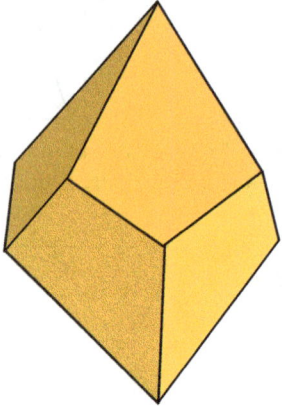

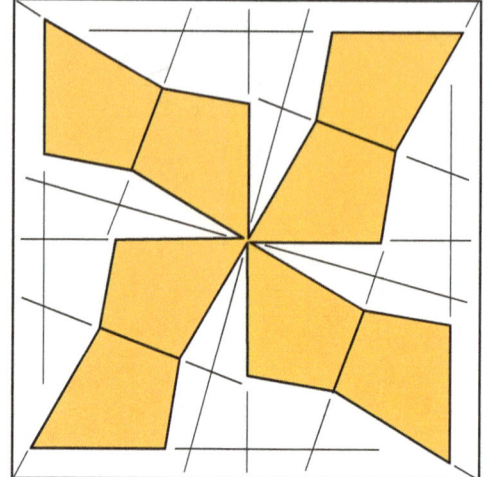

Trapezohedra are beautiful shapes composed of kite-shaped faces staggered symmetrically. Represented through origami, these shapes present challenges to design and fold. The results are stunning.

A square trapezohedron is composed of eight identical kites. For this model, the angles of each face are 60°, 100°, 100°, and 100°. Square symmetry is used.

1

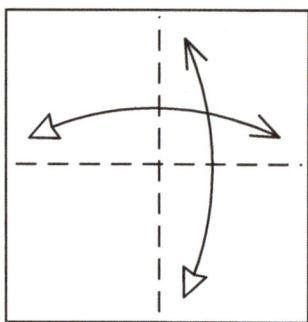

Fold and unfold.

2

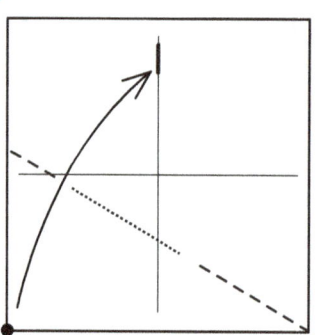

Bring the corner to the line.

3

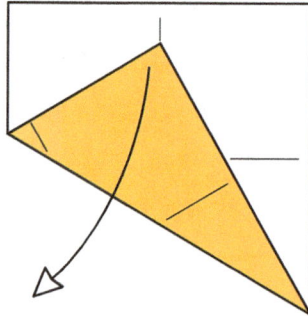

Unfold and rotate 180°.

4

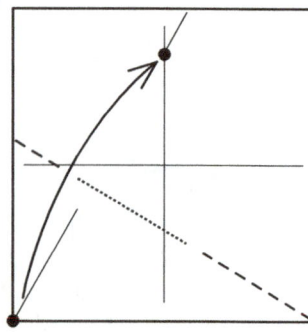

Repeat steps 2–3 three more times.

5

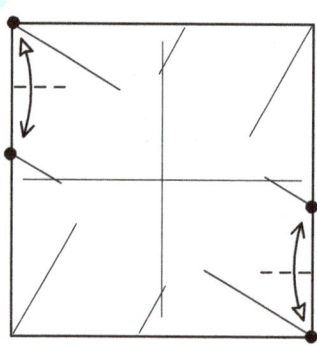

Fold and unfold on the edges.

6

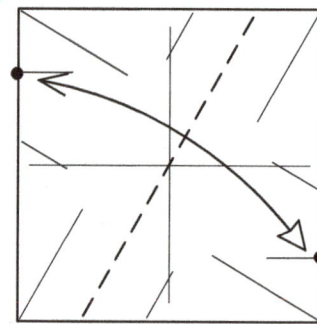

Fold and unfold.

88    *3D Origami Platonic Solids & More*

**7**

Fold and unfold.

**8**

Fold and unfold at the top.

**9**

Fold and unfold on the left.

**10**

1. Fold and unfold on the left.
2. Fold and unfold.
Rotate 90°.

**11**

Repeat steps 8–10 three more times.

**12**

1. Fold and unfold at the top.
2. Fold and unfold on the right to find the 1/4 mark of the thin strip near the bottom.

**13**

Bring the bottom right corner to the landmark at the top. Fold and unfold on the left.

**14**

Fold along a line from the landmark on the left to the 1/4 landmark on the right. Crease on the left side.

**15**

Fold and unfold both layers.
1. Valley-fold along a hidden crease.
2. Mountain-fold along the crease.

*Square Trapezohedron* 89

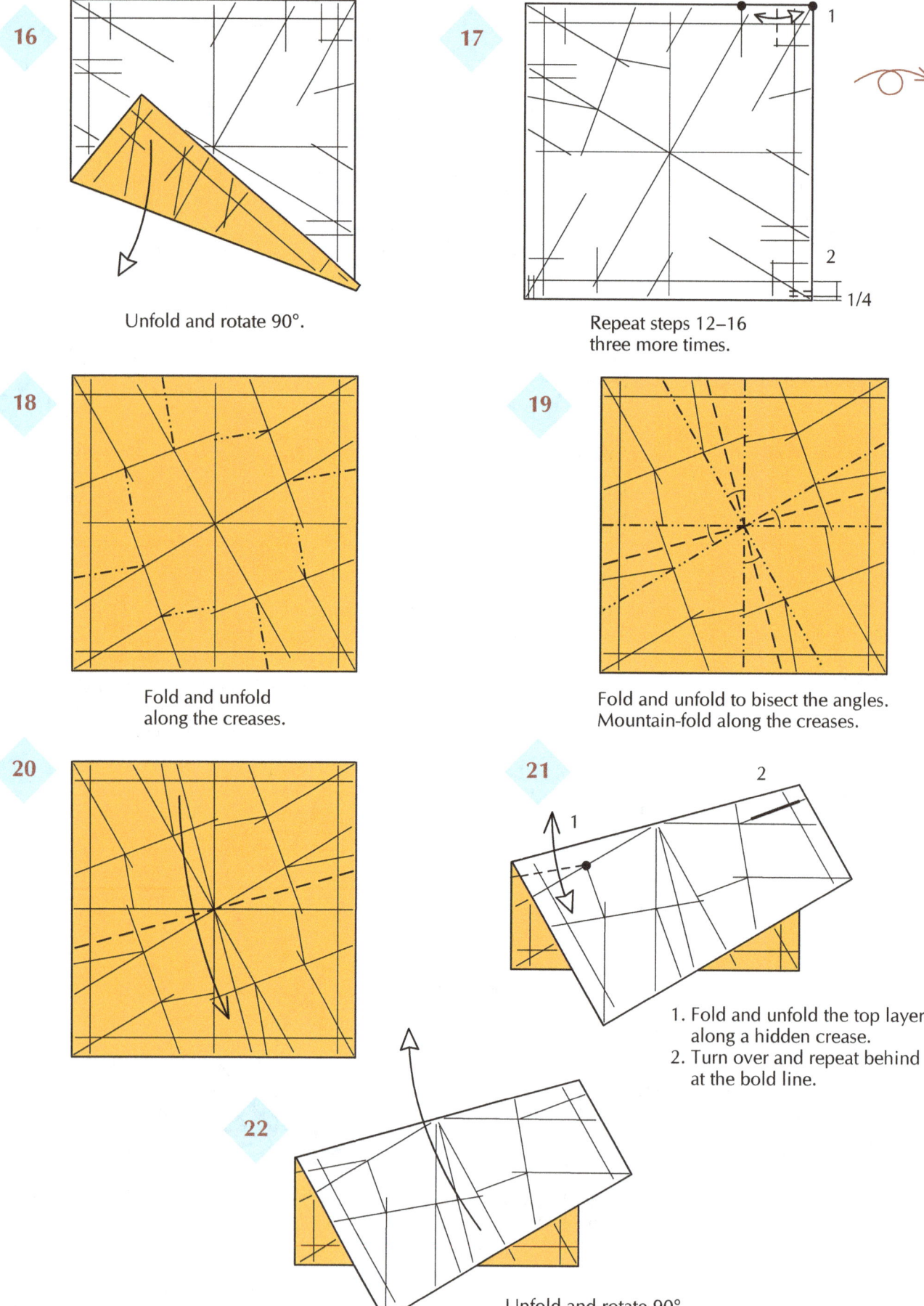

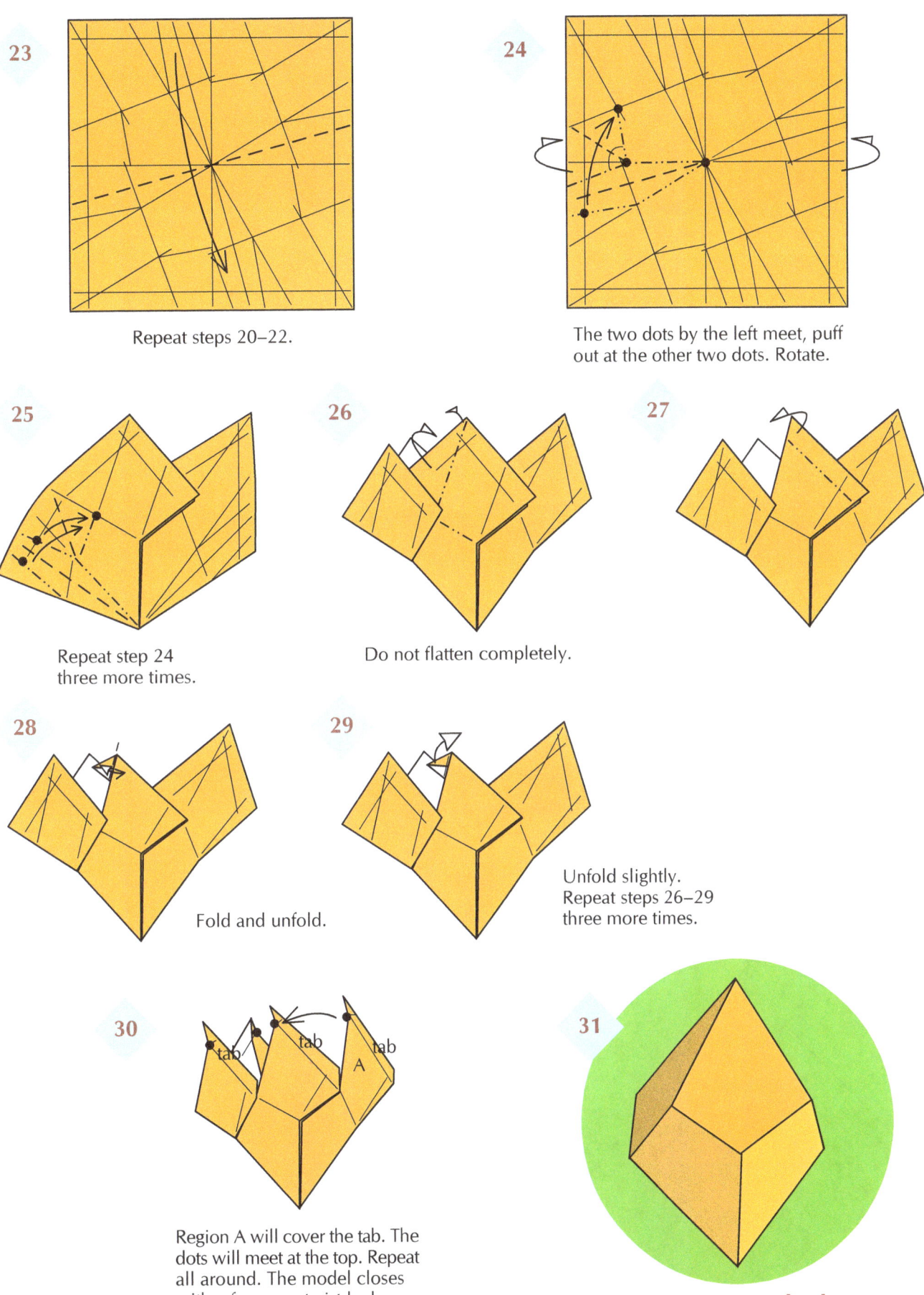

# Hexagonal Prism

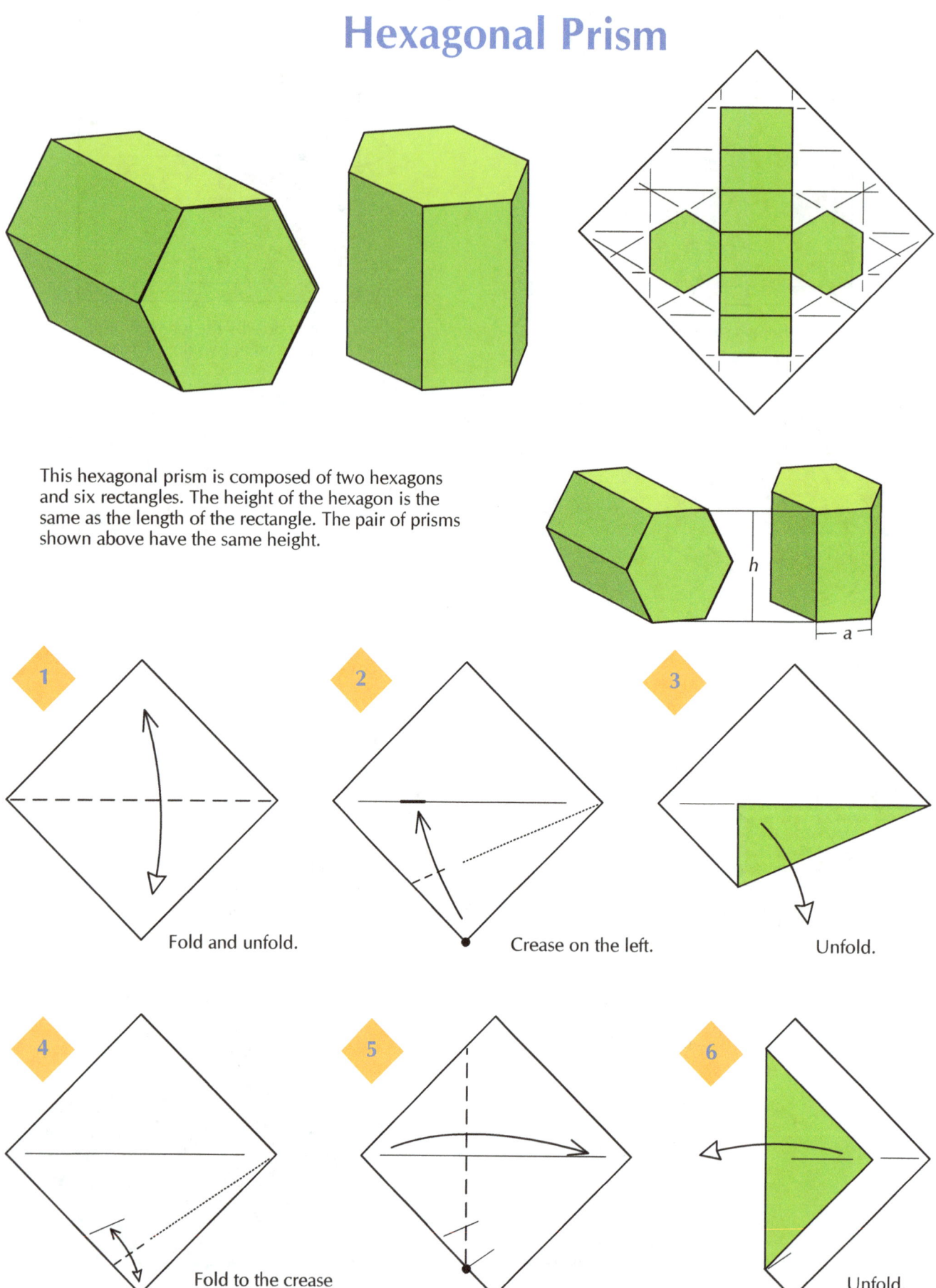

This hexagonal prism is composed of two hexagons and six rectangles. The height of the hexagon is the same as the length of the rectangle. The pair of prisms shown above have the same height.

1. Fold and unfold.
2. Crease on the left.
3. Unfold.
4. Fold to the crease and unfold.
5. 
6. Unfold.

92   3D Origami Platonic Solids & More

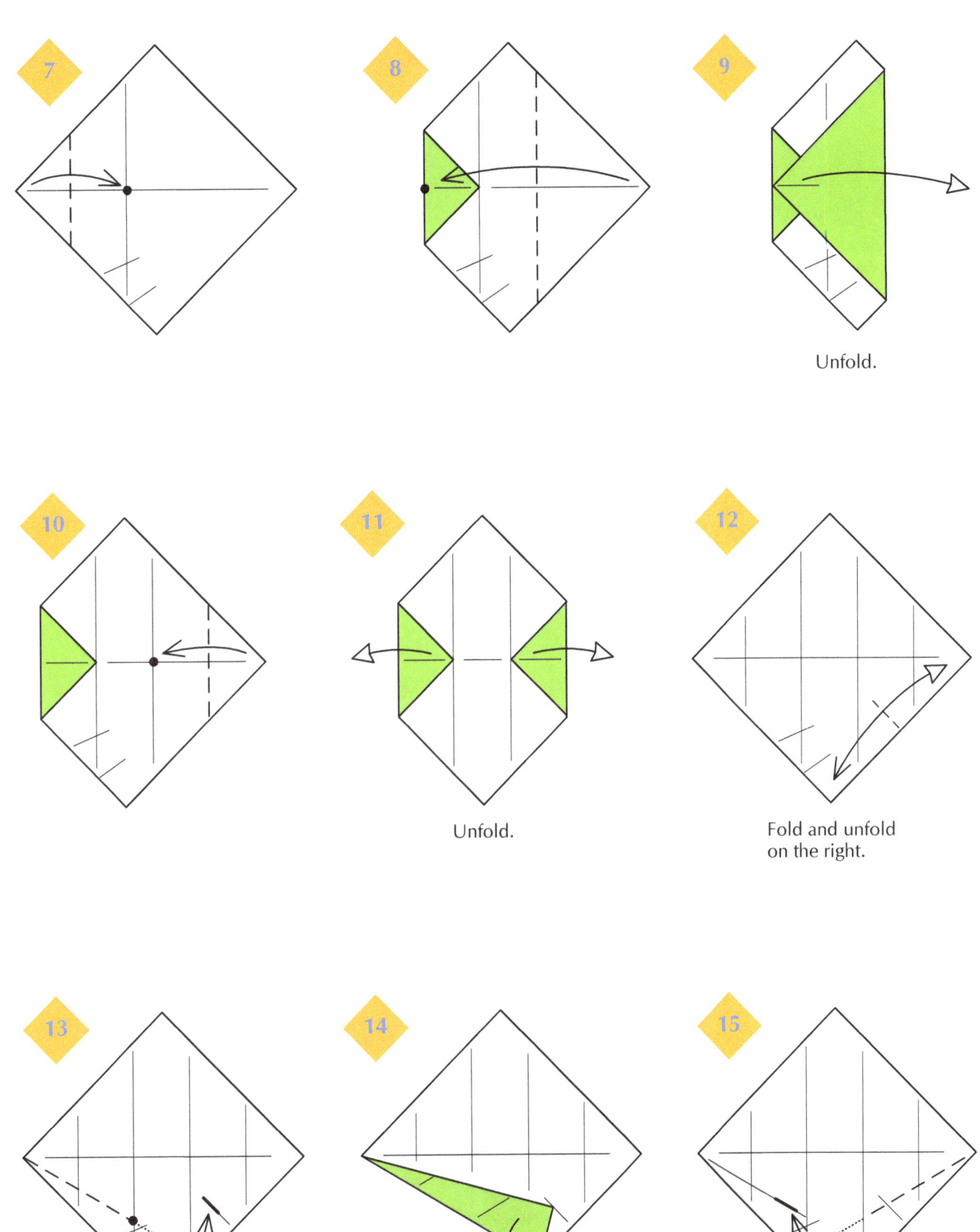

Hexagonal Prism 93

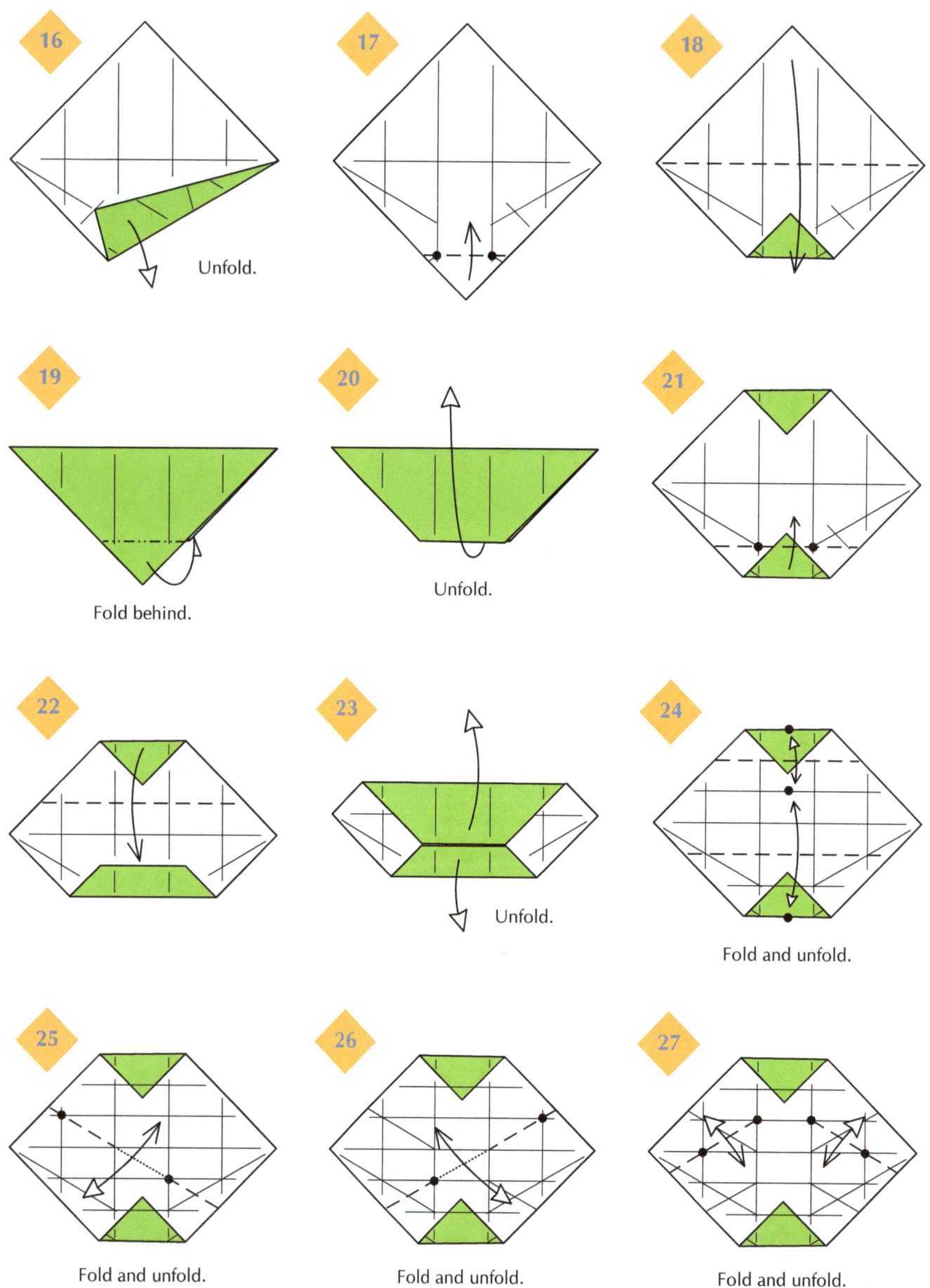

94   *3D Origami Platonic Solids & More*

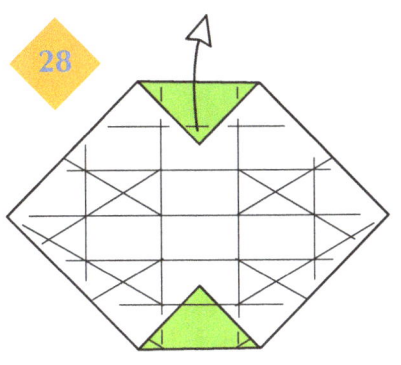

Unfold.

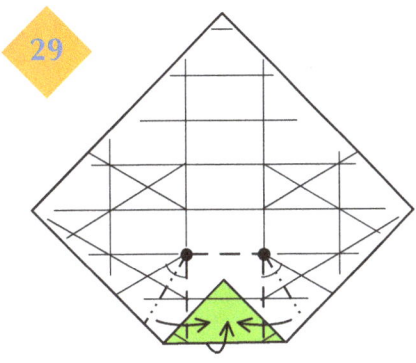

Push in at the dots and bisect the angles. Rotate to view the side.

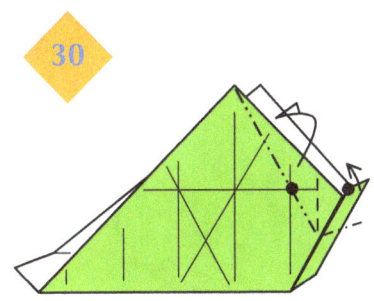

The dots will meet. Repeat behind.

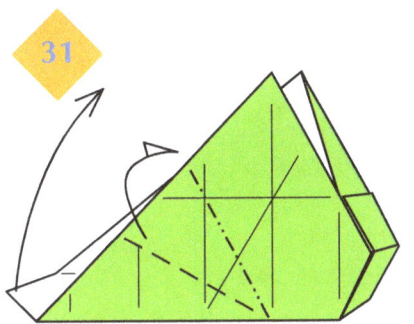

Repeat behind.

Repeat behind.

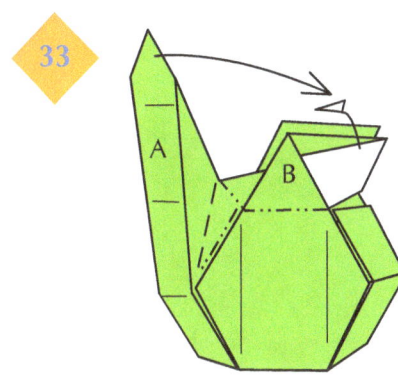

Region A will cover B. The dots will meet. Repeat behind.

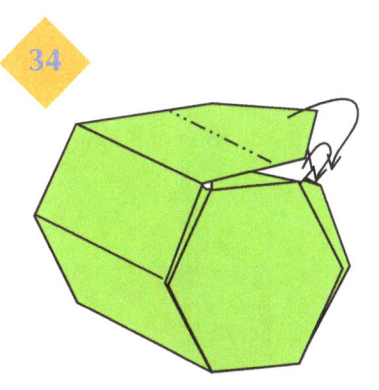

Tuck three tabs inside the pocket.

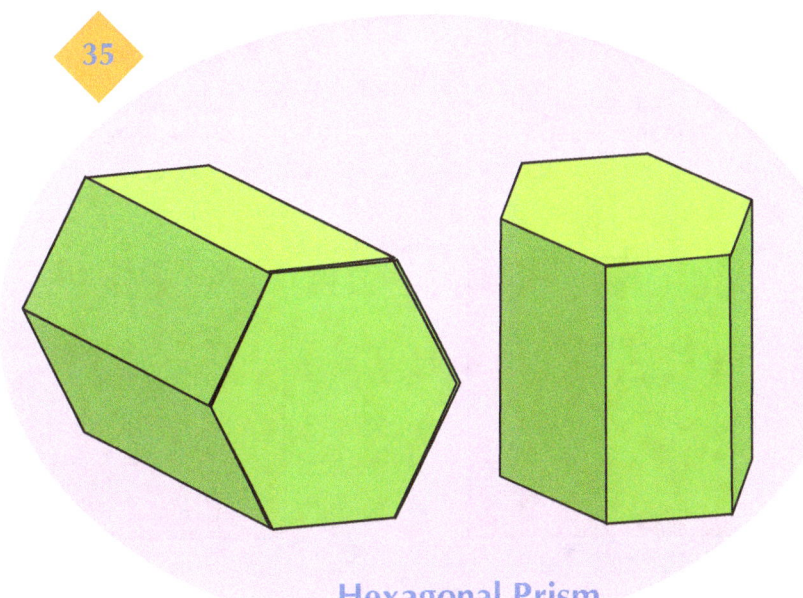

**Hexagonal Prism**

Hexagonal Prism 95

# Triangular Antiprism

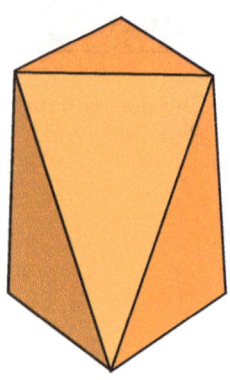

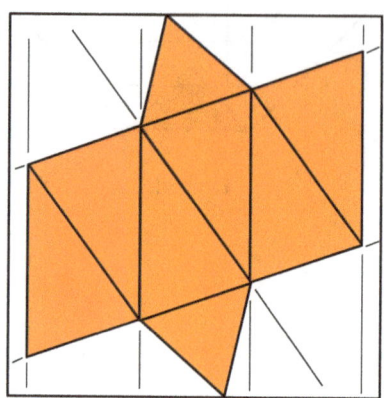

A triangular antiprism is composed of 6 isosceles triangles and two equilateral triangles. In this one, the angles of the isosceles triangles are 36°, 72°, and 72°. The triangles form a band wrapping around.

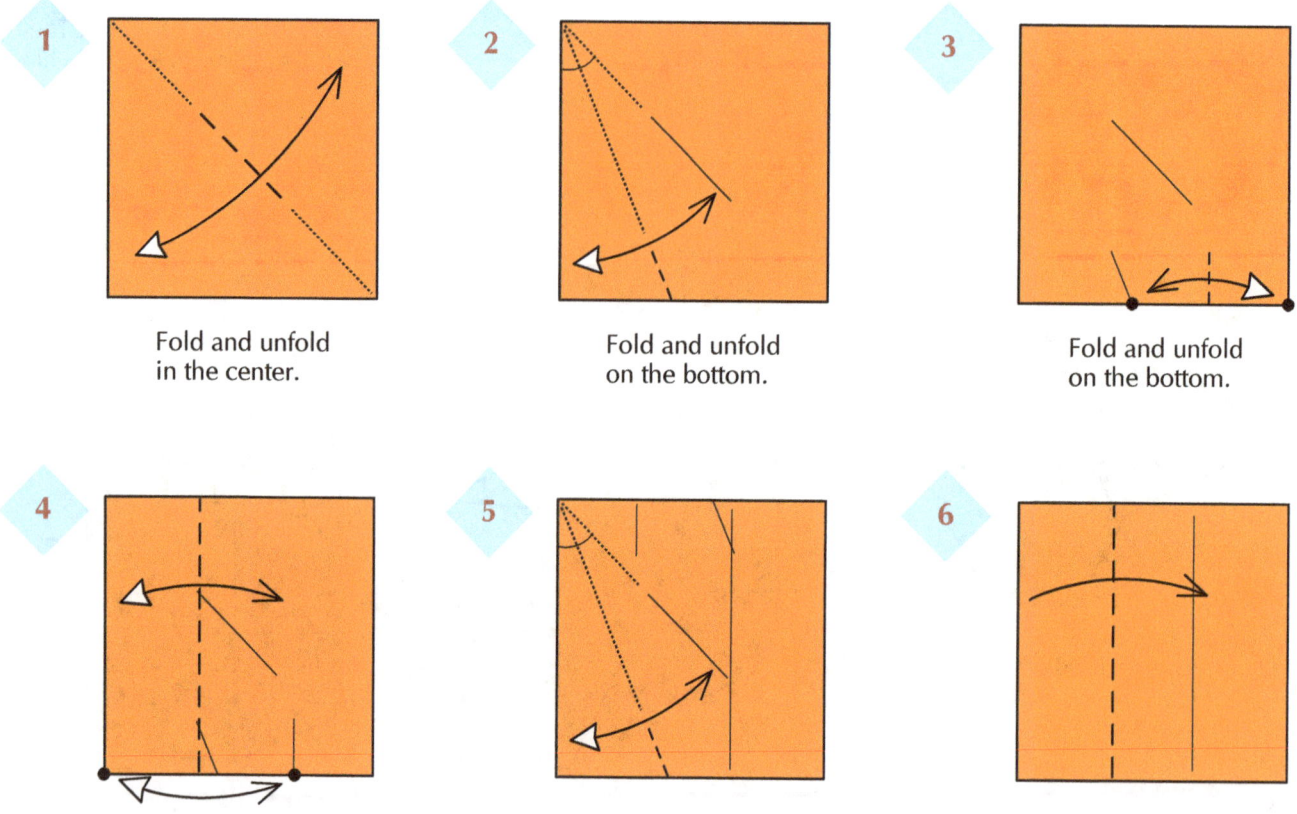

1. Fold and unfold in the center.
2. Fold and unfold on the bottom.
3. Fold and unfold on the bottom.
4. Fold and unfold. Rotate 180°.
5. Repeat steps 2–5.
6. Fold on the crease.

96   3D Origami Platonic Solids & More

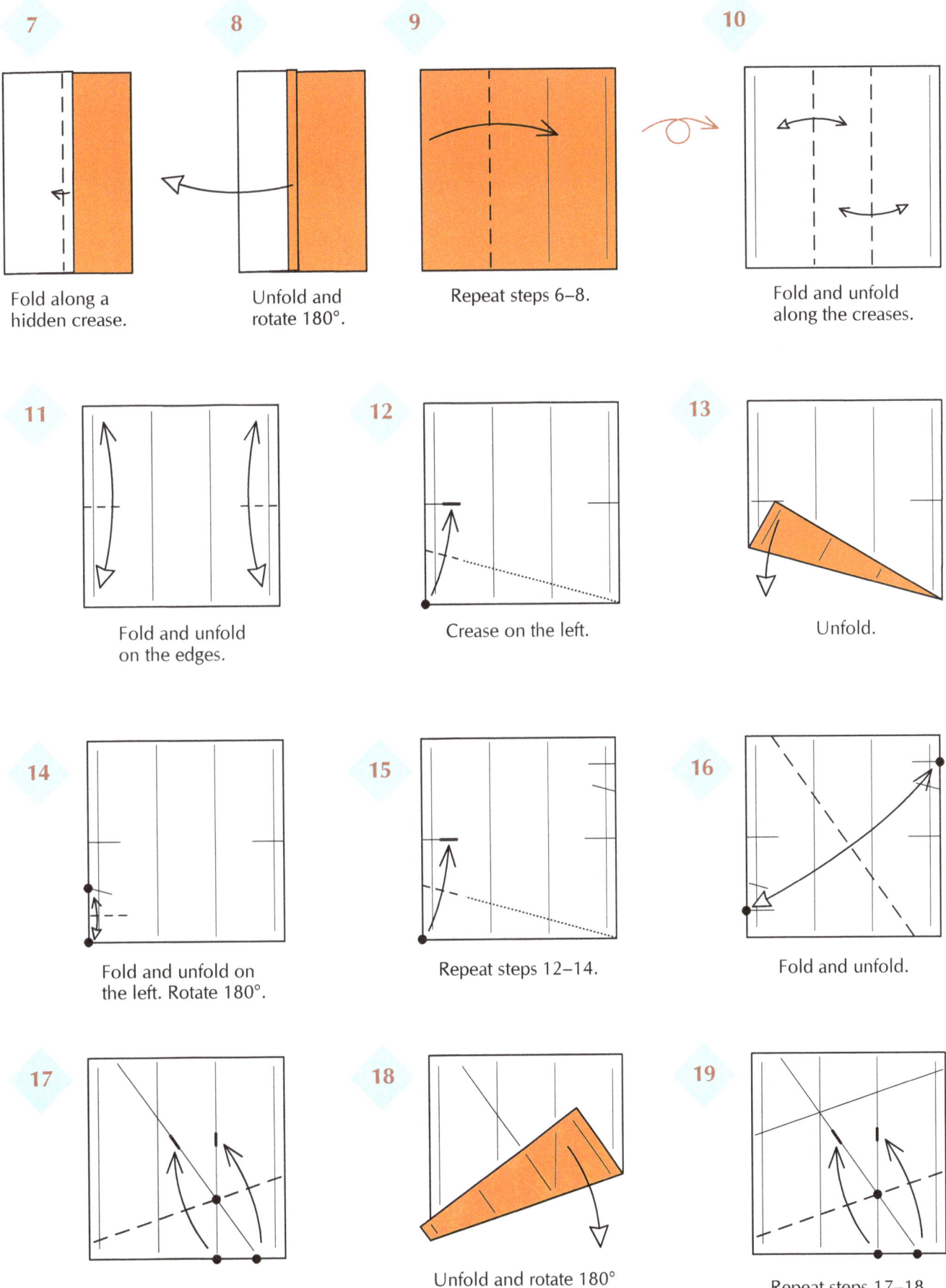

Triangular Antiprism 97

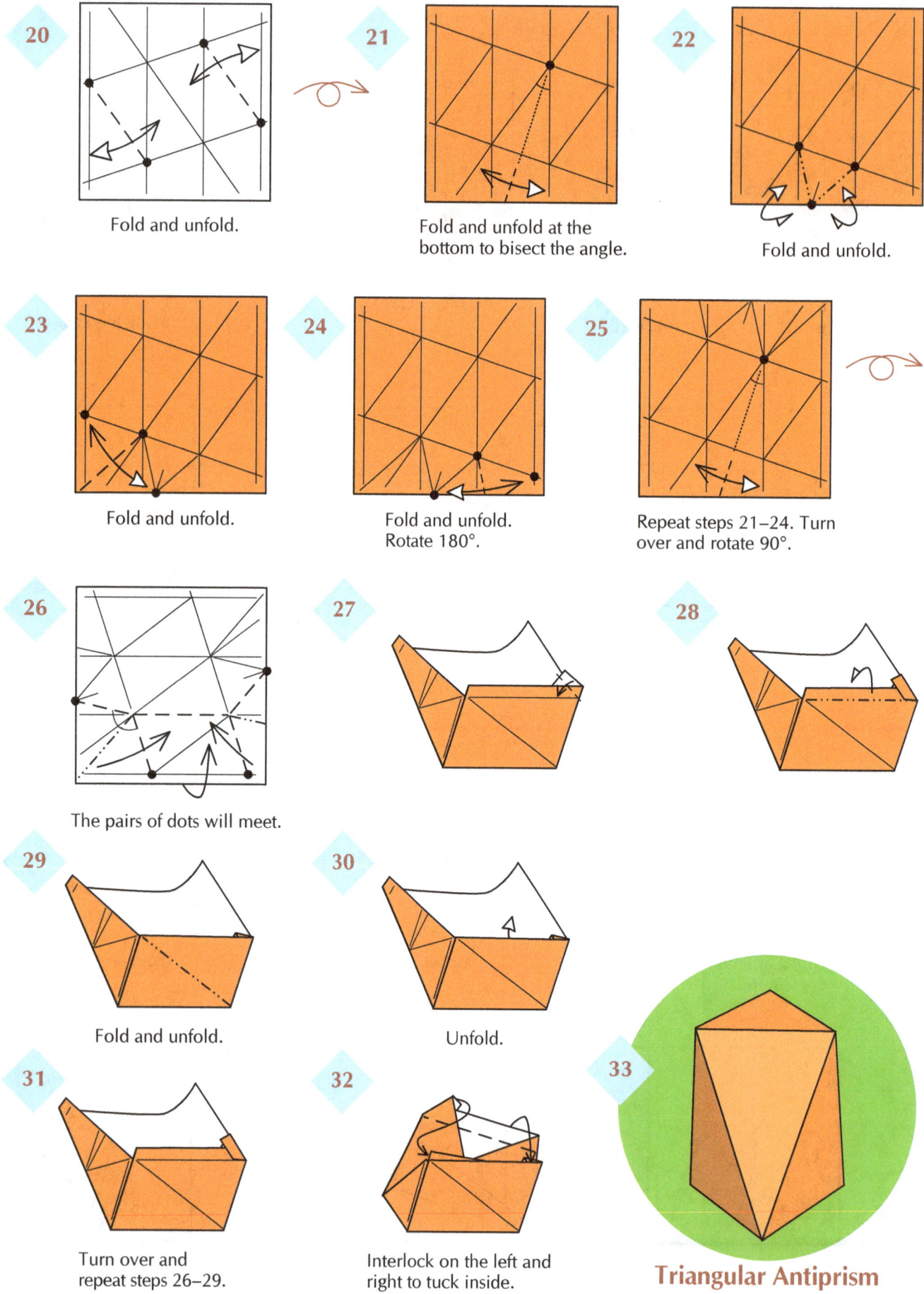

98  3D Origami Platonic Solids & More

# Dodecahedra

Dodecahedra are polyhedra with twelve faces. This collection includes a hexagonal dipyramid, hexagonal trapezohedron, and pentagonal antiprism. The triakis tetrahedron and rhombic dodecahedron are Catalan Solids whose faces are identical for each solid.

This group highlights the variety of polyhedra that each have twelve faces.

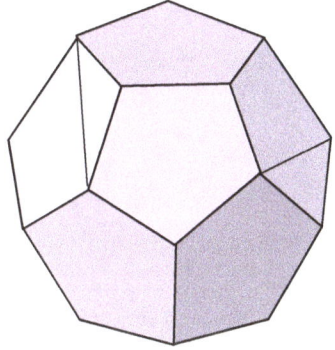

Dodecahedron

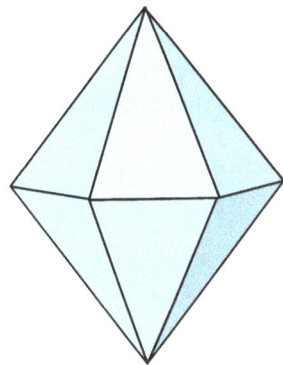

Hexagonal Dipyramid

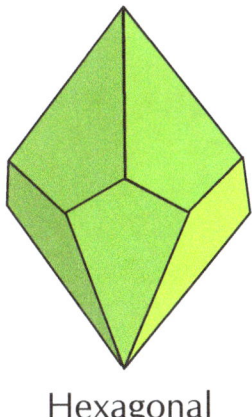

Hexagonal Trapezohedron

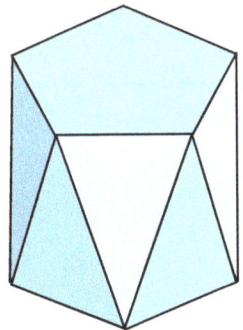

Golden Pentagonal Antiprism

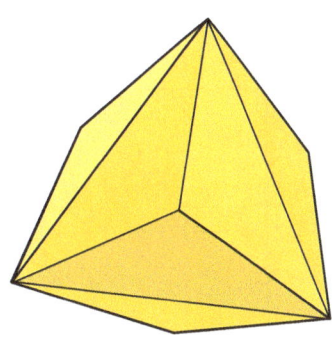

Triakis Tetrahedron

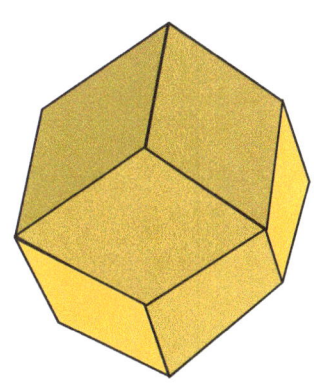

Rhombic Dodecahedron

*Dodecahedra*

# Hexagonal Dipyramid

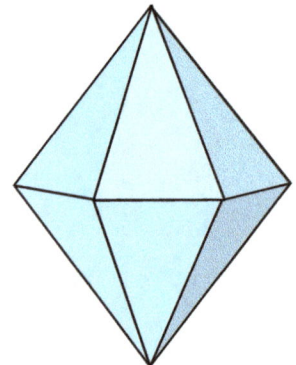
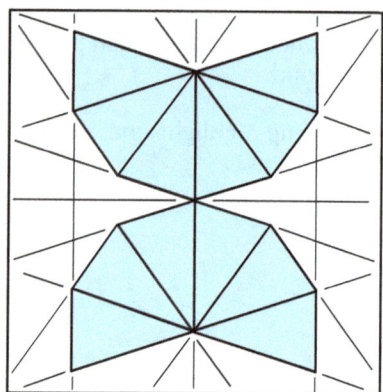

A hexagonal dipyramid has twelve triangular faces. The angles of each triangle are 36°, 72°, and 72°. Odd symmetry is used.

1. Fold and unfold.

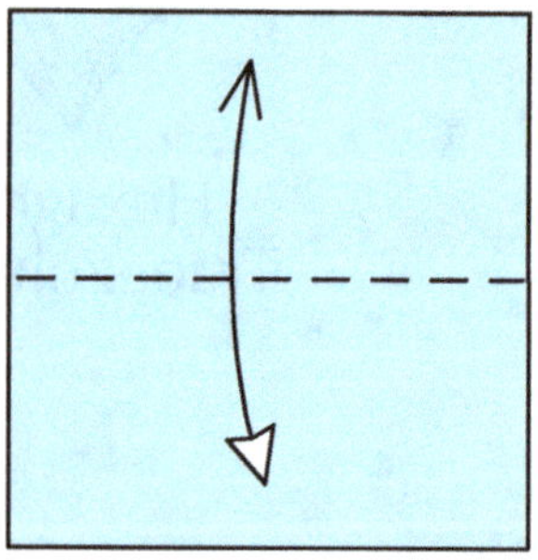

2. Fold and unfold by the right.

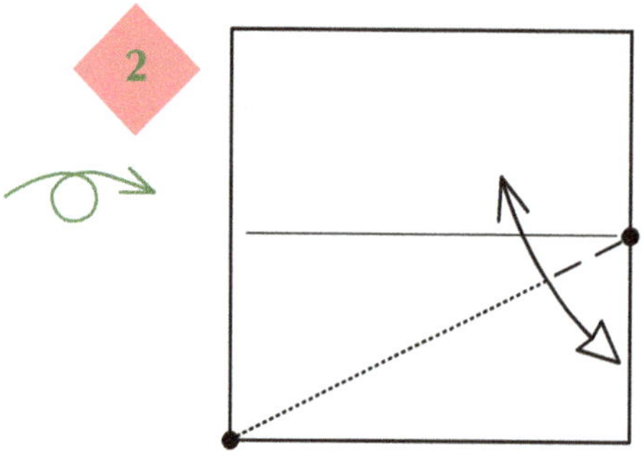

3. Fold and unfold on the top to bisect the angle.

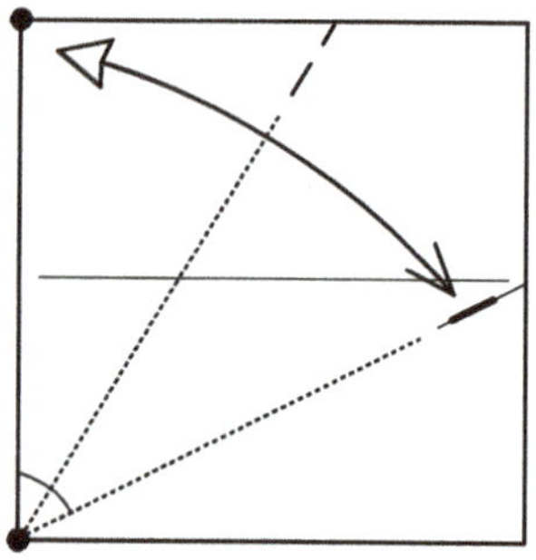

4. Fold and unfold in the center.

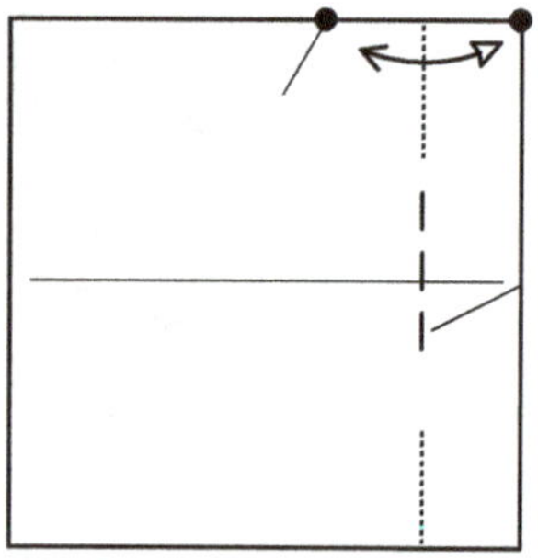

5. Bring the corner to the crease. The 18° angle is exact.

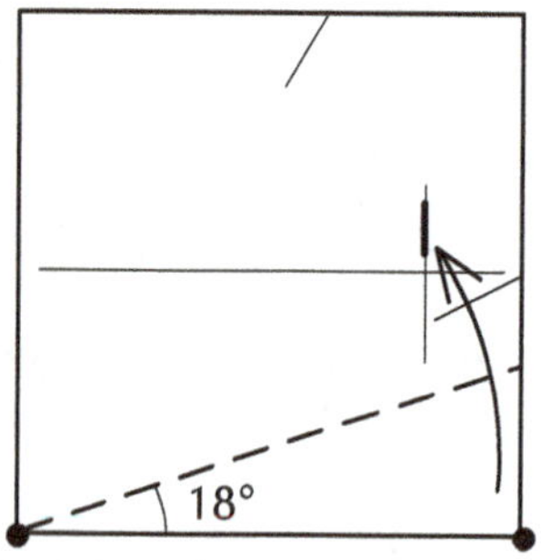

6. Unfold.

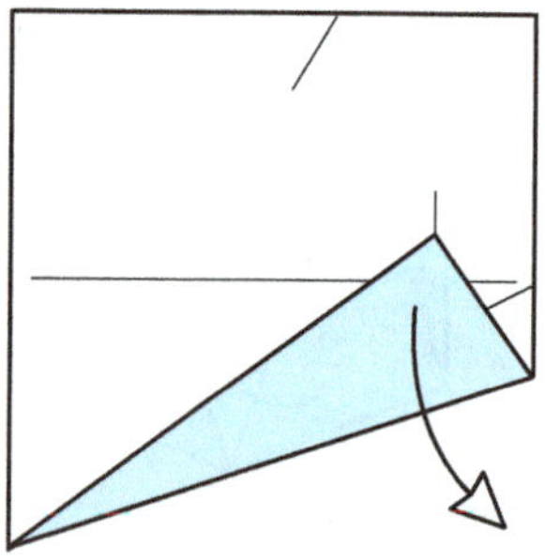

100   *3D Origami Platonic Solids & More*

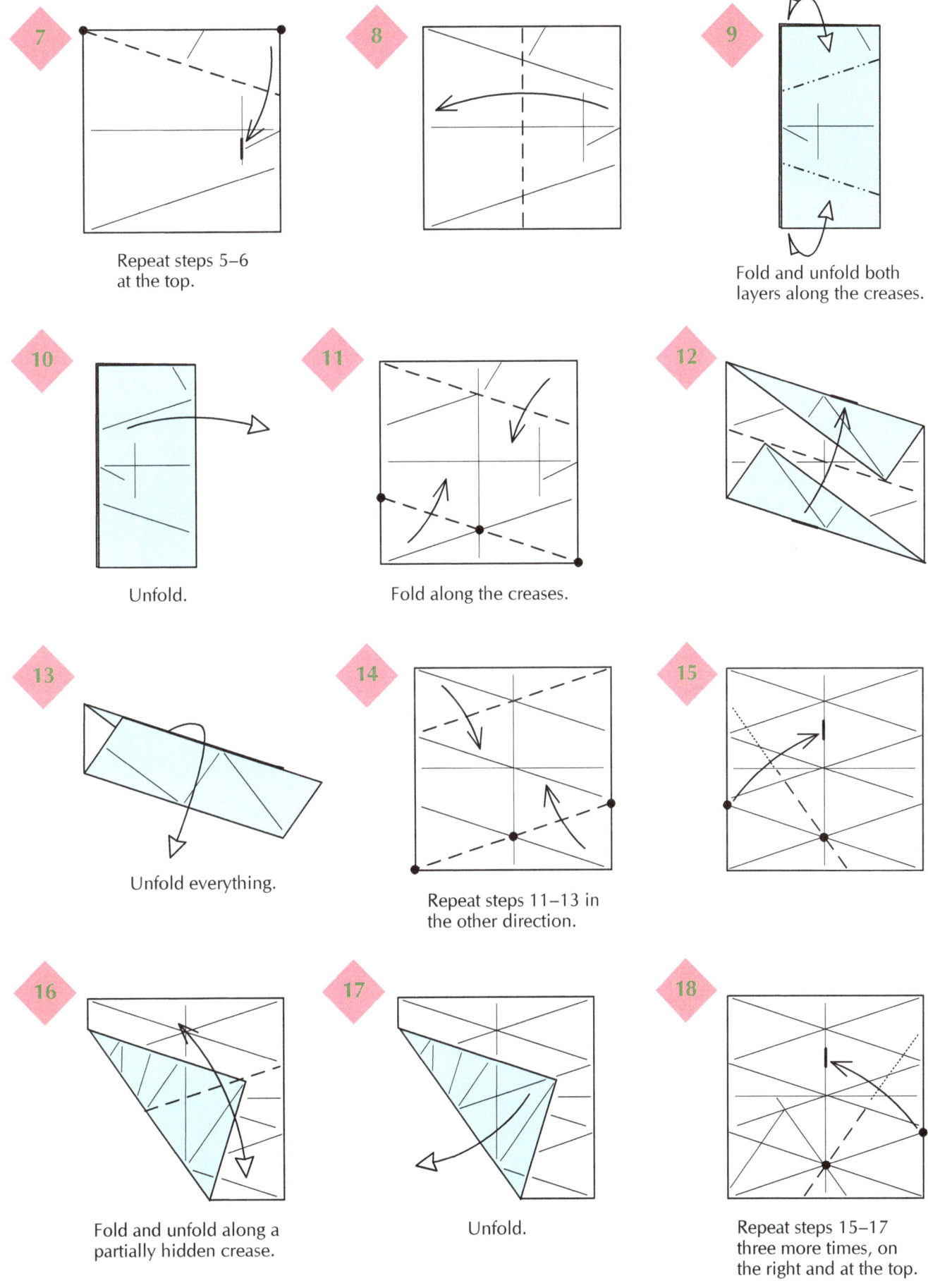

Hexagonal Dipyramid 101

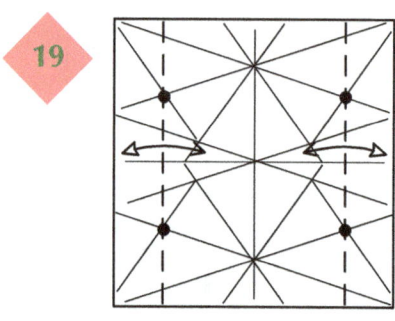

19

Fold and unfold.

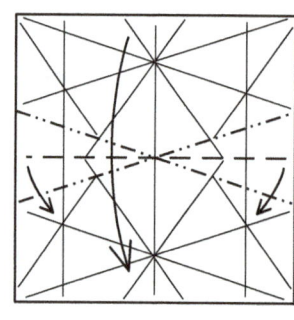

20

Fold along the creases.

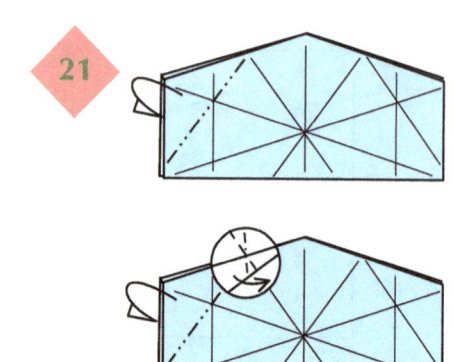

21

Inside view. Fold the inside layers together for this spine-lock fold. Turn over and repeat.

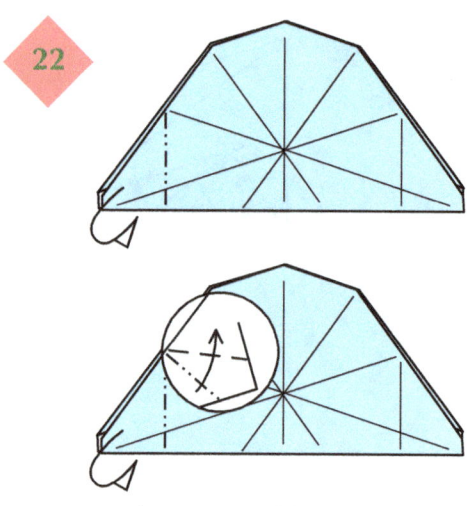

22

Inside view. Fold the inside layers together for this spine-lock fold. Turn over and repeat.

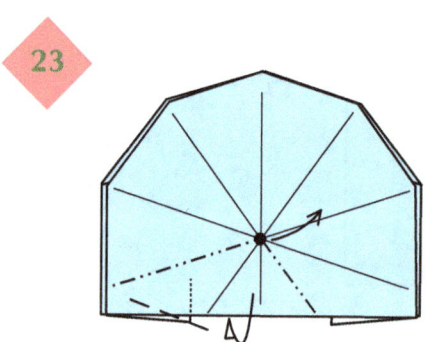

23

Puff out at the dot and fold along the creases. Turn over and repeat.

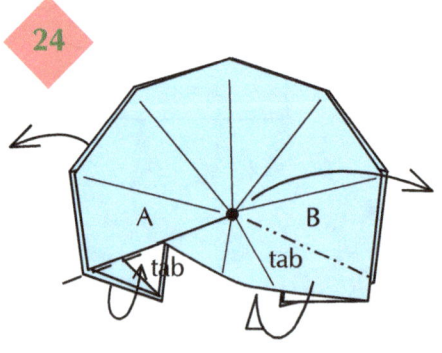

24

Bring the dot to the right and the one behind to the left. Follow regions A and B into the next step. Fold all the layers of each tab.

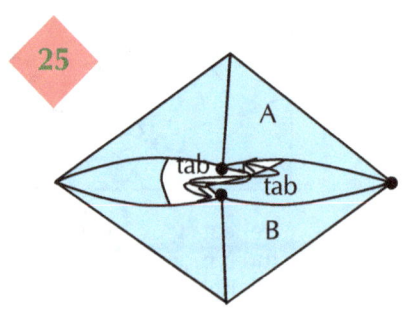

25

Tuck the two tabs into each other so the center dots meet.

26

**Hexagonal Dipyramid**

102   3D Origami Platonic Solids & More

# Hexagonal Trapezohedron

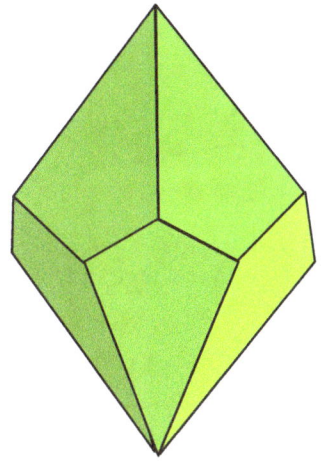

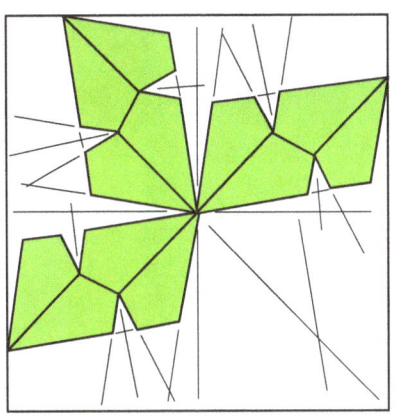

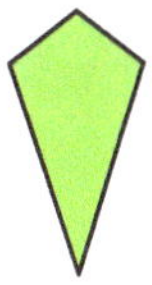

A hexagonal trapezohedron has twelve kites staggered symmetrically. The angles of each of the twelve faces for this trapezodedron are 36°, 108°, 108°, and 108°. The crease pattern shows 3/4 square symmetry.

1. Fold and unfold.

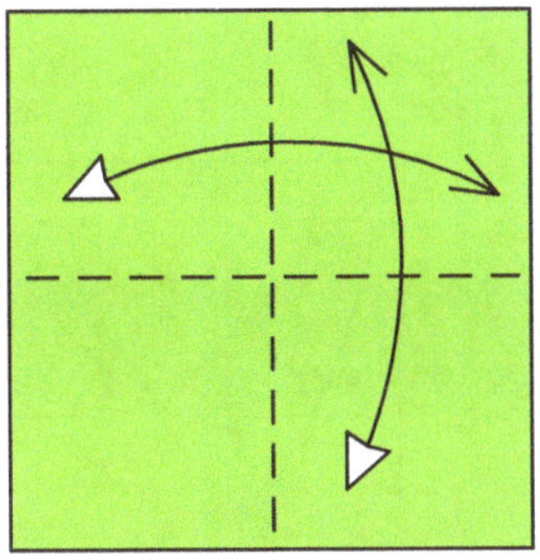

2. 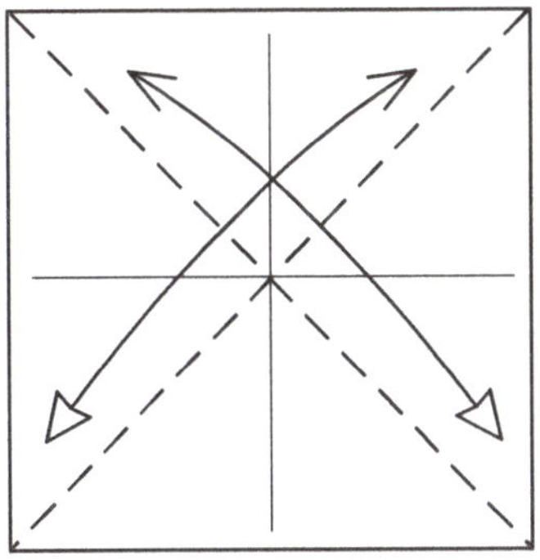 Fold and unfold.

3. Fold and unfold on the left.

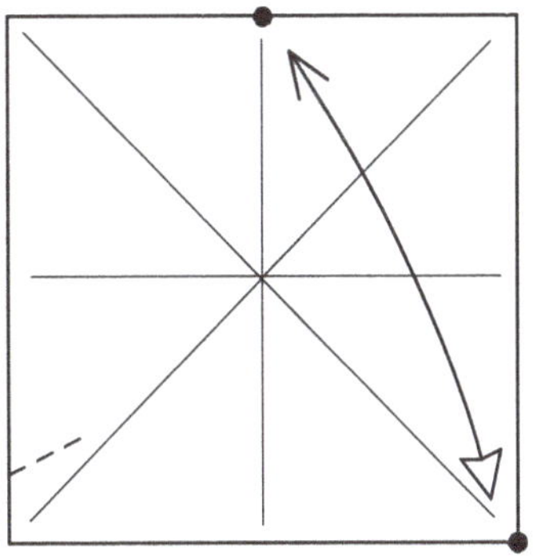

4. Fold and unfold on the left.

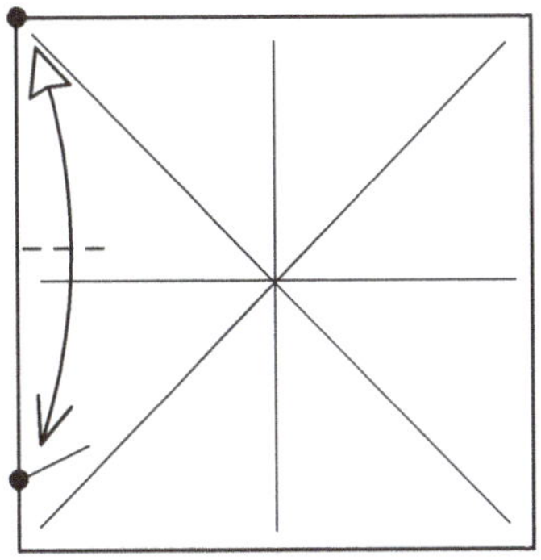

5. Fold and unfold at the bottom.

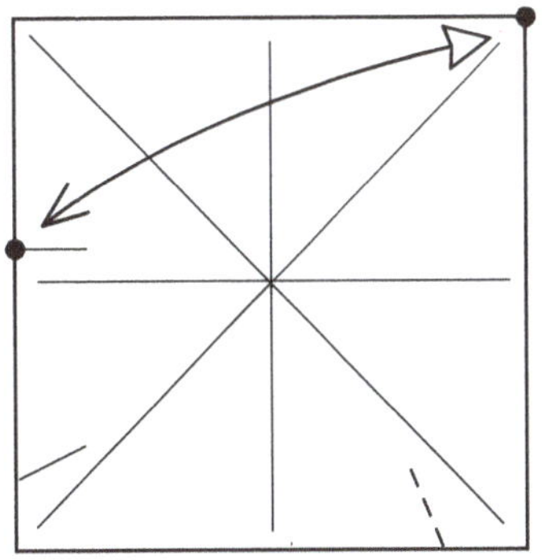

6. Fold and unfold at the bottom. Rotate 180°.

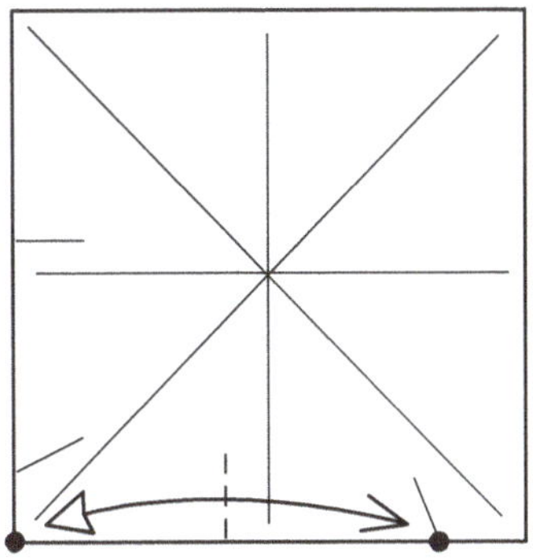

Hexagonal Trapezohedron 103

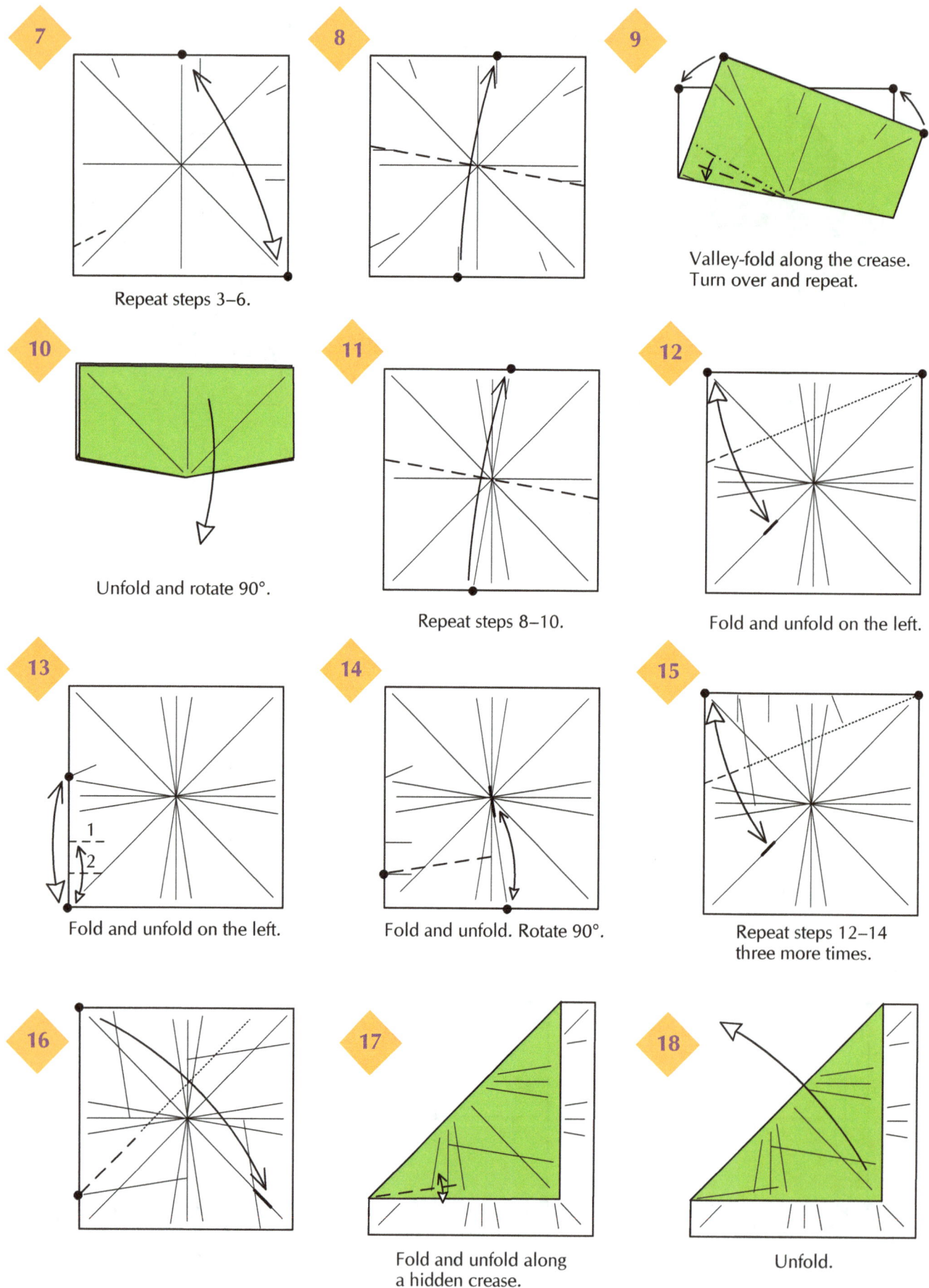

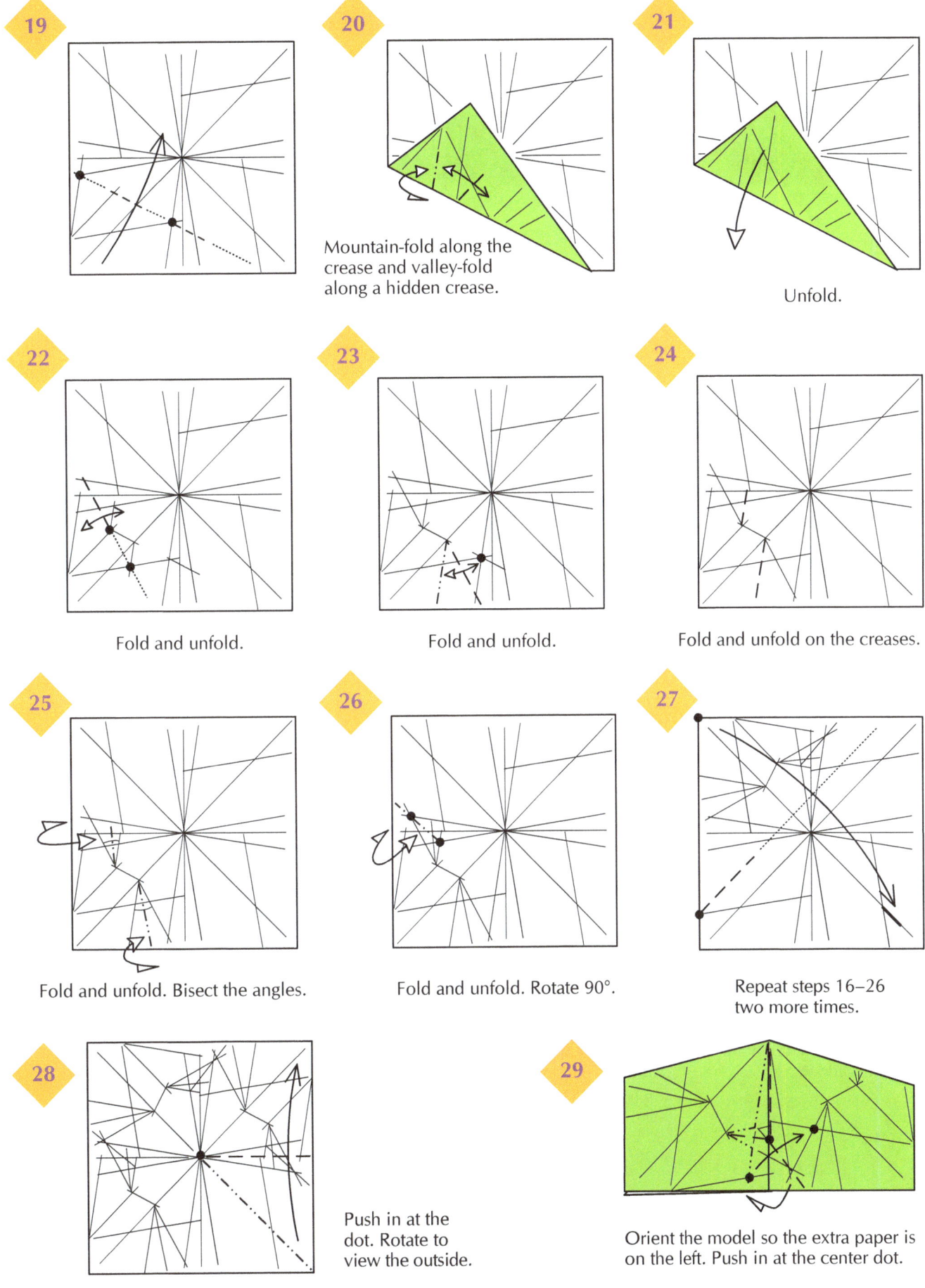

**20.** Mountain-fold along the crease and valley-fold along a hidden crease.

**21.** Unfold.

**22.** Fold and unfold.

**23.** Fold and unfold.

**24.** Fold and unfold on the creases.

**25.** Fold and unfold. Bisect the angles.

**26.** Fold and unfold. Rotate 90°.

**27.** Repeat steps 16–26 two more times.

**28.** Push in at the dot. Rotate to view the outside.

**29.** Orient the model so the extra paper is on the left. Push in at the center dot.

Hexagonal Trapezohedron 105

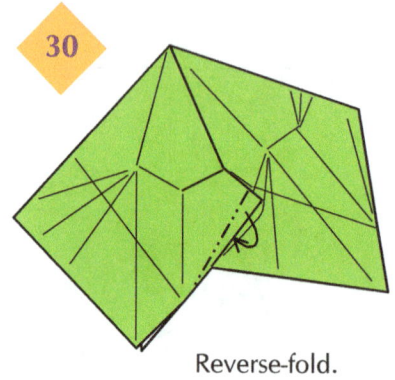

30. Reverse-fold.

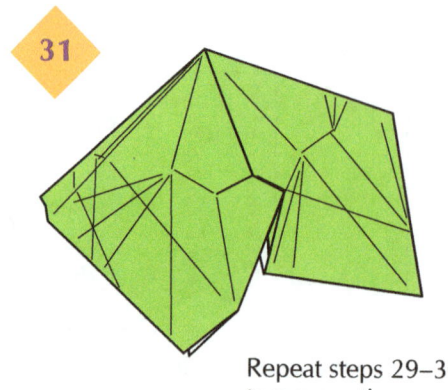

31. Repeat steps 29–30 two more times.

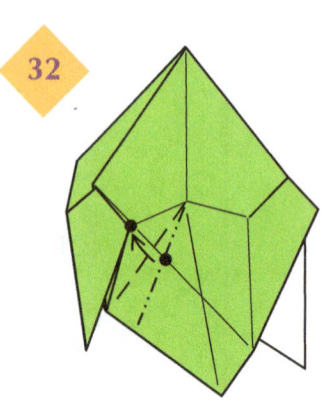

32.

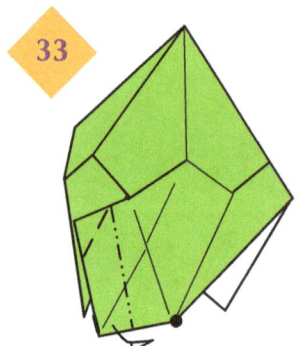

33. Fold the edge to the dot.

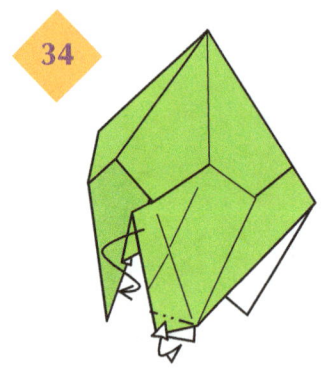

34. Fold and unfold at the bottom. Bring the darker paper to the front.

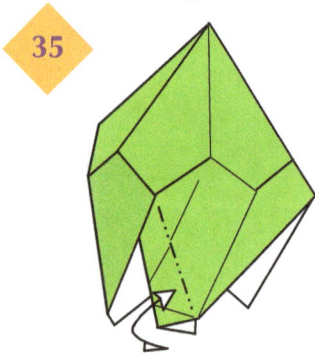

35. Fold and unfold.

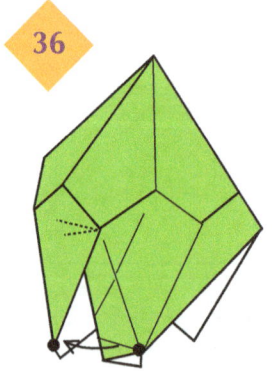

36. Little valley and mountain folds are hidden.

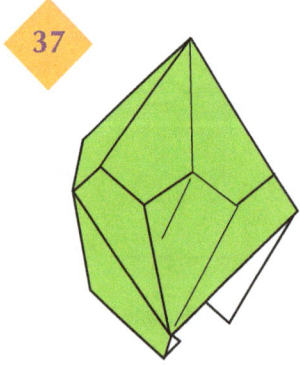

37. Repeat steps 32–35 two more times. The model closes with a three-way twist lock.

**Hexagonal Trapezohedron**

106   *3D Origami Platonic Solids & More*

# Golden Pentagonal Antiprism

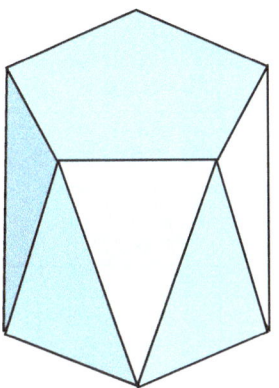
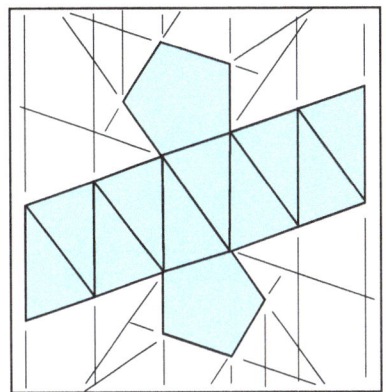

A pentagonal antiprism is composed of 10 triangles and two pentagons. In this one, the angles of each triangle are 36°, 72°, and 72°. The triangles form a band wrapping around.

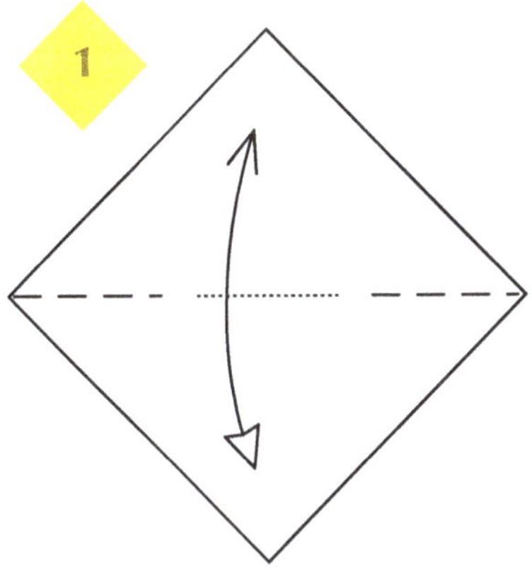

1. Fold and unfold.

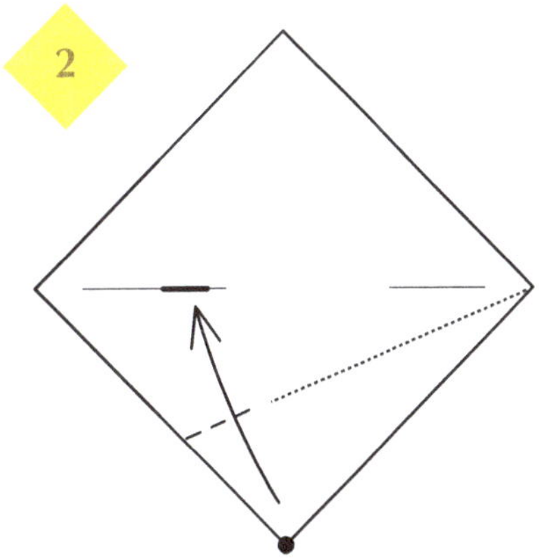

2. Crease on the left.

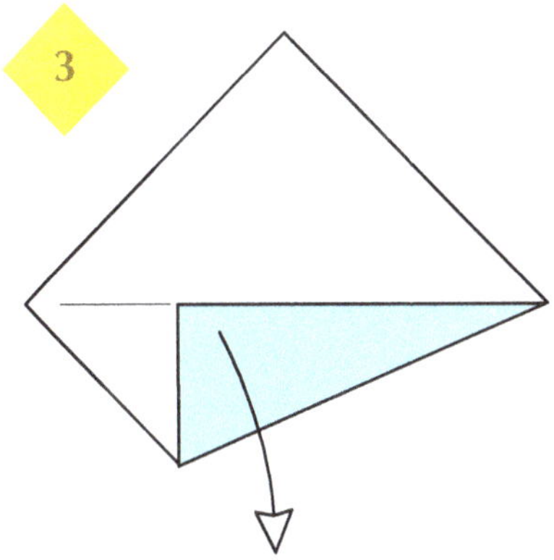

3. Unfold.

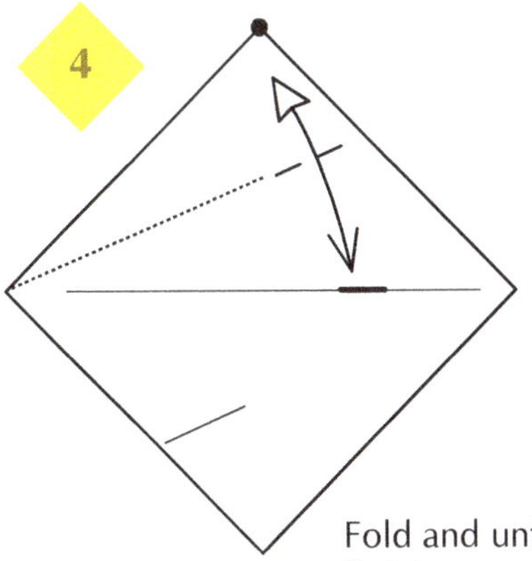

4. Fold and unfold. Rotate.

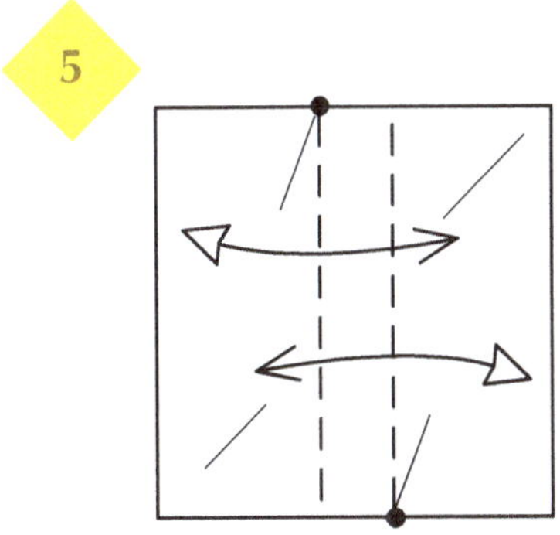

5. Fold and unfold.

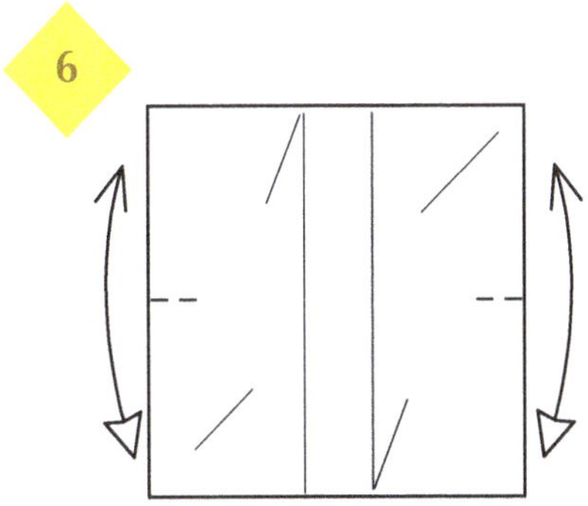

6. Fold and unfold in half at the edges.

*Golden Pentagonal Antiprism* 107

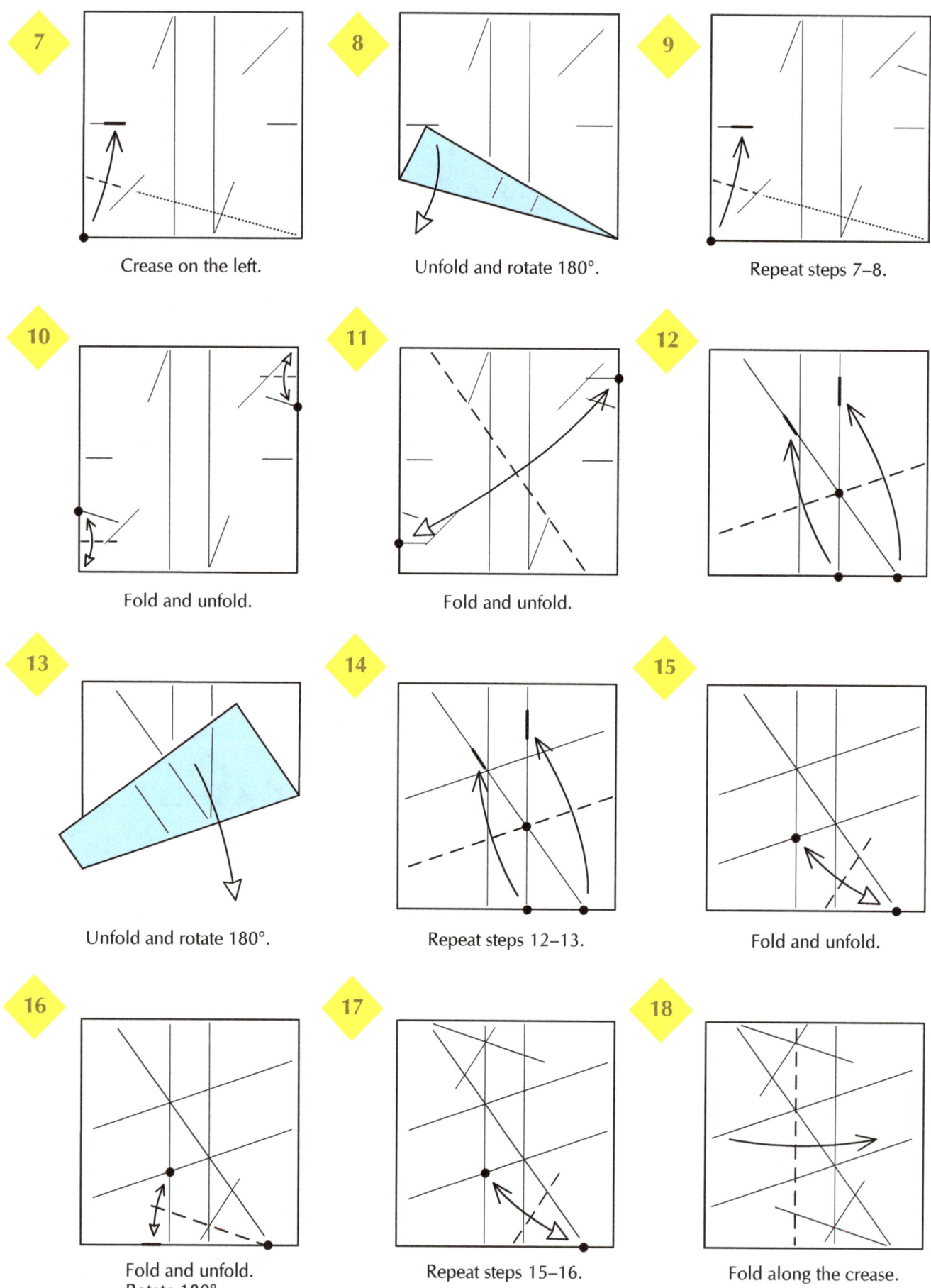

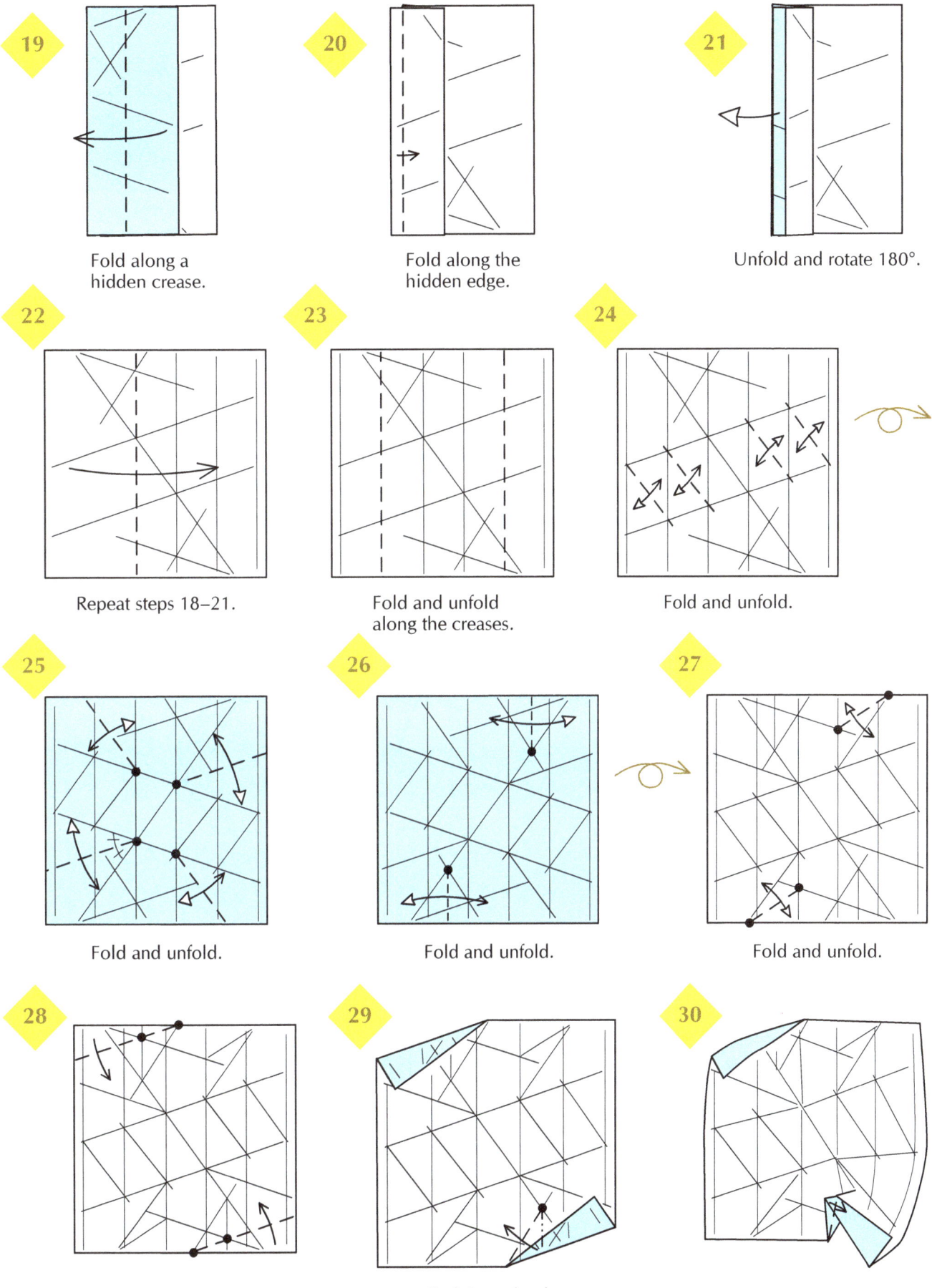

Golden Pentagonal Antiprism

**31** Repeat steps 29–30 above. Rotate to view the outside so the dot is front and center.

**32** Push in on the valley line. Fold along the creases. Turn over and repeat.

**33**

**34** Tuck inside by wrapping around the layers.

**35** Unfold to step 33.

**36** Repeat steps 33–34.

**37** Refold steps 33–34 behind.

**38**

**Golden Pentagonal Antiprism**

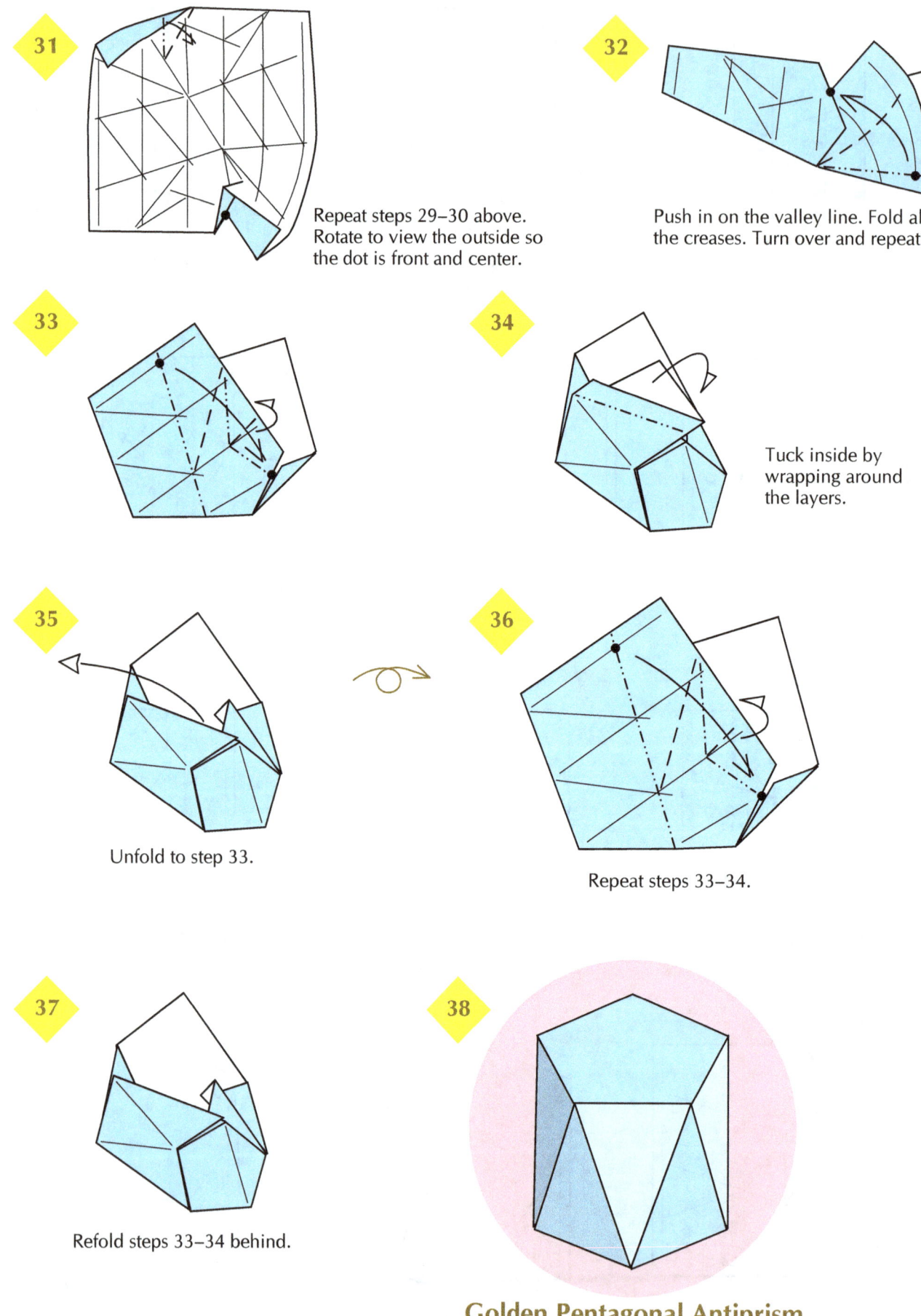

110   *3D Origami Platonic Solids & More*

# Triakis Tetrahedron

The triakis tetrahedron is a Catalan solid composed of twelve triangular faces. The sides of each triangular face are proportional 3, 3, and 5. The crease pattern shows 3/4 square symmetry.

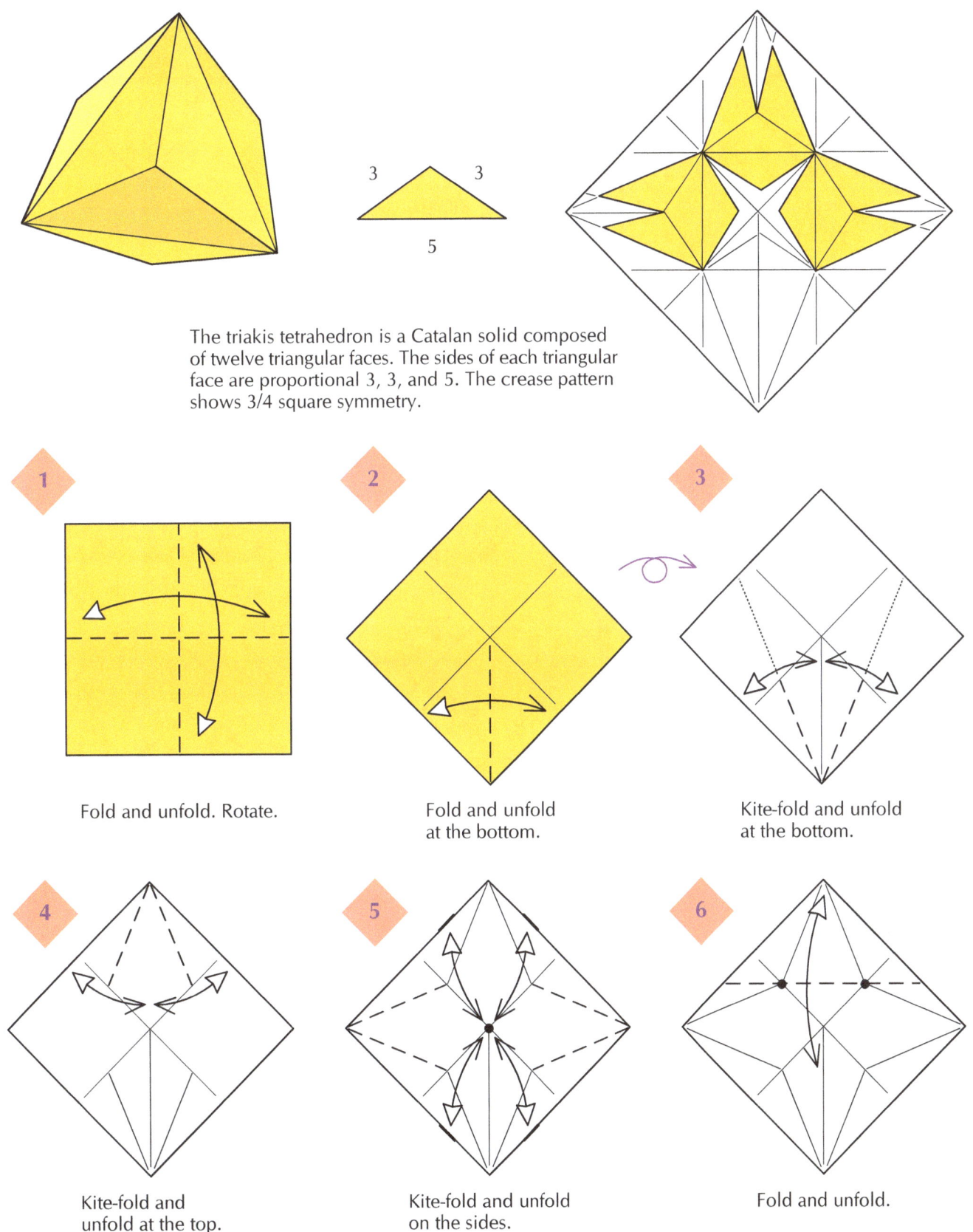

1. Fold and unfold. Rotate.
2. Fold and unfold at the bottom.
3. Kite-fold and unfold at the bottom.
4. Kite-fold and unfold at the top.
5. Kite-fold and unfold on the sides.
6. Fold and unfold.

Triakis Tetrahedron 111

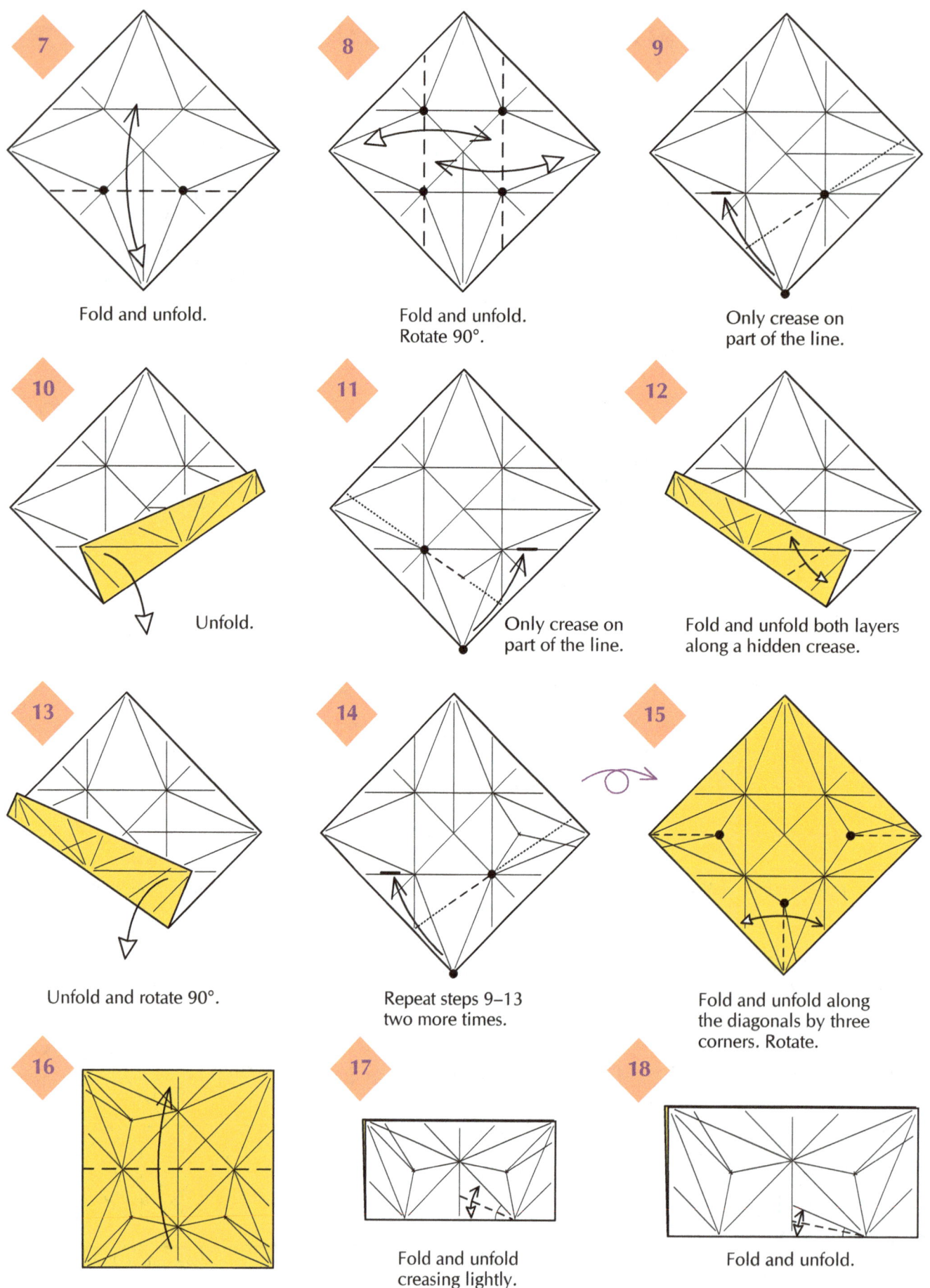

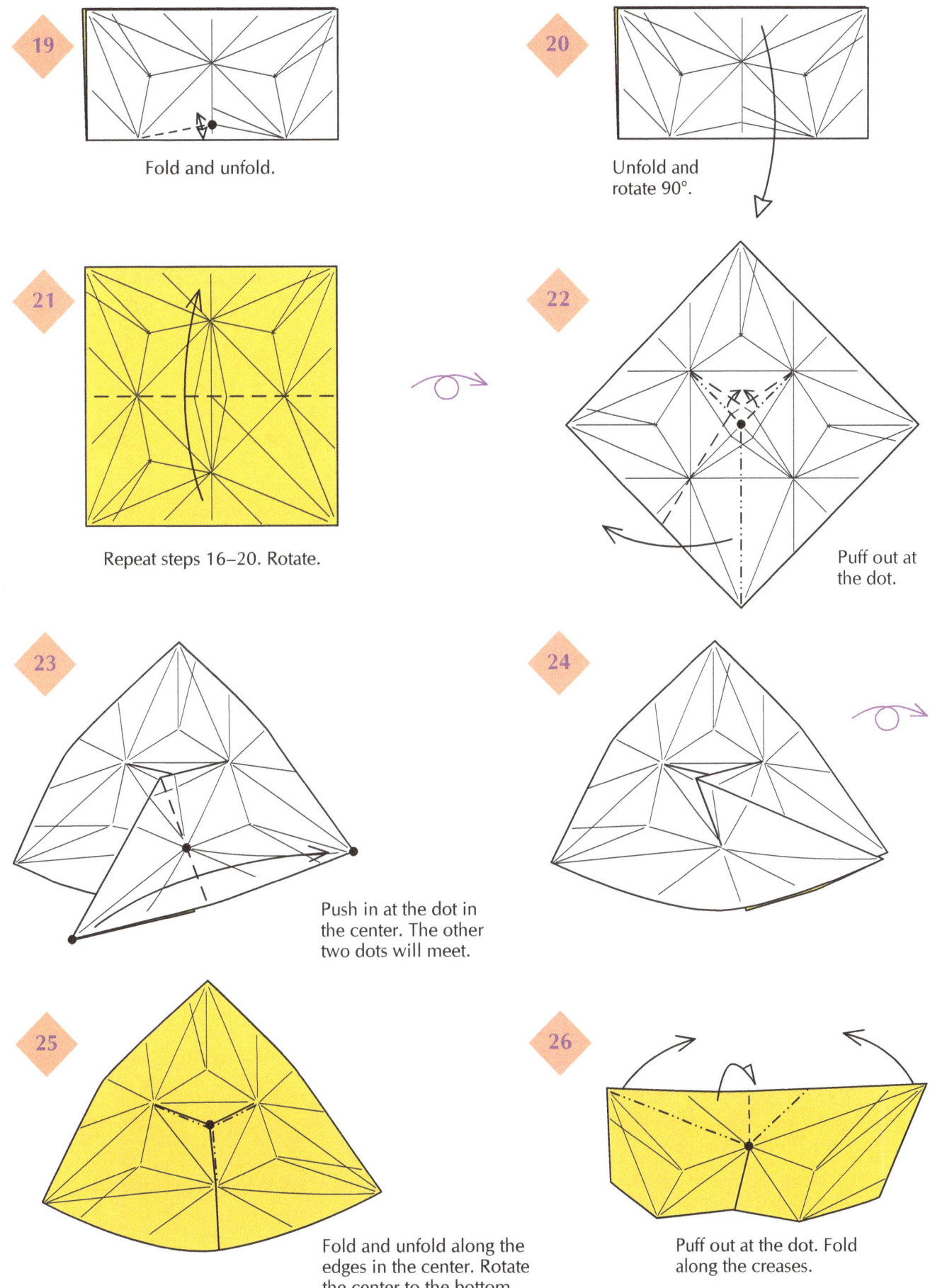

Triakis Tetrahedron 113

**27**

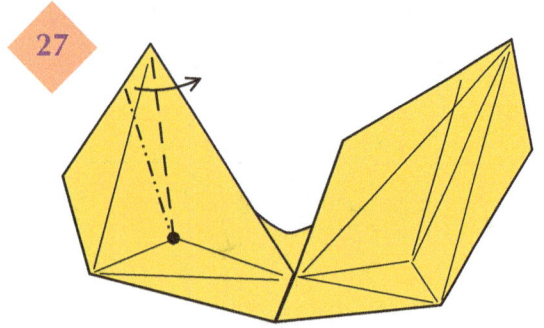

Puff out at the dot.

**28**

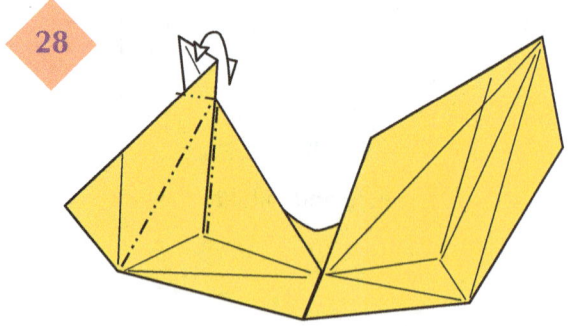

Fold and unfold at the top and along the crease and edge.

**29**

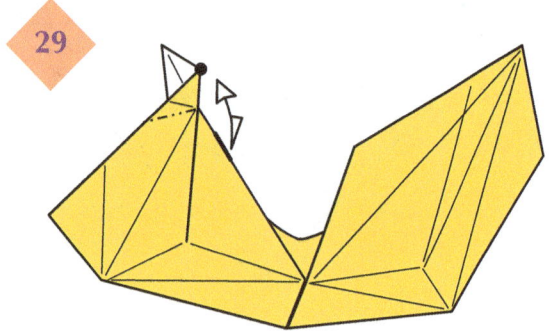

Fold and unfold. Rotate.

**30**

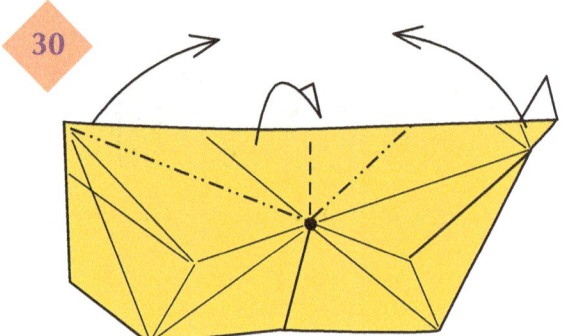

Repeat steps 26–29 two more times.

**31**

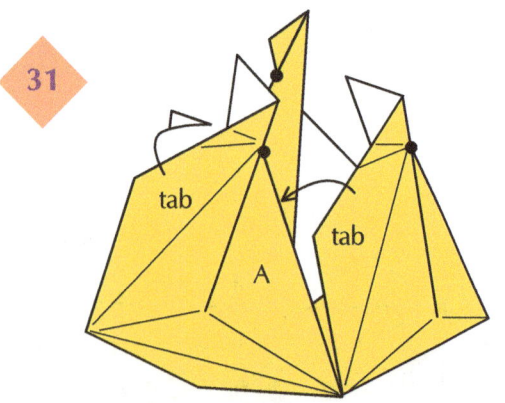

Tuck the tab behind region A. Continue all around. The three dots will meet. The model closes with a three-way twist lock.

**32**

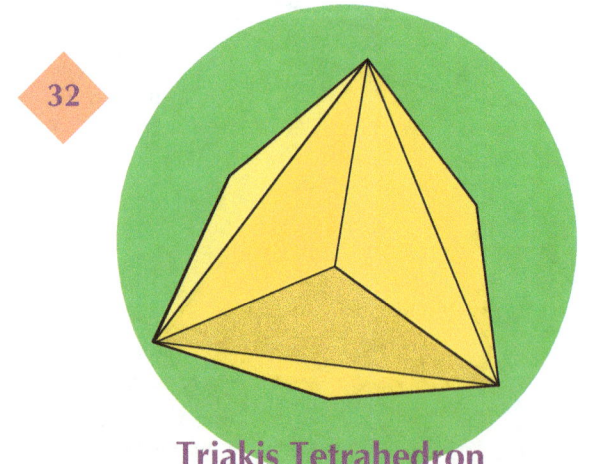

**Triakis Tetrahedron**

114    3D Origami Platonic Solids & More

# Rhombic Dodecahedron

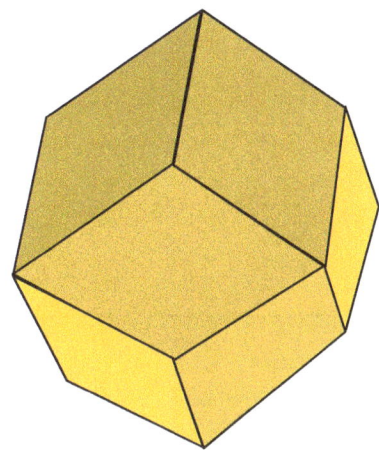

The rhombic dodecahedron is composed of twelve sides, each with diagonals proportional to 1 and √2. The model uses square symmetry and closes with a twist lock.

1. Fold and unfold.

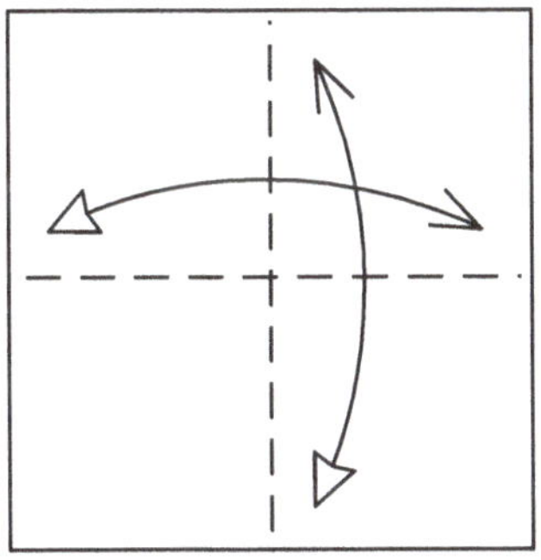

2. Bring the edge to the center and crease at the bottom.

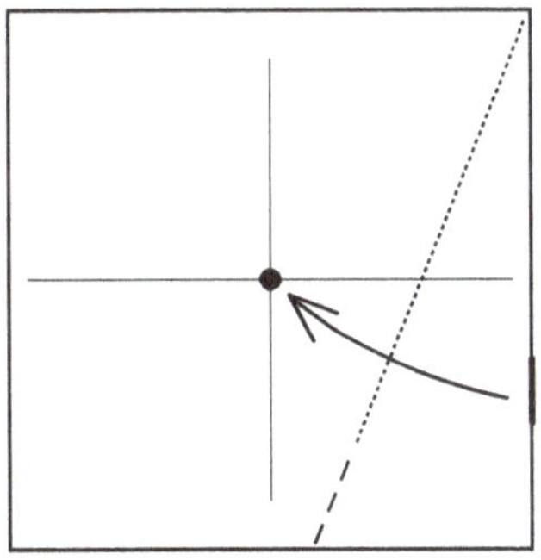

3. Unfold and rotate 180°.

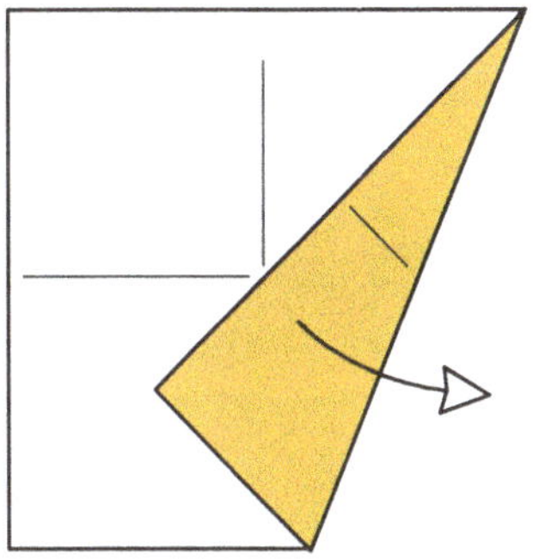

4. Repeat steps 2–3.

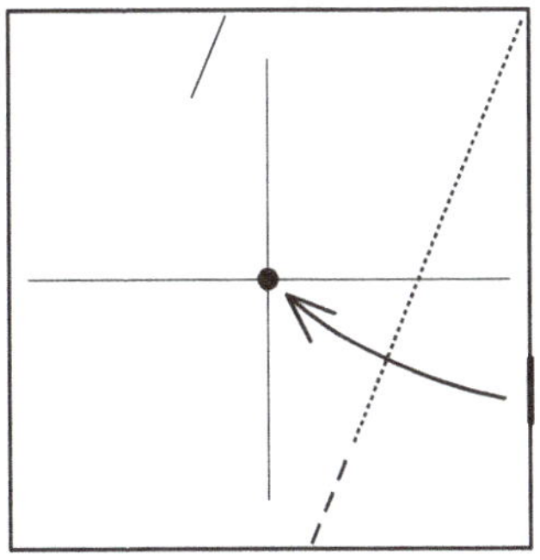

5. Fold and unfold. Rotate 90°.

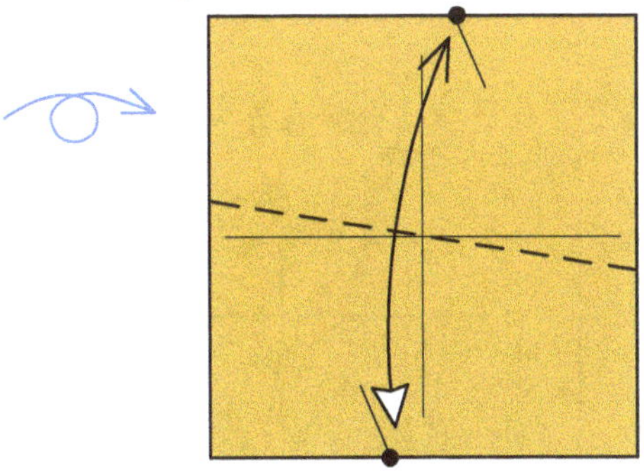

6. Fold and unfold.

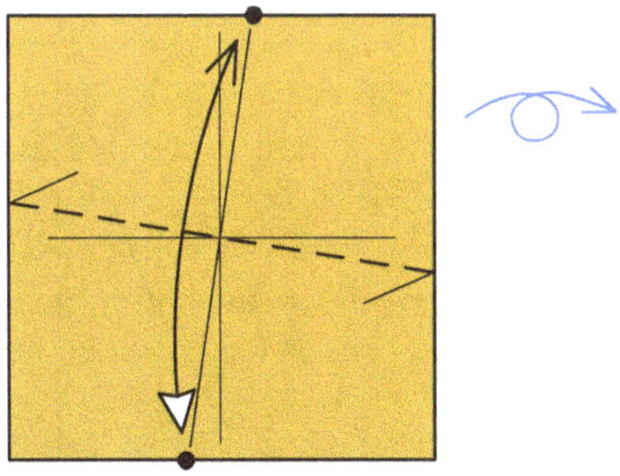

*Rhombic Dodecahedron* 115

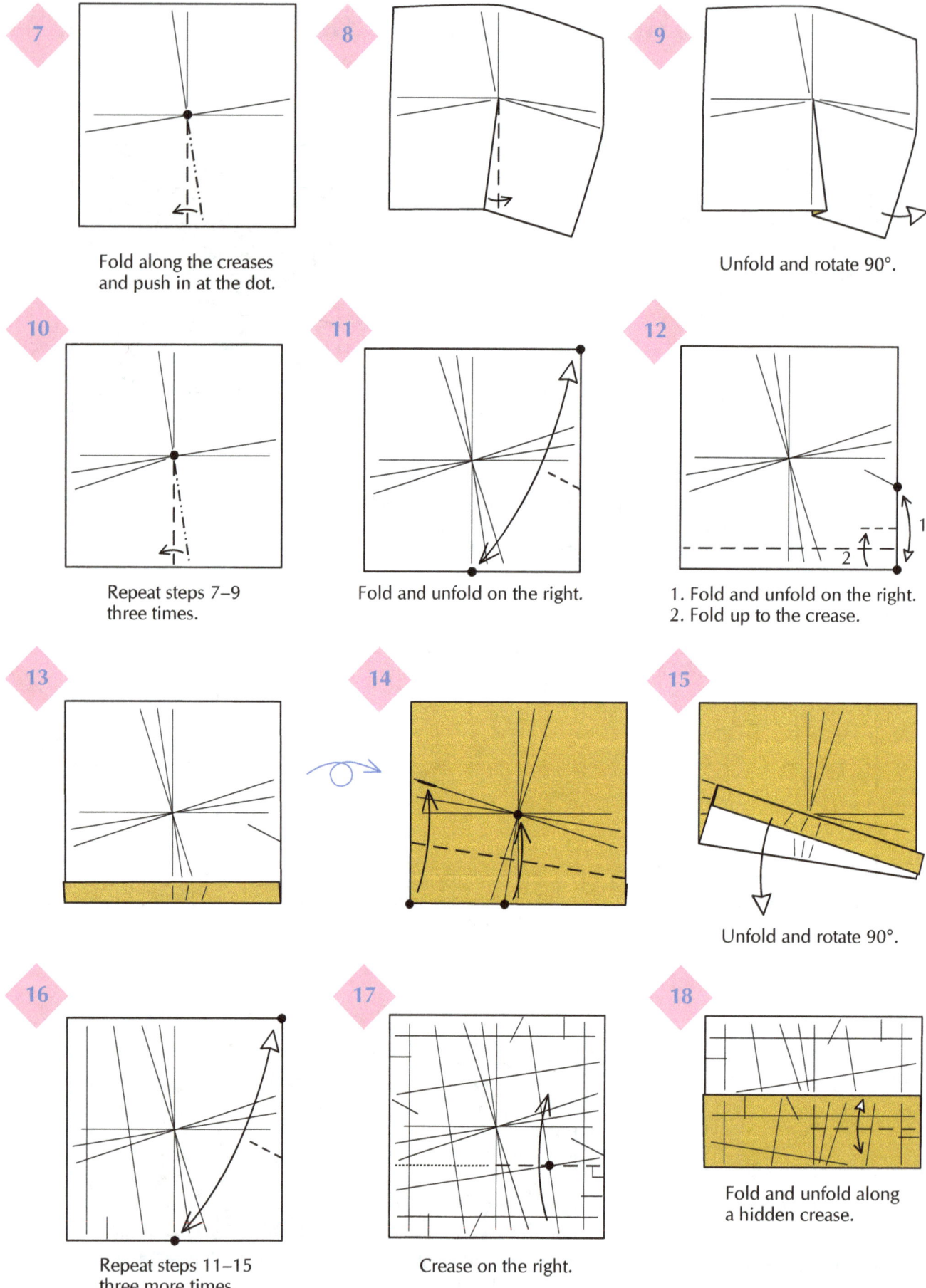

116    *3D Origami Platonic Solids & More*

| | | |
|---|---|---|
| **19** | **20** | **21** |
| Unfold. | Fold and unfold in the center. Rotate 90°. | Repeat steps 17–20 three more times. |
| **22** | **23** | **24** |
| | | Unfold and rotate 90°. |
| **25** | **26** | **27** |
| Repeat steps 22–24 three more times. | Fold and unfold on the bottom. | Fold and unfold on the bottom. Rotate 90°. |
| **28** | **29** | |
| | Repeat steps 26–27 three more times. | Fold and unfold on the top. Rotate 90°. |

*Rhombic Dodecahedron*

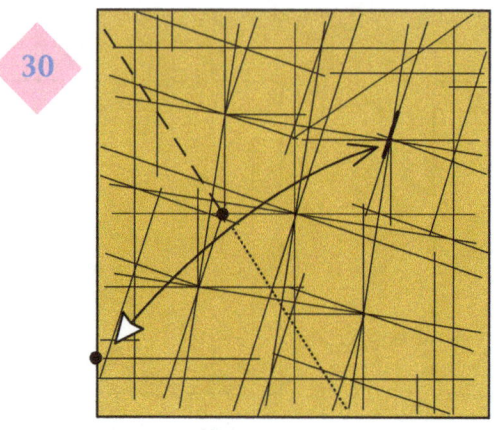

Repeat step 29 three more times.

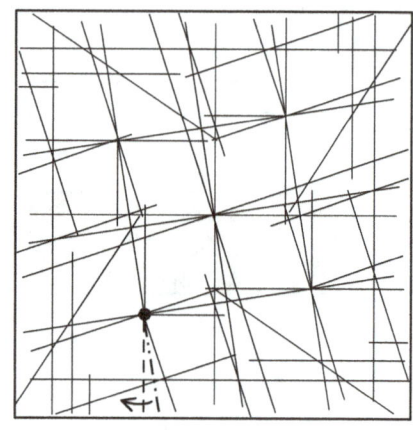

Fold along the creases and push in at the dot.

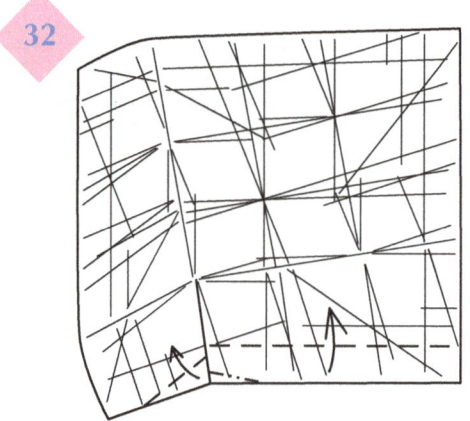

Valley-fold along the creases. Rotate 90°.

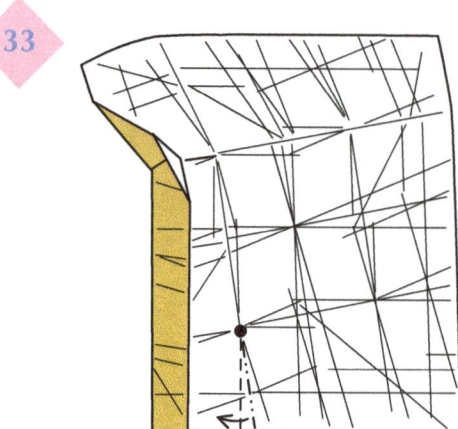

Repeat steps 31–32 three more times.

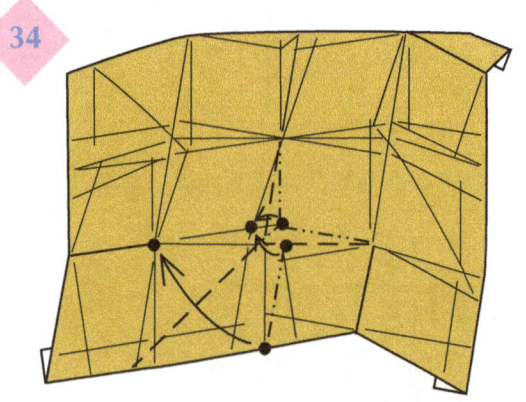

The groups of dots will meet.

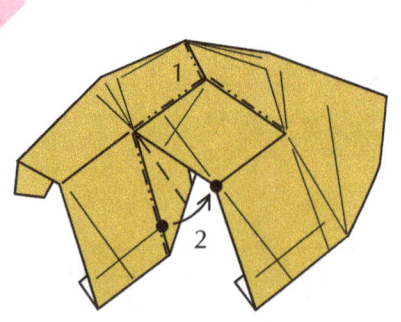

1. Fold and unfold along the edges.
2. The dots will meet.

118   *3D Origami Platonic Solids & More*

36.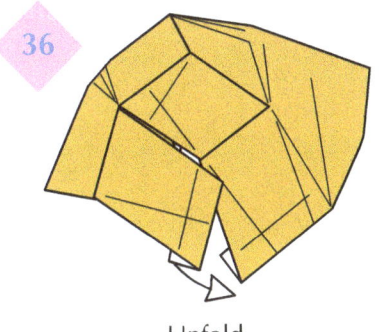
Unfold.

37.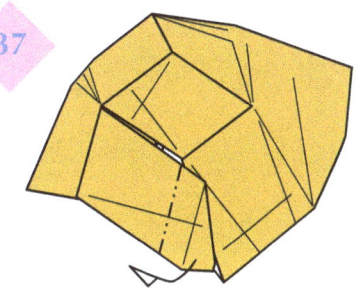
Fold along the crease.

38.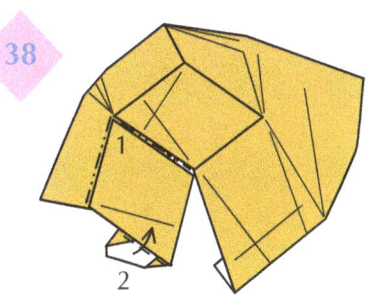
1. Fold and unfold along the edges.
2. Valley-fold.
Rotate 90°.

39.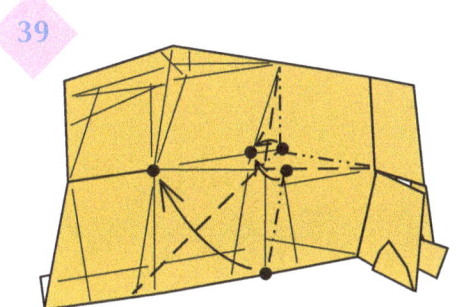
Repeat steps 34–38 three more times. Rotate the top to the bottom.

40.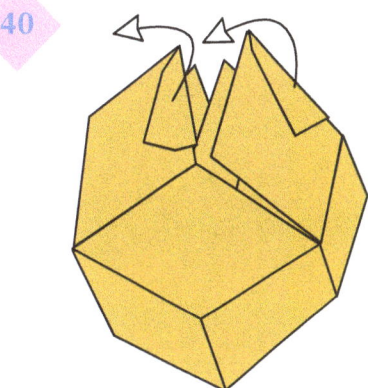
Unwrap the four tabs at the top.

41.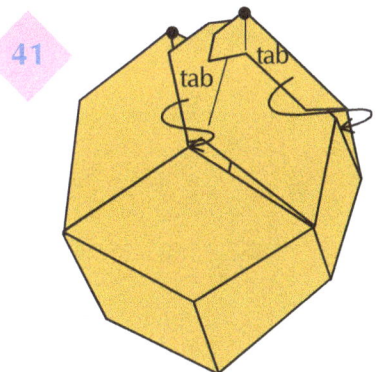
Tuck the four tabs inside to lock and close the model with a twist lock.

42.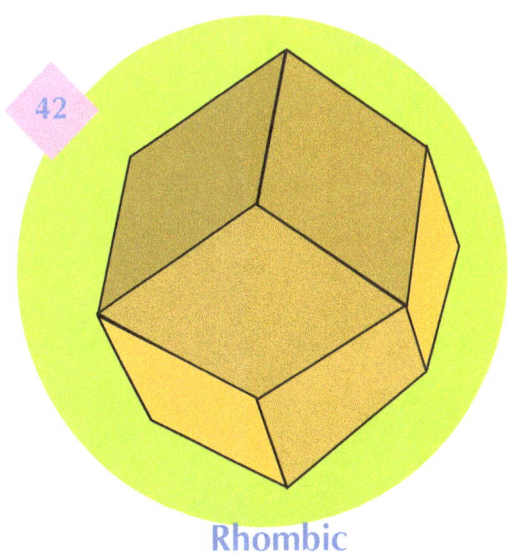

**Rhombic Dodecahedron**

*Rhombic Dodecahedron*